When Two Spines Align: Dressage Dynamics

When Two Spines Align: Dressage Dynamics

Attain Remarkable Riding Rapport with Your Horse

Beth Baumert

Foreword by Axel Steiner,
FEI 5* and USEF Dressage Judge

TRAFALGAR SQUARE
North Pomfret, Vermont

First published in 2014 by
Trafalgar Square Books
North Pomfret, Vermont 05053

Copyright © 2014 Beth Baumert

All rights reserved. No part of this book may be reproduced, by any means, without written permission of the publisher, except by a reviewer quoting brief excerpts for a review in a magazine, newspaper, or website.

Disclaimer of Liability
The author and publisher shall have neither liability nor responsibility to any person or entity with respect to any loss or damage caused or alleged to be caused directly or indirectly by the information contained in this book. While the book is as accurate as the author can make it, there may be errors, omissions, and inaccuracies.

Trafalgar Square Books encourages the use of approved safety helmets in all equestrian sports and activities.

Library of Congress Cataloging-in-Publication Data
Baumert, Beth.
 When two spines align, dressage dynamics : attain remarkable riding rapport with your horse / Beth Baumert.
    pages cm
  Includes index.
  ISBN 978-1-57076-695-4
  1. Dressage. I. Title.
  SF309.5.B385 2014
  798.2'3--dc23
                          2014010775

Book design by Lauryl Eddlemon
Cover design by RM Didier
Typefaces: Source Sans Pro, Roboto Slab

Printed in China

10 9 8 7 6 5 4 3 2 1

Contents

Foreword by Axel Steiner ix

Preface xi

Introduction: The Possibility of Magic 1
Solving the Freedom vs Control Enigma 2
How Riders Work 4
How Horses Work 4
How Two Spines Meet in Balance 5

Part I: How Riders Work 7

Chapter One: The Seat—The Place Where Two Spines Meet 9
The Balanced Seat 9
The Weight Aids 13
Aids That Send One Message 17
   Exercise: Find the Floor of Your Seat 18
Essential Information about the Seat 20

Chapter Two: An Introduction to Powerlines . 21
Positive Tension: The Easy Way to Be Strong 21
Powerlines Channel the Horse 22
Supple Joints Make Supple Powerlines 25
   Exercise 1: Find Your Vertical Powerline 26
   Exercise 2: Find Your Connecting Powerline 26
   Exercise 3: Find Your Spiraling Powerline 27
   Exercise 4: Find Your Visual Powerline 27
   Exercise 5: Strengthen Your Core with the "Bridge" 28
   Exercise 6: Strengthen Your Core with Push-Ups from the Forearms 28
   Exercise 7: Keep Your Powerlines Supple 29

Essential Information about Positive Tension and Powerlines 29

Chapter Three: The Vertical Powerline—Power to GO 31
The Rider's Foundation 31
Posture Checklist for Your Vertical Powerline ... 32
"In Front of the Leg"—The GO Button 36
   Exercise 1: Strengthen Your Vertical Powerline .. 36
   Exercise 2: Pedal to Strengthen Your Vertical Powerline 37
   Exercise 3: Turn-on-the-Forehand to Help the GO Aids 38
Essential Information about the Vertical Powerline 40

Chapter Four: The Connecting Powerline—Suppleness to STOP 41
Posture Checklist for Your Connecting Powerline . 42
Making the Connection 44
A Well-Executed Half-Halt 45
Use the Hands Last 48
    Exercise 1: Who's Drawing on Whom? 49
    Exercise 2: Half-Halts to Minimize the Use
    of Your Hand 50
Essential Information about the
Connecting Powerline 51

Chapter Five: The Spiraling Powerline—Flexibility to TURN 53
Bending and Turning 54
Posture Checklist for Your Spiraling Powerline . . . 57
    Exercise 1: Confirm the Turning Aids 58
    Exercise 2: Triangles for "Throughness" 59
Essential Information about the
Spiraling Powerline 60

Chapter Six: The Visual Powerline—Connecting to the Outside World 61
Posture Checklist for Your Visual Powerline 62
Influence on the Horse's Longitudinal Balance . . . 62
    Exercise 1: Steer with Your Eyes 64
    Exercise 2: Increase the Power and Focus
    of Your Eyes 64
Essential Information about the
Visual Powerline 65

Chapter Seven: Clear Aids for Communication 67
Aids for Three Purposes 67
Whole-Body Riding 75
Passive Aids—Freedom for Him and Control
for You 77
    Exercise 1: Circles for Shaping and Figure Eights
    to Put Your Horse "In Front of the Leg" 78
    Exercise 2: Whip Control for the Rider 79
    Exercise 3: "In Front of the Leg": A Whip
    Exercise for the Horse 79
    Exercise 4: Listening and Action Aids:

    The Prompt Leg-Yield 80
    Exercise 5: The Square Serpentine 81
Essential Information about the Clear Aids 83

Part II: How Horses Work 85

Chapter Eight: Balance Issues 87
Understanding Balance Improves It 87
Longitudinal Balance 88
Thrust, Reach, and Engagement 89
Half-Halts and Transitions for Coordinating
and Connecting 94
The Circle of Energy and the Circle of Aids 95
Lateral Balance 99
    Exercise 1: Get Your Horse's Pushing Engine
    in Gear 102
    Exercise 2: Connect Your Horse in
    Shoulder-Fore 104

Exercise 3: Transition for Throughness 104
Essential Information about the Horse's
Balance Issues 106

**Chapter Nine: How the Horse's Weight
Distribution Changes** 107
Improve Balance by Suppling
and Strengthening 107
   *Exercise 1: Ask Yourself: How Is My Horse's
   Weight Distributed?* 113
   *Exercise 2: Ask Yourself: How Round Is
   My Horse?* 113
   *Exercise 3: Ask Yourself: Is My Horse Heavy
   in My Hands?* 114
   *Exercise 4: Ask Yourself: How Long Should
   My Horse Be?* 115
Essential Information about Weight
Distribution 116

Chapter Ten: Impulsion and Engagement 117
Timing the Aids to Maximize Freedom 117
Timing the Aids for Thrust, Reach, and
Engagement 118
   Exercise 1: Timing and Free "Boing" 120
   Exercise 2: Building Impulsion in the Trot ..121
   *Exercise 3: Feeling the Moment of
   Engagement* 122
Essential Information about Impulsion
and Engagement 123

Chapter Eleven: Leverage for Collection 125
The Science of Leverage 125
Finding Collection 127
   Exercise 1: Shoulder-In for Collection 130
   Exercise 2: Rein-Back 131
   *Exercise 3: Überstreichen Asks: Are You
   in Balance?* 133
Essential Information about Collection 134

Chapter Twelve: Transitions 135
Connecting and Collecting Your Horse 135
Connecting and Collecting Transitions 136
Have a Clear Idea 142

*Exercise 1: Clean Transitions That Are
Connecting Then Collecting* 144
Exercise 2: Energy Conversion 145
Exercise 3: Retaining the Rhythm 146
Exercise 4: Looking for the Possibility 147
Essential Information about Transitions.......148

Chapter Thirteen: Half-Halts 149
Connecting and Collecting Your Horse 149
What the Heck Is a Half Halt? 149
   Exercise 1: How to Do a Half-Halt 156
   Exercise 2: Half-Halts for Smooth Transitions ..157
   Exercise 3: Asking Your Horse to Wait for You ..158
   *Exercise 4: Using Halts to Improve Your
   Half-Halts before Corners* 159
Half-Halts That Make the Neck Long and
the Back "Through" 160
Essential Information about Half-Halts 161

Part III: How Two Spines Meet in Balance ..163

Chapter Fourteen: Rhythm 165
Speaking Your Horse's Language 165
   Exercise: Working with a Metronome 169
Essential Information about Rhythm 170

Chapter Fifteen: Energy 171
Monitoring and Regulating Power 171
   Exercise: Organizing the Energy 175
Essential Information about Energy 176

Chapter Sixteen: Flexion of the Poll 177
The Key to a Supple Back 177
   Exercise: Monitor and Regulate the Flexion ..179
Essential Information about Flexion 180

Chapter Seventeen: Spinal Alignment 181
The Key to Straightness 181
Alignment of Two Spines 181
   Exercise: Threading 185
Essential Information about Spinal Alignment ..186

Chapter Eighteen: The Bend................187
Bend Control Is Horse Control 187
Bending and Turning for a Perfect Circle 187
Common Problems on a Circle 191
   Exercise 1: Know the Feeling of a
   20-Meter Circle 196
   Exercise 2: Turning and the 12-Meter Corner ...197
   Exercise 3: Theodorescu Serpentines..........199
Essential Information about Bend 200

Chapter Nineteen: The Height of the Neck ...201
"Throughness" by Nature 201
   Exercise 1: Finding the Falling-Down Neck 204
   Exercise 2: Fixing a Hanging-Down Neck......205
Essential Information about the Height
of the Neck..................................206

Chapter Twenty: The Length of Stride 207
Shortening in a Forward Way 208
   Exercise: Lengthen and Shorten the Stride
   on a Circle................................209
Essential Information about the Length
of Stride....................................210

Chapter Twenty-One: The Line of Travel 211
Controlling Your Path for Perfect Balance 211
   Exercise 1: The Shifting Shoulder-Fore 213
   Exercise 2: The Spiraling Circle 214
Essential Information about the Line of Travel ..214

**Chapter Twenty-Two: Figures and
Movements**..................................215
A Long-Term Training Plan 215
   Opposing Qualities Exercise 1: Training Level..216
   Opposing Qualities Exercise 2: First Level......217
   Opposing Qualities Exercise 3: Second Level...220

   Opposing Qualities Exercise 4: Third Level.....221
   Opposing Qualities Exercise 5: Fourth Level ...223
Essential Information about Figures
and Movements..............................224

Conclusion: The Probability
of Magic....................................225

Photograph & Illustration Credits............227

Index......................................229

Foreword
by Axel Steiner

I've had the pleasure of knowing and working with Beth Baumert and her daughter Jennifer for many years. Beth has honed her skills, not only in the saddle, but also as a trainer and coach. With many years as the technical editor for *Dressage Today* (the leading dressage magazine in the United States), Beth has had access to some of the top trainers and riders in the world. In her search to clarify some of the more difficult aspects of training dressage horses, she attended European shows, conducted countless interviews, and has built strong trusting relationships with some of the best trainers in the world. The collection of this priceless gained knowledge is the basis for this book.

Beth and I agree that a balanced and supportive seat is the foundation for a successful horse/rider partnership. In the first chapter, she tackles this quite complicated subject by expertly explaining the dynamics of the way the rider balances, and the use of positive tension in establishing the Powerlines that shape and channel the horse's energy so he can properly balance himself and the rider.

She continues, in the next section, to discuss the same subject from the horse's point of view, again giving many examples and suggested exercises.

In the last section, she masterfully marries the earlier subjects into one, and demonstrates the magic of two spines aligning for the common good of horse and rider.

This is a book that needs to be read slowly, and then reread over and over. With each subsequent reading, you will find increased understanding of this fascinating subject: This book is truly timeless. I can humbly admit that this book clarified some subjects even for me, after a lifetime of being involved with dressage. It is the equivalent of countless clinics given by some of the best in the world.

Dressage is a journey of many individual dances with our horses. I hope you enjoy learning the dance steps so carefully outlined and illustrated here.

Axel Steiner
FEI 5* Dressage Judge for 25 Years (Retired)
Current USEF "S" Dressage Judge
USDF "L" Program Faculty Member

Preface

I'm deeply grateful to trainers who share their knowledge with passion and generosity out of their pure love for horses. My appreciation began in earnest in the early 1970s, when I rode with George Morris. It didn't take long to figure out he was a genius. In addition to his scientific understanding of equitation, he really cared that his horses and his riders understood him—down to the finest detail. And he had a passion for passing on his knowledge.

In those days, Morris held a clinic specifically for teachers where I became fully aware that "Science comes before art can begin." To Morris, there was no horse or rider detail that was irrelevant. The complex whole with its bazillion factors sifted smoothly through his analytical mind. This insight was life-changing for me: "Technique comes before art." My fascination with the science of equitation began on that weekend.

Later, in the 1980s, Sally Swift further fed my curiosity about how horses work, how riders work, and how they can best work together. It was in the early days when she was exploring equitation herself, coming up with the images found in her famous book, *Centered Riding,* which was published by Trafalgar Square Books in 1985. I remember sitting around a table and reviewing, with fascination, the drawings that would later appear in that book. I think that Sally Swift, more than anyone else on the planet, has been responsible for improving the comfort of horses.

Because my fascination was now a full-blown obsession, I took the position of technical editor with *Dressage Today* when the magazine began in 1994. Through *Dressage Today,* I could legitimately call whatever rider I wanted in the whole world, and ask, "How do you do that?" It was great. Over the years I talked with Hubertus Schmidt, Henk van Bergen, Kyra Kyrklund, Steffen Peters, Isabell Werth, the late Dr. Reiner Klimke, his children Ingrid and Michael Klimke, Monica Theodorescu, George Williams, Guenter Seidel, Arthur Kottas, Bo Jena, Lilo Fore, and countless others. I talked to judges—Axel Steiner, Stephen Clarke, and others. I went to clinics, symposiums, and the Global Dressage Forums held at Joep, Tineke, and Imke Bartels' stable in Hooge Mierde, the

Netherlands. And I had the advantage of working with good horses and riders at my own stable in Connecticut.

This book is my interpretation of the path taken by the great riders and judges I spoke with through the years, who were so generous with their techniques and ideas. There were no national boundaries when it came to sharing knowledge. They all impressed me with their attention to detail. They were endlessly picky about their riding. As Hubertus Schmidt once said to me, "Everyone knows how important it is to get the horse on the outside rein, but most riders are too easily satisfied with the quality of that detail." When Hubertus Schmidt pays extra attention to that detail on a 20-meter circle, maybe the rest of us should too!

During a weekend symposium in Arizona, Isabell Werth reminded us, "inside leg to outside rein" at least a thousand times. When I asked her about it, she replied, "I said it as often as I think of it myself when I'm riding."

Details, details. The greatest respect and gratitude goes to all those riders, trainers, and judges I met through *Dressage Today* who wanted their articles to be perfect.

Like George Morris, they were generous in sharing their knowledge and cared that our reader-riders understood. They are all great horsemen with that passion for perfection, and lucky for us, an eagerness to pass their knowledge on.

Many thanks to my primary trainers who formed my thinking and riding in the first place—the late Walter Christensen and his student, Volker Brommann.

Many thanks go to those who read the manuscript: George Williams, whom I think of as America's dressage theory guru; my daughter, Jennifer Baumert, who spent decades thoughtfully training horses with me; Annie Morris, a trainer at my farm in Connecticut who also epitomizes thoughtful riding (her horses—and mine—are blessed to have such a rider); Susie Holic (a kind, knowledgeable horsewoman and amazing editor for IBM); Patricia Lasko, my editing partner at *Dressage Today*; and, of course, the editors at Trafalgar Square Books, Caroline Robbins, Martha Cook, and Rebecca Didier. They're the best there is.

Beth Baumert

Word Choices

For purposes of simplicity in these pages, I refer to the horse as "him" and the rider as "her." No disrespect is intended to men and mares. I'm very fond of both.

INTRODUCTION

The Possibility of Magic

Magical moments happen on the back of a horse. They don't always happen, but they can—when horse and rider become one. Their two spines meet in perfect balance, their minds meet in perfect understanding, and they move in perfect harmony.

Riders can search for this magical feeling or they can live without, but most of us, once we experience it, fall prey to its charming addiction, and choose to go for it. Once we get that feeling of harmony, we want it again and again.

The magic occurs when the horse is worked (both physically and mentally) in a way that honors his nature. That is, he is helped to use his body with "integrity," and he works freely and willingly for his rider while the rider has control of the balance. This is what I call "Dressage Dynamics," and when these dynamics are at work, the horse's muscles are physically used in a way that supples and strengthens but also preserves him. Mentally he feels free and unconstrained. This is true for horses of all types and disciplines as you can see from the photos on the pages that follow.

Intro 1 There's a little magic going on here! German Olympian Ingrid Klimke is aboard FRH Butts Abraxxas competing in Aachen, Germany, in 2010. Ingrid and "Braxxi" won the European Championships in 2011 and team gold medals at the Olympic Games in 2008 and 2012. This partnership is filled with joy. Braxxi freely works for Ingrid, and Ingrid's in the driver's seat!

The system of Dressage Dynamics is based on laws of nature that are fixed and dependable, and they, in theory, determine how horse and rider work in harmony.

Solving the Freedom vs Control Enigma

In everyday riding life, a problem commonly arises as a result of the conflict of interest between the horse that inherently wants to feel free and the rider who wants to have control. Too many riders find themselves compromising at this fundamental juncture. They give the horse a little freedom and they take partial control—a poor compromise.

Riders who are able to preserve the spirit of freedom in their horses are inevitably the ones who garner the prizes. Indeed, hunter judges reward the horse that looks free and has a quiet enthusiasm controlled invisibly by a beautifully balanced rider. Dressage judges also reward the freedom of the horse's movement when they evaluate the horse's gaits on their "freedom and regularity." This freedom is what makes horses beautiful.

On a deeper level, it's not about prizes. Riders who incorporate Dressage Dynamics in their riding are the most satisfied riders because they honor the inner nature of their horses, and they enable their horses to reach their potential. Fortunately, the horse is a herd animal by nature and happy to be under the control of a skilled rider. But what *is* a skilled rider?

Intro 2 Klaus Balkenhol and his beloved Goldstern—one of the most famous partnerships of all time. Goldstern, a Westfalen gelding, was purchased in 1981 as Klaus' Dusseldorf police horse for 6700 Deutsch Marks. Klaus had an American-like rise to fame with Goldstern. He was hard to miss as he competed in uniform, and his performances were always marked by such harmony. At the Barcelona Olympic Games in 1992, Klaus and Goldstern won team gold and individual bronze medals; at the World Equestrian Games in The Hague, team gold and individual silver; and another team gold at the Atlanta Games in 1996. Their winnings can't be counted, but the real victory is in this partnership that was so heartfelt. This photo was taken in 2001 at the Balkenhol family farm in Rosendahl when Goldstern was in his twenties. It looks as if the work is his own idea, but Klaus has perfect control.

introduction

Intro 3
This is a study in focus! Anne Kursinski, a five-time Olympian for the United States, is pictured here with Champ 163, a Holsteiner stallion, competing at Aachen in 2008. They are clearly of the same mind and body. Champ has the freedom to do his job, but Anne is at the helm. Although Anne had only had Champ for a short time, they nabbed the alternate position for the 2008 Olympic Games in Beijing where Americans won team gold.

How Riders Work

Part I (p. 7) is about how you can become a balanced and effective rider. Centuries of experience training horses have given us a collective equestrian knowledge that tells us how a rider should sit. Some riders are born with a feel for balance, but most of us spend thousands of hours trying to figure out how to balance in the saddle. In the process, we learn that a loss of balance creates tension, which inevitably prevents the ability to feel. The tense rider can't feel her horse and the tense horse can't feel his rider. All horses and riders have experienced this loss of balance and tension. However, as balance improves, feeling and timing return, along with effective communication and harmony.

In theory, riding in balance is easy, but the cavorting horse challenges the rider's seat and position. I'll show you how to use positive tension and pathways of energy that I call "Powerlines" to enhance and improve the effectiveness of your aids. With effective positive tension and Powerlines, you can use your aids with sensitivity at the right place, with the right intensity, and at the right time. Your aids will balance your horse so he feels free to work for you.

Intro 4 No need to ask if these two are having fun. This is the ideal picture of freedom with control, taken at a Pony Games event in Lamotte Beuvron, France.

How Horses Work

Part II (p. 85) is about the horse's balance and, specifically, how to help him overcome his coordination challenges. He has two issues:

First, he is crooked by nature, so the skilled rider helps him carry himself straight and aligned. Second, as a four-legged creature, the horse is eager with his front legs but innately unconscious about his hind legs. His natural inclination to do too much with his front end and not enough with his hindquarters puts him out of balance.

introduction

I'll show you how to develop positive tension and Powerlines in your horse. With supple positive tension, the horse is able to accept half-halts and transitions that slow down his front end, lift his torso, and encourage his hind end to thrust, reach, and carry so that he becomes straight, coordinated, and balanced.

However, just being in balance isn't the end goal. It's the place where you can begin the great adventure of developing your horse into the best athlete possible.

How Two Spines Meet in Balance

Part III is (p. 163) about developing a collected, athletic balance by regulating and monitoring qualities of your ride that give you control—without sacrificing your horse's feeling of freedom. These qualities are your horse's rhythm, energy, flexion, alignment, bend, height, and length of neck, and finally his line of travel. All these aspects of your ride balance your horse and make him supple and strong. They

Intro 5 Horses can feel free even when they're not going anywhere! Courtney King Dye is riding the Dutch stallion Idocus here at Aachen in 2007. This piaffe is active, supple, and rhythmic. Idocus doesn't feel even slightly constrained. This is Dressage Dynamics at work: The horse feels free even in high collection, and he's invisibly controlled by a perfectly balanced rider.

THE POSSIBILITY OF MAGIC 5

enable half-halts, transitions, figures, and movements to develop your horse into an athlete that starts to carry more of his weight with his hindquarters. A byproduct of this collected balance is a lightness of the horse's forehand. In this balance, he looks as if he's working on his own—as if the movements were all his idea.

Whereas this book dares to make promises of harmony and even the possibility of magical moments, it's really all about techniques of balancing where horse and rider spines meet. When the center of gravity of a balanced rider is directly over the center of gravity of a balanced horse—and the horse's hind foot steps under that place where two spines meet—the horse can carry himself and his rider in balance.

In these pages, I hope you can resolve the freedom versus control riddle for yourself. You can look at the underlying mechanics of how your body works, how your horse's body works, and what unites you in a partnership in which you are the leader of a dance that makes normal horses beautiful, and beautiful horses magnificent.

PART I • DRESSAGE DYNAMICS
How Riders Work

When you and your horse are in balance, it feels as though the horse is performing on his own. To an observer, the horse looks free and unconstrained despite being controlled by the aids of a rider, who sometimes can be quite small. This freedom is what makes the horse beautiful.

When there's a loss of balance, there's tension that prevents the ability to feel. All horses and riders have experienced this loss of balance and subsequent tension. But when they regain their balance, they can relax and the rider's ability to communicate is enhanced. Feeling and timing both improve.

In this part, How Riders Work, I explain the dynamics of how the rider balances. I explore the rider's seat and her use of positive tension to make supple and strong pathways of energy—"Powerlines"—that shape and "channel" the horse's energy so that he can balance (see p. 21). This simple system, Dressage Dynamics, gives your horse his freedom and gives you control.

how riders work

CHAPTER ONE

The Seat
The Place Where Two Spines Meet

The place where two spines meet is where the central nervous systems of horse and rider come together. It's a very sensitive area, but many riders, even after years of riding experience, have no idea how influential the seat can be. It's like the mind; we're not aware that we use such a small percentage of it.

The seat gives the weight aid, which is the only aid that a rider can't remove completely. She can release the rein, and she can take away her leg, but her weight is always there. However, the rider's weight can be regulated when and *only* when her seat is balanced (fig. 1.1).

The Balanced Seat

Three factors make a "balanced seat."

1 The Flexible Floor: The rider sits on the "floor" of her seat—that is, the triangular space within her two seat bones and pubic bone.

2 Supple Strength: The floor of the seat is flexible but stable and strong so it can follow the horse's motion with control. When a rider is learning, this takes mental discipline as well as physical strength and suppleness.

1.1 Courtney King Dye is riding Idocus at Gladstone, New Jersey, in 2007. Even with her tailcoat, one can somehow see how perfect her seat is; it is part of the horse's back at the place where two spines meet. Her elastic elbows connect her soft hands to her seat and back. These mechanics connect the horse's hindquarters to the bit from back to front and from front to back.

3 Building Blocks: The rider's body parts are like building blocks (see fig. 1.5, p. 13). Her bottom building blocks, her feet, should be directly under her, supporting her seat and upper body.

1 The Flexible Floor

The "floor of your seat"—the triangular space within your two seat bones and the pubic bone—moves as the horse's back and the correctly fitted saddle move (fig. 1.2). The multi-dimensional flexibility of your pelvis enables the floor of your seat to follow the horse's back with sensitivity. Surface follows surface. Your pelvis makes tiny three-dimensional movements. It can, for example, move each hip up, forward, down, and back. Independent from this, your pelvis can also be tilted in relation to your spine with your tailbone pointed down and forward, or back and up.

When you follow the horse's back with the floor of your seat, you're in the best position to grow tall in your *front* (fig. 1.3). This frontline is responsible for a rider's self-carriage in the same way that the horse's topline carries him. By anchoring your pubic bone and keeping your frontline tall, you stabilize your *core:* the 29 pairs of muscles that surround your center of gravity enabling you to move in a coordinated, controlled way.

2 Supple Strength

"Suppleness of the seat" refers not only to its looseness but also to its stability, which is based on core strength. The seat shouldn't be so loose that it's "out of control." Riders don't usually realize when their undisciplined seats slosh, slide, and shove. Some think that "using the seat" *means* shoving every stride. However, horses find a "noisy" seat distracting, annoying, or intolerable, so they "tune out" and simply ignore it.

While "using the seat" *does* imply that the rider is *doing* something, she should never move more than the horse's back moves until she gives an aid. Your passive seat follows the horse. When a rider who has been sloshing and shoving in the saddle with insensitivity for years makes an attempt at being perceptive and educated with her seat, it's amazing that the horse usually listens immediately.

1.2 The floor of the seat is the triangular space within the two seat bones and the crotch bone. By concentrating on her supple hips, the rider can follow the horse's back quite precisely with the floor of her seat.

how riders work

1.3 At the 2011 North American Young Rider Championships, Rachel Chowanec rides the PRE gelding Embrujado XI ("Mouse") owned by Lendon Gray. Lendon sent Rachel and Mouse to train with me at my Connecticut barn for three years. This photo clearly shows the elastic front of Rachel's body, from her anchored seat to her sternum to the crown of her head. This elastic frontline is as important to the rider as the elastic topline is to the horse. Mouse is using his body with great integrity—that is, in a "horse-friendly" way.

A PEEK INTO PART II: "How Horses Work"

Reach and Roundness

Reach is what gives horses their attitude of forwardness. Horses reach with their hind legs, they reach with their front legs, and they reach through the neck for the bit. The direction of the horse's reach is extremely important to the quality of your ride. By nature, the horse's reach to the bit is forward and downward (fig. 1.4 A), and in riding, it's key that we retain that forward and downward attitude under saddle. With his hind legs, the horse should ideally reach forward and downward, stepping to a point directly under his center of gravity. It's important that we help him do this so he can carry himself (and you) with greatest ease (see p. 100 on straightness and shoulder-fore).

The horse's *roundness* is a result of the reach of his hindquarters combined with his reach in front. If you visualize the front of your horse's spine (his neck) reaching forward and downward, and the tail end of his spine also reaching forward and downward, it's easy to see how and why the middle of his spine (his torso and back under your saddle) naturally comes up. It's also easy to see that the front legs can reach more freely when the torso and back are up. In this round shape, the horse builds a "bridge" of muscle that carries him and relieves his legs of unnecessary strain. Dressage Dynamics ideally enables the horse's natural posture to develop under the weight of a rider by using laws of nature to make the work easy and exhilarating.

1.4 A I love how the Oldenburg stallion Noble Champion reaches toward the bit. It's too bad we can't see his hindquarters because it looks as if he moves with great integrity. I'll bet his left front hoof is directly under his nose and his hind foot is stepping directly under his center of gravity. As a result of his great balance, he looks mentally relaxed too, which is evident in his alert but content eye. Energy flows through the base of his neck to his relaxed mouth, and his whole countenance is pleasant.

1.4 B My student Annie Morris is warming up the Hanoverian mare, Weltdancer ("Dancer"). Notice how Dancer reaches in the same way that Noble Champion reaches in hand. As Annie asks Dancer for more engagement of the hindquarters, Dancer will become rounder: Her croup will be a little lower as her hind legs bend more, and her back and torso will be higher. As a result of the torso being higher, the neck will lift proudly, and she will be more "closed" in her frame.

12 WHEN TWO SPINES ALIGN: DRESSAGE DYNAMICS

3 Building Blocks

Everyone knows how easy it is to stay balanced on a horse at a standstill or a walk. You simply need to keep your feet under your seat and your head on top as if you are standing or walking on the ground. This vertical, ear-shoulder-hip-heel alignment is important because it gives you stability based on gravity, and you can always depend on gravity. The dynamics of how you ride your horse can tap into this law of nature that never fails us; gravity grounds us to the center of the earth.

But when in motion, the thrust of the horse challenges the rider's vertical self. (Chapter Two—p. 21—is about how the rider can stay with her horse's motion.) When you learn to *follow* your horse and *not* use your seat in the walk, trot, and canter, it will be easy to learn *how* to use it. Do the exercise at the end of this chapter (p. 18). When your building blocks are in place, and your seat can follow your horse's back with sensitivity, you're in a position to use your seat with sophistication (fig. 1.5).

1.5 When it comes to towers, we know how important the foundation is! The rider's body is like a tower and her body parts are like building blocks. The rider's base of support is directly under her so it supports her seat and upper body.

The Weight Aids

When your riding position is balanced, you are able to regulate the weight in your seat. You can make your seat very light while remaining in the saddle, or you can make your seat heavier by adding weight to one or both seat bones.

The amount of weight needed in the seat depends on the circumstances. For example, if you want your horse's topline to become "rounder" (longitudinally supple) during your warm-up, you might *lighten* your seat. The light seat invites the horse's back to come up, and he uses his entire topline with more integrity. But, when the horse's back is already round and he is well connected or collected, you can sit more heavily, which causes your horse's hind legs to bend and engage more, thus making him rounder behind and under the saddle.

Your seat (weight) aids can also influence the horse's direction and line of travel. When you step into your right stirrup (without leaning), your horse follows your weight to the right. Imagine that you're balancing a book on your head, and the book starts to slip to the right. Your automatic instinct would be to step right. Your horse responds to subtle weight shifts in the same way.

The seat aids also regulate the length of the horse's stride, his rhythm, and *tempo* (the speed of his rhythm). In the rising trot, for example, the seat lifts and falls exactly with the timing of the horse's diagonal footfall. The same rhythmic emphasis is used in the sitting trot. Your seat bounces the horse as you would bounce a ball, developing energy and elasticity. Here's *The Official Instruction Handbook of the German National Equestrian Federation—The Principles of Riding* description of how the seat achieves that:

> "The rider seems literally to 'sit the horse on the bit,' creating and maintaining his desire for free, forward movement."

"A correct seat of itself acts as a positive influence on the horse's movement and posture, because the relaxed elasticity of the rider's spine, together with a deep seat and soft embracing leg contact, are stimulating the horse's back movement and impulsion. The rider seems literally to 'sit the horse on the bit,' creating and maintaining his desire for free, forward movement. Thus the rider is able to control the horse and to keep the elastic 'spring' in all paces, even in collection."

When you "sit the horse on the bit," your seat absorbs the energy and motion of the horse and then returns it to him in a Circle of Energy (see sidebar on p. 16). When the Circle of Energy is working, the seat is sometimes *passive* and sometimes *active*. Here's how it works:

1 The Passive Seat

The *passive* seat follows the movement. You'll practice following with a passive seat in the exercise on page 18. This seat is actually a "non-message." You don't add or subtract anything. You listen and absorb the motion and energy of your horse, and follow the saddle very precisely with the floor of your seat. You feel the energy flow forward from your horse's hindquarters, through his back and through your center of gravity toward your hand. The Circle of Energy (see p. 16) then returns the energy to the horse's grounded hind leg. Even though the seat is passive, the energy still flows in the same way it does when the seat is active.

The passive seat makes an active seat "audible" to the horse. If you can't achieve a passive seat, your intentional aids are cushioned in noisy static. But, when your seat melds with the horse's back, he wants to lift it and *follow your seat.* Then you start to be the leader of the dance.

2 The Active Seat

With the *active* seat, you ask your horse for either less or more: less or more energy, length of stride, or tempo of stride. The energy continues to circle and recycle in the same way. You continue to absorb your horse's motion and energy, which continues to flow from your center of gravity *toward* the hand and return to your horse's grounded hind foot in half-halts. Your active seat, together with your leg, activates the horse's back and hindquarters. Some people correctly call the active seat a "driving" seat, but the word "drive" has a harsher connotation than is usually intended. It implies "more" but the active seat can ask for more or less.

Connecting and Collecting Half-Halts

Throughout this book, I'll explore the half-halt as a method of rebalancing your horse to connect him and collect him. The half-halt uses both the passive and the active seat: The seat rides the horse forward and back, adjusting the length of stride, increasing (or decreasing) the tempo, or developing more (or less) energy. These half-halts shape your horse's energy, perpetuate it, and balance it, and they connect your horse's hindquarters to the bit and close (or open) his frame.

When your horse is working with suppleness through his back and stepping under his center of gravity, you can "bounce" him into bigger or smaller strides. Instead of a sustained aid, the half-halt sends a timely impulse to the horse. (For more information on half-halts, see pp. 94, 149, and 161.)

Focus on Your Seat

An amateur rider in her fifties went with her trainer on a horse-shopping trip. Her well-trained Grand Prix horse was getting older so she was looking for a younger one. It had been a long time since she had ridden young horses, but she was required to do so again and again on the trip and was, understandably, quite nervous. Every time she got on a new horse, her trainer said, "Just *trust* your seat." For a whole week, she trusted her seat—with good results. When she came home, friends remarked on how well she was riding her older horse. "The young horses taught me to trust my seat," she said. "Who would think that the young horses would help me with my Grand Prix horse? It's supposed to work the other way round!"

Concentrate on your seat more often, and trust that you can ride from that place. Even if you have a technically perfect position, your mind has to help you ride from your center. Focus on riding from your seat.

Listen with your seat too. What is it telling you? What is your horse saying? The seat connects you to your horse at a place where you can communicate most successfully—where two spines meet.

A PEEK INTO PART II: "How Horses Work"

Circle of Energy and Circle of Aids

Even though we can't see energy, it is a real force that we can control. Here's what we know about how horses and riders use energy.

When horses and riders are in harmony, they share their energy. That is, the rider absorbs the horse's energy and the horse absorbs the rider's energy in motion.

Experienced riders recycle the common energy with half-halts to keep it balanced and contained—and to economize. Riding recycled energy requires less effort.

When energy is recycled, it travels in a circle within the horse-and-rider unit. This Circle of Energy covers ground in the same way that a bouncing ball covers ground when a basketball player dribbles it down the court.

A rider can "shape" energy in the horse in the same way that a basketball player can shape the path of the ball either in short, quick bounces or in long, ground-covering bounces. The horse and rider's Circle of Energy can shape the horse into a closed, collected frame with short, high strides or into a long, thrusting frame with low, ground-covering strides.

How does the Circle of Energy begin? The rider closes her leg and can feel the energy thrust from one pushing hind leg and then the other, in rhythm. Riders can feel the energy travel over the horse's topline in a "pathway of energy" and go to the bit as the horse reaches for it. The rider feels the energy—in the form of weight—land in her hand. This weight would become heavy if it didn't recycle.

After the energy goes to the bit, how does it recycle and go back to the hindquarters? The rider's half-halts cause the horse to balance back instead of leaning on the bit. They cause the horse to "push away from the bit." He "bounces" lightly off the bit into self-carriage. At the moment of pushing away, the weight gets transferred back to whichever hind leg is on the ground and "engaged" (carrying weight). Then, in the next stride, the hind leg pushes off again, sending the energy through the forward pathway again (see p. 45).

Technically, in every stride, there's a tiny forward "Go" aid and a tiny half-halting "Whoa" aid: Go-and-Whoa-and-Go-and-Whoa-and…. That's the rhythm of riding horses when the circle of energy is working.

What, then, is the Circle of Aids? The rider's aids travel on the Circle of Energy. When the Circle of Energy is ideal, we say the horse is "through" because the energy goes through his entire body, and he responds to very small aids in a whole-bodied, self-perpetuating way.

Aids That Send One Message

The seat aids should work together with the leg and rein aids to give the horse a single, coordinated message. However, this doesn't always happen! Here are some examples of seat and leg aids giving contradictory messages: When the legs are "whispering" and the seat is "shouting," the horse is inclined to be hollow in his back; the energy from the hind legs is inadequate, and the shouting seat prevents that energy from going through the horse's back. When the legs are "shouting" and the seat is "shoving," the horse has too much energy and doesn't know what to do with it.

The seat aids must also work with the rein aids to give a single coordinated message. It's a common mistake, for example, for a rider's overactive seat and leg to ask the horse to cover more ground while her hand is asking him to cover less ground.

Contradictory messages are almost always caused by the rider giving unconscious aids or misunderstanding the influence of her position and aids.

The seat, leg, and hand should act as a single, consistent aid that improves the horse's balance.

The Horse's Responsibility

As you become more sophisticated in using your seat, you will realize that the horse has a responsibility, too, because the seat aids (and the others, as well) only work effectively when the horse is moving forward in a clear and steady rhythm; he is supple, he reaches for and accepts contact with the bit. These three qualities are the requirements of Training Level dressage, and they balance the horse. Maintaining these requirements is the horse's responsibility, but it's your responsibility to tell him that it's his responsibility. When your horse is balanced under the place where two spines meet, his back is supple and receptive to your seat.

EXERCISES

EXERCISE
Find the Floor of Your Seat

Purpose This exercise will help you gain control over the "floor" of your seat. Your horse will feel for your seat and start to listen to it. You might be surprised at how effective your very small aids will become.

Directions Pick up a relaxed but active walk in a comfortably connected frame, and look onto your line of travel.

Step 1 Feel for the "floor" of your seat—the triangular area within the two seat bones and the pubic bone. *Follow* the saddle very specifically as the horse moves. Be passive, not moving more than the horse's back moves. Be sure the floor of your seat doesn't jostle around or move more than the saddle. It might take a while before you feel you're successful, but be persistent. If your horse hesitates or stops, don't punish him, but quietly close the legs to encourage him onward. His misunderstanding is to be expected. Soon, your horse will give you a very clear rhythm.

Step 2 Look down. Notice that it isn't physically possible to follow with the floor of your seat when your head is down. Now, look up. When your head is correctly balanced on top of the spine, the pelvis is, once again, able to follow the motion of your horse's back. A well-carried head puts the trajectory of your eyes on the horizontal line of travel.

Step 3 When your horse is giving you a consistent walk, ask for bigger strides by closing your legs and following with your hips. Your horse's back will carry your seat forward in a motion similar to a wave coming to shore. As you follow with your hips into larger strides, they will move in a slightly larger wave. Then, ask for smaller strides by half-halting and following with a smaller wave. (For specific directions on the half-halt, see pp. 94, 149, and 161.) Your lower legs might need to remind your horse to keep the energy and the tempo going so he doesn't misinterpret the smaller movement of your seat as wishing for inactivity.

Step 4 Ask for canter. With your seat, feel all three beats of the canter, and follow smoothly.

1.6 U.S. Olympian Steffen Peters makes riding look so easy. Here we see him riding the Dutch gelding Grandeur at the Los Angeles Equestrian Center in 2001. Steffen provides his horses with supple boundaries within which they feel free but balanced. Chapter Two (p. 21) explains how you can develop these supple boundaries.

Step 5 Make a transition to trot: Interrupt the canter rhythm with your seat and thighs, then follow the movement of the trot with the floor of your seat. This takes very little rider movement.

Step 6 Follow passively with the floor of your seat, then ask for smaller strides with your seat. Your horse will probably think he should walk, but that should be *your* decision. Ask him to wait and take smaller trot strides until you specifically half-halt and make walk strides with your seat.

Step 7 Follow passively with the floor of your seat in walk. When you want to halt, half-halt and immobilize your seat.

Some riders coordinate their aids and use their position in such a way that they look like they aren't doing anything at all, and yet they're incredibly effective. U.S. Olympic medalist Steffen Peters demonstrates how to influence a horse passively with a soft but strong position (fig. 1.6). You only need to see a still photo to know how his horses feel about his aids. They're so soft that the horse can't resist them. However, a supple-yet-strong rider position sets boundaries that are clear and help the horse to balance. You'll see how in the next chapter.

Essential Information about the Seat

- The seat can give an accurate weight aid only when it is balanced.

- Three qualities make up a balanced seat:
    1 You sit on the *floor* of your seat—the triangular space within the seat bones and the pubic bone.
    2 The floor of the seat can follow the saddle because it is flexible but stable, too.
    3 Your legs support your seat and upper body.

- The seat influences the horse's direction, energy, frame, suppleness, and rhythm.

- There are two kinds of seats:
    1 The *passive (following)* seat gives no aid. Your skill at being passive makes an active aid more understandable to the horse.
    2 The *active* seat asks the horse for more or less movement.

- Half-halts combine the passive and active seat to *connect* and *collect* your horse.

how riders work

CHAPTER TWO

An Introduction to Powerlines

Positive Tension: The Easy Way to be Strong

When your body is *open*, your muscles are stretched, and you're in a state of *positive tension*—that is, *tension with suppleness* (fig. 2.1). In contrast, when your body is *closed*, the muscles are clenched, and you're in a state of negative tension. Lack of tension or slack relaxation also has the effect of closing the body. The state of your muscles is reflected in your posture.

Elastic *positive tension* enables the rider to be soft, supple, and strong, so her body can become a powerful conductor of energy. Riding with positive tension is much easier than riding with muscles clenched. In the photos (figs. 2.2 A & B), you can see that positive tension is

2.1 Annie Morris shows us that positive tension is physically supple and stretchy. It is also mentally positive. Negative tension is contraction.

2.2 A & B (A) Positive tension is joyous. (B) Angela Krooswijk rides Flash, a Westfalen gelding. Positive tension is obvious both physically and mentally with this Dutch pair. Angela and Flash have had a very successful partnership under the guidance of Dutch trainer Coby van Baalen. I hoped to capture some of her joy when I put her on the cover of this book. (In competition, that beautiful hair gets tucked away!)

AN INTRODUCTION TO POWERLINES 21

mental as well as physical. Horses and riders with *positive mental tension* have a positive outlook along with increased awareness and mental acuity.

Powerlines Channel the Horse

The rider's elastic, upright strength creates *pathways of energy* that I call "Powerlines," through which energy can flow. The rider's Powerlines are absolutely straight. They stabilize her position. And, as energy goes through them, they channel the horse's energy and sculpt (shape) his body by providing supple but solid boundaries within which the horse can balance easily. In this situation, the horse can stay in a frame that's comfortable and yet one that stays underneath his rider's seat.

If the horse follows his own path instead of his rider's, he goes "out of bounds" and "runs into" the rider's stretchy, firm Powerlines. If that isn't enough to put the horse back on the rider's path, the rider must give an active aid to remind her horse to stay "within bounds."

When a rider uses active aids unnecessarily, the horse may challenge her—sometimes negotiating, leaning on the aids, or overreacting to them. However, when a horse runs into a Powerline, he is less likely to challenge it, because he actually caused the aid to happen through his own actions—not the rider's. As a result, the aid is more likely to be perceived as an "absolute truth."

2.3 Annie demonstrates all the Powerlines well. Her stretchy, elastic Vertical Powerline goes from ear, shoulder, hip, to heel, and she uses it as a Spiraling Powerline as she turns slightly to the left. Her elastic Connecting Powerline goes from her elbow to the bit. Her Visual Powerline points the way. Her positive tension throughout provides a supple box within which her horse Dancer can play.

The rider has four primary Powerlines:

The *Vertical* Powerline: The line from ear, shoulder, hip, to heel helps the horse *go forward* by putting him in front of the leg (for more on this Powerline, see "The Vertical Powerline—Power to GO," p. 31).

The *Connecting* Powerline: The line from the elastic elbow and lower back to the bit helps the rider to connect the horse, collect him, and *slow him down* (for more, see "The Connecting Powerline—Suppleness to STOP," p. 41).

The *Spiraling* Powerline: Although straight, this vertical line spirals to help the rider *steer* through a turn (for more, see "The Spiraling Powerline—Flexibility to Turn," p. 53).

The *Visual* Powerline: The rider focuses on an object, which helps to balance her horse on her *line of travel* (for more, see "The Visual Powerline—Connecting to the Outside World," p. 61).

Whether you're short or tall, you can maximize your effectiveness on a horse when you use all the "verticality" you have. To find your Vertical Powerline, do Exercise 1 found at the end of this chapter (p. 26). (You can do this exercise anywhere not just on the horse.) It shows you that your Powerlines are all about using everything you have, from the soles of your feet to the crown of your head (fig. 2.3).

To find your Connecting Powerline and your Spiraling Powerline, do Exercises 2 and 3 (pp. 26 and 27). To find your Visual Powerline, do Exercise 4 (p. 27).

how riders work

Riding Out of Balance

Powerlines stabilize the position of the rider, but let's look at how Mother Nature is inclined to challenge these Powerlines. Riders can fall out of balance in four ways: *Longitudinally*, they can fall *behind the motion* or they can be *in front* of it. *Laterally*, they fall *left* or *right*.

One by one, let's look at what you can do about these problems.

Longitudinal Imbalance

1 Falling *behind the motion* is a common occurrence because the thrust of the horse naturally throws the rider back, even when she's in a perfect position to begin with. Sometimes, a rider leans back because she is pushing the horse forward incorrectly. This behind-the-motion position of the rider is like a mild, but perpetual, version of the jumping rider who gets "left" at the fence. Anyone who has felt this helpless "kite-in-the-wind" feeling remembers how impossible it is to change her position. The behind-the-motion rider is always stiff and unable to make voluntary, clear aids. She causes her horse to be stiff, too.

2 The rider can also make the mistake of being *in front of the motion*. This problem is less damaging to the horse, but can be dangerous. Typically no one falls off the back of a horse, but plenty have gone over the front.

2.4 A To be laterally balanced you must put 50 percent of your weight on each side of the horse. This young Pony Games rider makes that looks simple!

(continued on p. 24)

AN INTRODUCTION TO POWERLINES 23

(continued from p. 23)

Lateral Imbalance

On a curved line to the left, centrifugal force "throws" the rider to the outside (to the right). As the rider's weight gets thrown onto her right foot, she is forced to compensate by collapsing in the rib cage to the left. Also, the innate crookedness of the horse's body can make a rider crooked. As long as she conforms to her horse's anomaly, she'll never be able to correct it. Riders can also do other strange variations of lateral twisting that are difficult to categorize, and it's not useful to do so.

The rider who aligns her spine precisely with her horse's aligned spine is on the road to effectiveness and harmony. When the spines are aligned, 50 percent of the rider's weight falls to the inside of the horse and 50 percent to the outside (figs. 2.4 A & B). This makes the rider able to be stretched and strong, as she is when she is standing tall with good posture. This stretched and strong positive tension enables energy to flow through the rider as it flows through her horse, and it helps her keep her balance.

Use your Powerlines to stay balanced over the center of gravity of your horse. For this, you need a horse that is in a consistent, self-perpetuating working pace to begin with. Remember "The Horse's Responsibility" (p. 17)? The horse must also have positive tension in his body. His commitment to rhythm, suppleness, and contact is a prerequisite for the rider being able to stay balanced.

2.4 B It's surprisingly difficult to find a photo in which the rider carries her weight equally left and right but Lynne Maas comes very close.

2.5 British Olympic medalist Carl Hester rides the Dutch stallion, Uthopia ("Uti") at the European Championships in 2011. Notice how positive tension enables Carl's position to channel Uthopia freely forward in extended trot.

Core Muscles

Powerlines are stabilized by supple but strong core muscles that surround your center of gravity. Twenty-nine pairs of muscles make up your stable core that connects your seat to your Powerlines, and enables you to move in a coordinated, controlled way. The core muscles keep you balanced when the laws of nature tend to throw you out of balance. Exercises 5 and 6 at the end of this chapter strengthen the core (p. 28).

how riders work

Supple Joints Make Supple Powerlines

The rider's Powerlines need to be supple: relaxed yet controlled, flexible yet strong. Suppleness occurs in very small places, for instance, in joint capsules. But the effect of supple joints isn't small. When all the rider's joints are supple the rider appears to move very little, or not at all. She is fluid and melds with her horse easily. When joints are not supple but instead are uncontrolled, they move too much, resulting in gross (visible) movement.

All joints have "end" positions and "middle" positions. Ideally, your heel, for example, should be able to spring down in motion with the help of gravity so your ankle can act as a shock absorber. But, when your heel is thrust down completely, your *ankle* joint is in an *end* position where it can't be supple (fig. 2.6). When the ankle is locked in an end position, it can't be flexible and absorb motion. It makes the entire

2.6 When a joint—the ankle, for example—is in an "end" position, it can't be flexible. This stiffness reverberates throughout the rider's entire body. Rachel demonstrates this with her heels too far down.

AN INTRODUCTION TO POWERLINES   25

rider stiff. This little stiffness reverberates up through the rider's whole body and can cause a bobbing head, flapping elbows, slouching shoulders, collapsing ribs, and other postural abnormalities.

However, when a joint is in a *middle* position, it can absorb concussion. Imagine both ankles absorbing motion equally, left and right. When they do, your Vertical Powerline is straight. This Powerline encourages the horse to be in front of your leg and go forward when you ask him to. When all your Powerlines are "supple," they can shape your horse's body and balance him on his line of travel. He feels free to move in relaxation. Try Exercise 7 to help you develop supple joints (p. 29).

EXERCISES

EXERCISE 1
Find Your Vertical Powerline

Purpose To give you a powerful vertical presence that uses gravity to make you supple and strong.

Directions To find and strengthen your Vertical Powerline, imagine yourself in a riding stance in a small boat, facing the bow (fig. 2.7). Your feet are grounded as if you were riding. Now, turn on the imaginary engine and start to go forward in your boat. The sea may be slightly rolling and you'll need to go with the motion. Your body should automatically assume a tall stature from your feet to the crown of your head. This Vertical Powerline is strong, but also supple. Your hips, knees, and ankles move in a way that keeps you balanced.

2.7 To find your Vertical Powerline, imagine standing in a boat when the seas are slightly choppy. Notice how your joints are supple to accommodate the movement. This image gives you a feeling for your Vertical Powerline; it's a powerful vertical presence that uses gravity to make you supple and strong.

This is the way to ride a horse—with a supple, strong Vertical Powerline. This strength enables you to be coordinated and strong enough to sit in balance no matter what the horse is doing.

EXERCISE 2
Find Your Connecting Powerline

Purpose Made famous by Finnish Olympic medalist Kyra Kyrklund, there is probably no better way of getting the right feeling for the connection.

Step 1 Stand at a halt. Ask a friend or your trainer to push the back of your upper arm forward toward the bit.

Step 2 Resist the push very slightly so your arm feels elastic (fig. 2.8). This causes you to engage muscles in your upper back in the area of your shoulder blades (that lie flat against your back) and the back of your armpits. These are the muscles that create a connection from the elbow to the bit—a connection in which the hand can influence the horse without pulling back. It feels like the energy flows from your elbow to the bit without backward influence. In this situation, you can stop or slow the energy by fixing your hands or closing your fist—not by pulling back.

EXERCISE 3
Find Your Spiraling Powerline

Purpose To help you stay compact and controlled as you turn through corners and bent figures. In the process, it will keep your horse compact and controlled too.

Directions Imagine you are standing in the same small boat as in Exercise 1. Now you want to steer it to the right, so you spiral (like an old-fashioned barber pole) to the right, which puts a little more weight toward your desired direction of travel—in the right foot. This is exactly what you do in the saddle, too. When you spiral to the right, more weight automatically transfers to your right inside stirrup, and your right inside seat bone becomes just a tad heavier. Your horse steps under your weight and turns.

Sit straight on both seat bones so you don't abandon your horse on the outside (left). When you imagine being in your small boat, it's easy to keep your outside foot down because you wouldn't last long if you lifted it!

EXERCISE 4
Find Your Visual Powerline

Purpose To give you a sense for how influential your line of vision is to the balance of your horse (see also fig. 6.2, p. 63). Try this at the beginning of your ride:

Step 1 Sit with the floor of your seat down, the crown of your head high, and your line of sight horizontal to the ground. At a walk, go around your entire riding space in this posture, once to the left and once to the right.

2.8 This exercise is a favorite of Kyra Kyrklund's. Annie resists the pressure on the back of her arm, which engages the muscles in her upper back but keeps her forearms pliable enough to channel the energy from back to front. This exercise gives you a feeling for your Connecting Powerline.

Step 2 In this same posture, pick up trot and go around once to the left and once to the right.

Step 3 Now do the same in canter. This exercise for your Visual Powerline only takes a few minutes, but self-discipline in the beginning of your ride can improve the balance for your whole ride.

EXERCISE 5
Strengthen Your Core with the "Bridge"

Purpose To strengthen the core muscles that coordinate your seat and your Powerlines. In this exercise, your body will arc into the shape of a bridge.

Step 1 Lie flat on your back with your knees bent, feet placed the width of your shoulders apart, arms at your sides, palms down.

2.9 Annie shows us the Bridge pose that strengthens her core muscles.

Step 2 Push through your heels and lift your hips to a height that aligns them with your knees and shoulders (fig. 2.9). Hold to the count of three and lower them to the ground. Repeat. Increase the duration of the pose and the repetitions as you feel comfortable.

EXERCISE 6
Strengthen Your Core with Push-Ups from the Forearms

Purpose To strengthen your core without stressing your wrists as normal push-ups do.

Step 1 Lie on your stomach. Place your elbows directly under your shoulders and clasp your hands (fig. 2.10).

2.10 Annie demonstrates the modified push-up that strengthens her core muscles.

Step 2 Lift your body in alignment and hold for a count of five. Lower yourself and repeat. Increase the duration of the pose and the repetitions as you feel comfortable.

EXERCISE 7
Keep Your Powerlines Supple

Purpose To enable your movement to be subtle and soft.

Directions When you ride, minimize your gross (visible) motor movement. Concentrate on the small spaces within the joints of your fingers. Feel the spaces between your ribs. Concentrate on all the small places within your body, and know that those are the places that make you supple.

Essential Information about Positive Tension and Powerlines

- Positive tension in your body is elastic and supple. It creates Powerlines through which energy flows. Powerlines help to "sculpt" the horse. They create positive tension, channel his energy, and put him in a shape that balances him. There are four Powerlines for you to use:

    1 The Vertical Powerline helps you ask your horse to go forward. It puts the horse in front of the leg.

    2 The Connecting Powerline helps you connect your horse, collect him, and slow him down.

    3 The Spiraling Powerline helps you steer.

    4 The Visual Powerline gives you a "magnetic" ability to accurately follow your line of travel.

- Positive tension is also mental. You feel it as a positive outlook with increased awareness and mental acuity.

- When the horse is balanced within your Powerlines, he feels free to move in relaxation.

CHAPTER THREE

The Vertical Powerline
Power to GO

When it comes to building a tower, the bottom block is a big deal. The tower has to be balanced and centered over that foundation. The rider's "tower"—her Vertical Powerline—is in three-dimensional motion, so that bottom building block—the rider's foot—had better be under her "tower" in such a way that it is prepared to let the body "spring" in a forward direction with supple joints (see fig. 1.5, p. 13).

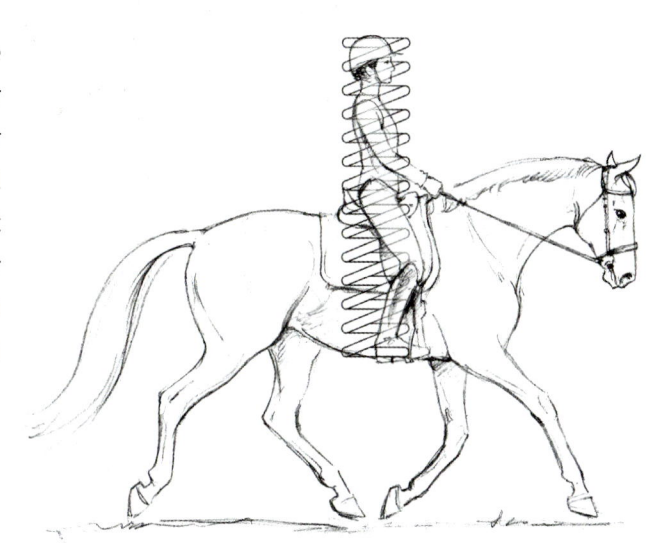

The Rider's Foundation

The rider's *feet* serve as that extremely important bottom building block, and when the rider is vertically aligned, she has the same reference to the ground as when she is standing on it. This "stance posture" is grounded to the earth and balanced according to the law of gravity. The great thing about gravity is you can always depend on it. When your feet are directly below your center of gravity, your weight is supported and in self-carriage. You're in a perfect position to ask your horse to be responsive to the leg.

On your horse, you feel as stable as if you were standing on solid ground, but you are active, like a vertical spring with flexible ankles, knees, hips, and elbows (fig. 3.1). As long as you can stay vertically aligned, balanced, grounded to the earth, and supple, you won't need to use muscular strength to stay on your moving horse. You *do,* however, need *core* muscular strength to stay vertically aligned and balanced when the horse's movement becomes challenging.

3.1 The rider's body is like a tower of building blocks, and her foot is the bottom building block. That bottom building block needs to support the rider's body so that the body can spring in a forward direction with supple joints. The rider's Vertical Powerline is elastic and can enable the rider to "bounce" her horse forward.

3.2 Rachel reviews her "Posture Checklist" as she rides. There's not too much to complain about here, but her hands look a bit flat, so I'd like to see her forearms turned so her thumbs are up. Also, her heels might be too far down—or I suspect they aren't in the bottom of her boots.

Posture Checklist for Your Vertical Powerline

Pelvis

Find your Vertical Powerline bit by bit (fig. 3.2). Begin with the *seat*. Sit on the "floor of your seat," the little triangle that is within the two seat bones and the pubic bone. If your saddle fits your horse and you, it positions the floor of your seat horizontally to the ground. You want this little triangle to follow the lowest point in the saddle. Focus on the *pelvis*. A supple pelvis (in the *middle* position, see p. 25) allows the floor of your seat to follow the motion of the horse with precision. But, the rider's pelvis is positioned incorrectly when it is:

1. Too much on the crotch (an *end* position).
2. Too much toward the tailbone (an *end* position).

In these positions, efficient communication with the horse is impossible.

From the floor of your seat, reach up gently through your spine so the crown of your head is closer to the sky, as if you were a puppet on a string. Thinking about that string makes your head high, your tailbone low, and your feet deep. The top and bottom of your spine stretch gently in opposition. Think of the crown of your head as your poll. This is how you develop positive tension and become a positive rider (fig. 3.2).

Spine

Your *spine* doesn't end at your neck. It goes up into your head. When a rider looks down or juts her chin and head forward, her vertebrae collapse to an *end position*. Breaking at the base of the neck by looking down also prevents the energy from flowing "through" you, as you want it to flow "through" your horse. Just as you want your horse to use his entire spine in one piece, you want to use your spine in one piece, too.

Shoulders

Square, flat, low *shoulder blades* that lie close to your back align the spine so none of the vertebrae are in end positions. Flattened shoulder blades are felt in the back of the armpits, and they open the rider's frontline by broadening the area around the sternum. Your frontline is the elastic connection between your anchored pubic bone and your sternum. Your open frontline points your horse positively on his line of travel. Gravity works on the top of your shoulders so they fall softly down, making the elbows deep and elastic. In fact, your whole body oscillates rhythmically with the horse's movement and with your breath. You appear (to admiring spectators) to be still because you *are* still in relation to your horse's motion. The precise mechanics of your shoulders, shoulder blades, and elbows are critical to the Connecting Powerline that I'll talk about in the next chapter (see p. 41).

Abdominals

Your *abdominal muscles* connect the floor of your seat and the core muscles that surround your center of gravity to your sternum and entire shoulder girdle. This elastic mechanism stabilizes and coordinates your Vertical Powerline so you can connect and then direct your horse.

Hips

Next, focus on your *hip joint*, a ball-and-socket joint that unites the thigh and the pelvis. It has tremendous swiveling mobility. This looseness enables your seat to swing with the horse, but be aware that it needs to be controlled so your seat doesn't move around too much. When the knee and toe swivel out, it means the hip joint is too loose. Most problems with knee and toe "behavior" are caused by the hip joint, so "complaining" to your knee and toe doesn't help! An uncontrolled hip can also cause the heels to go too far forward so you lose your base of support.

When the knee pinches, the hip joint is too tight. A tight knee focuses the rider's weight on the horse's forehand where he is already inclined to be balanced. When the rider clings to the saddle, she's stuck in her horse's balance and can never influence him to a better balance. She's riding the *saddle* instead of the horse, which isn't nearly as much fun. Gravity isn't her friend because negative muscle tension is getting in the way and making her use her saddle as a frame of reference instead of grounding to the earth. The rider needs to keep her own balance based on gravity, and the horse gains his balance from the rider. The Vertical Powerline is like the pole of a merry-go-round horse.

> When the rider clings to the saddle, she's stuck in her horse's balance and can never influence him to a better balance.

Legs and Feet

Ideally, your *legs* hang loose but solid with the *knees* and *toes* pointing in the same direction controlled by the hips. Your knee falls down by virtue of gravity and supports you so you can give your leg aids from the flat of the calf, which ensures that you don't inadvertently use the spur. Horses respond to unskilled use of spurs with negative tension. Also, when a rider turns the toe out and uses the back of her leg, she loses her balance because her base is not supporting her. Then when the horse goes forward, the rider falls behind the motion, and the horse goes into a downhill frame. Using the flat of the calf keeps both horse and rider relaxed and balanced.

Gravity works on your *heel* as well as your knee; a supple ankle allows your heel to fall down *every* stride—not every other stride, as is common in the rising trot when the rider is tempted to clutch the horse's barrel at the sitting moment.

Your leg should let gravity do its thing and follow the horse's oscillating rib cage. The leg "falls down" into its place and "drives" as it sinks down. When you need to change this aspect of your riding, it will feel awkward until you get used to it. Although your legs should fall down, your stirrups shouldn't be too long. The legs can't be relaxed and flexible when they are stretched to an *end position*.

Be sure your *feet*—the bottom building blocks—are under your seat, but your weight shouldn't be centered on the stirrups. Look at the anatomy of your saddle: The stirrup leather falls directly below the stirrup bar, which is clearly in front of your seat. So the stirrup can't support the weight of the rider because it's not *under* the rider; it's *in front of* the rider.

When the rider carries her weight on the stirrup, her torso can fall behind the motion or she might need to pitch forward in an attempt to find her balance—causing her to look down. Let your weight fall on the *front* of your heels, which *are* under your seat. Then, rest the balls of your feet on the stirrups, relaxing the muscles on the top of your feet so your ankles can do their job as shock absorbers. Riders don't usually think of the muscles on the top of their feet, but when they are tense, the entire body loses its suppleness.

Centered Riding founder Sally Swift's advice was, "Ride with your bones instead of your muscles!" She wanted us to center our bones over the bottom building block. There's no negative tension (tight, closing, muscular tension) when you ride with your bones. When muscular strength isn't causing you to hold on to the saddle, you can be "independent" *in* the saddle and independent *from* the saddle—that is, free to use your aids with intention, free to use them in the specific place you want, with the specific intensity and at the specific time you want—in sync with the horse's movement.

When the energy is going "through" the rider, the soft motion of the rider's seat flows down through her legs and is echoed in her feet. Feet that move up and down with a relaxed, supple ankle are a clue that the rider has a good seat.

Begin each day with this Posture Checklist going from your seat to the crown of your head, then from your seat to the soles of your feet. Practice sitting well at the dinner table, at your computer, and at the wheel of your car. Then maintain this position on your horse at a halt, at a walk, at a canter, and finally the often-more-challenging trot. To increase the strength of your Vertical Powerline, do Exercises 1 and 2 on pages 36 and 37.

"In Front of the Leg"—The GO Button

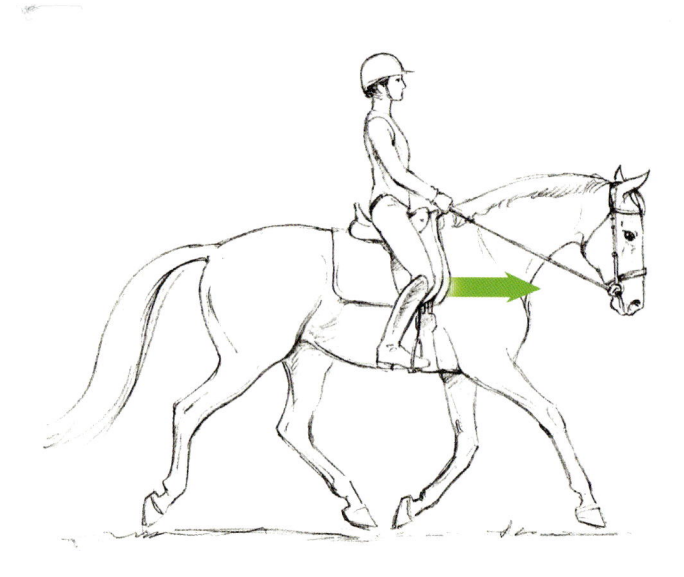

The term "in front of the leg" refers to the horse's ability—and willingness—to react to the rider's leg aid immediately. Being in front of the leg is not about speed, but it has a "starting-gate" quality. The horse that is in front of the leg does prompt transitions easily because the Circle of Energy (see p. 16) is working, and he is eager but relaxed. The horse being in front of the leg is a quality that all riders strive for; it's evidence of an eager horse stepping up to the plate to do his share in the name of harmony.

I'll talk about "in front of the leg" often throughout this book (see p. 70), but for now, know that maximizing the length of your Vertical Powerline is a prerequisite (fig. 3.3). When your leg is stretched and grounded to the earth, your horse feels your weight fall to a specific point, and it is this point that defines the place on the ground where your horse needs to step.

On the other hand, when the rider's leg is lifted up and is prodding, the horse can't feel it and he has no reference point on the ground—there is no definite leg for the horse to be in front *of*. He needs to use your bottom building block (your feet) as a reference point so he can step directly under your center of gravity. Be sure to step down into your feet when you ask for upward transitions so your horse can feel your Vertical Powerline and use it as a reference point for the place he should step. To confirm the "Go" aid, try Exercise 3 on page 38.

3.3 Maximizing the length of your Vertical Powerline gives you the ability to put your horse in front of the leg. When your leg is long and grounded to the earth, the horse is easily able to step in front it. The rider feels like her horse has the "green light."

EXERCISES

EXERCISE 1
Strengthen Your Vertical Powerline

Purpose To show you how easy it is to be strong when you use positive tension and Powerlines.

Directions Do a square halt next to your instructor or a friend.

how riders work

3.4 The Vertical Powerline is quite strong. I can't push Annie out of position, but the pressure I'm exerting has moved her horse!

Step 1 Make yourself vertically strong through the side that is closest to your friend. Send all your energy down through the sole of your foot so you feel grounded to the earth. Feel how your seat automatically deepens on that side.

Step 2 When you feel quite strong, ask your friend to reach above your elbow and try to push you away from her (fig. 3.4).

If you've effectively made a strong Powerline of energy, your friend will succeed in moving your horse, but not you. That's proof of the strength of positive tension. Lines of energy are much stronger than muscles. Maintain your length and strength while you ride.

EXERCISE 2
Pedal to Strengthen Your Vertical Powerline

Purpose To help put your horse in front of the leg in walk.

Directions To maximize your Vertical Powerline in walk, imagine that it's not too different from walking on your own two feet. Your legs support your hips, your torso

THE VERTICAL POWERLINE

and your head, just as they do when you're walking, and the energy goes down alternately—to the left, right, left, right. Try it.

Step 1 Step to the left and the right in the rhythm of your horse's walk. It might feel like you're pedaling a bike. As you do this for the first time, don't let your hips shift left and right. Your walking—or pedaling—movement is very subtle. It should be invisible to an observer; it should never result in gross shifting of weight. To help keep your base of support under you, Sally Swift suggested that the rider "pedal the bike" backward.

Step 2 When you're pedaling a bike, you never pull your foot up; you always push it down. Here's how it works on a horse: As your horse's hind leg leaves the ground, your leg on the same side naturally drops because the horse's rib cage swings away from it. In this phase of his stride, let your weight drop down into the stirrup. Then, as the other hind leg leaves the ground, let your weight drop down into your opposite stirrup.

Step 3 If you have a hard time feeling when a hind leg leaves the ground and you don't have a mirror in the arena, ask a friend to say, "Now, Now, Now," each time the inside hind leg leaves the ground.

Step 4 If this doesn't work, watch for the moment when your horse's inside shoulder is farthest back, which is the same as the moment that the inside hind leg leaves the ground. This is simply following the rhythm of the horse's movement; the rhythm is his language and it invites the rider to "speak" in the moment when the horse can best be heard. When you are successful in this pedaling exercise, your supple but strong Vertical Powerline will help keep your horse forward and "in front of the leg."

EXERCISE 3
Turn-on-the-Forehand to Help the GO Aids

Purpose Called the "Three Serpentine," this exercise helps put your horse in front of the leg in walk.

Directions Make a three-loop serpentine with half turns-on-the-forehand on the centerline. The turns will make your figure into the shape of a "3," and you do the entire exercise with the same flexion and bend (fig. 3.5). Your horse's walk should march in a rhythmic, eager but relaxed fashion.

Step 1 Starting at C, track right and listen for the marching rhythm of your horse's walk. Count 1-2-3-4, 1-2-3-4. Start your three-loop figure in walk.

Step 2 When you get to the centerline, keep your right flexion, do a momentary halt then make a half-turn-on-the-forehand from your right leg.

Step 3 Continue with the next loop to the right toward B and repeat your turn on the next centerline. You'll finish at A. Your horse's response to the leg should improve until he can do his turn without losing the rhythm—or the eagerness—of the walk.

Pay Attention:
During your turn, avoid the common mistake of leaning with your upper body to the inside. Keep your body aligned with the horse's.

- If your horse is sluggish to the aid and you feel he doesn't stay with you in the tempo, use short, light, quick aids with your lower leg or your whip until he is stepping with you. Your aids should be in the same tempo as the walk rhythm.

- Maintain the flexion to the inside so the action of your inside leg can send your horse to the outside rein.

- Once your horse is prompt to your inside leg aid, you'll feel the energy go "through" him and land in the outside rein (see sidebar, p. 16). Your horse should follow your rein aid to whatever length or height of neck you desire. His topline should stay round, he should stay bent to the right and relaxed.

Step 4 Do the exercise to the left to make a big backward numeral "3."

Step 5 Do the exercise in trot. From trot, you'll need to prepare for a transition to walk and then do the transition, so start your preparation to walk when you reach the quarterline, then walk, do your turn-on-the-forehand at the centerline and trot off. You should be having a "conversation" with your horse's hindquarters. From your horse's point of view, his hindquarters are "out of sight and out of mind." The hindquarters are also out of your sight but can never be out of your mind!

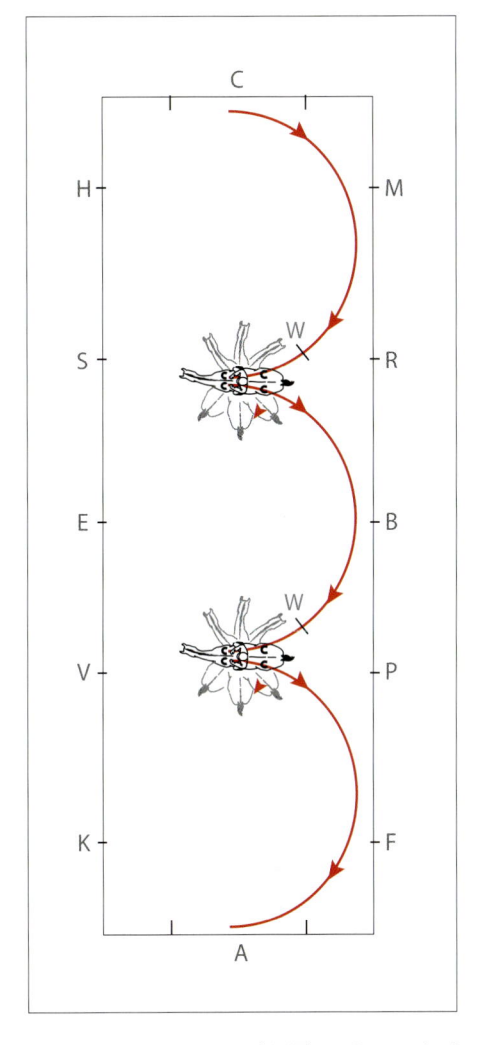

3.5 This "Three Serpentine" exercise enables the rider's Vertical Powerline to put the horse in front of the leg. Do accurate half-circles in your serpentine with half-turns-on-the-forehand on the centerline. Then ask your horse to step promptly forward again. Do this exercise in both directions.

Essential Information about the Vertical Powerline

- Your *feet* are the building blocks that provide the important foundation for your Vertical Powerline. They need to be positioned so that they support your body, which is grounded to the earth because of gravity.

- Use the Posture Checklist (p. 32) to develop a "stance posture" so that your feet are directly below your center of gravity, and the crown of your head reaches tall and your body is in self-carriage. In this stance posture, you're in a perfect position to ask your horse to be responsive to the leg.

- When you use *positive tension* to make a strong Vertical Powerline, your horse is inclined to be "in front of the leg" and is prompt to your aids to GO.

- The horse uses the depth of the Vertical Powerline as a reference point and steps directly under it and under your center of gravity.

how riders work

CHAPTER FOUR

The Connecting Powerline
Suppleness to STOP

The Connecting Powerline unites horse and rider. It's the straight line from the rider's elbow to the bit. The photo of U.S. Olympian Courtney King Dye in the first chapter shows this line very well (p. 9). It's been said that the rider's elbow is the most important joint in a rider's body. Here's why: The rider's elbow is elastically connected to her seat and back and also to the horse's sensitive mouth. It's the elastic link between the rider's Vertical Powerline (including the most important part—the seat) and her Connecting Powerline (including the most important part—the horse's mouth).

The elbow (and the entire Connecting Powerline) when uncontrolled, has the power to be rough on the horse. Sensitivity and skill are important in the building of trust. Within this Connecting Powerline, the horse shouldn't know where the rein ends and your hand begins. The passive rein, like the passive seat, follows—it follows the horse's mouth. The solid but soft, elastic texture is, ideally, the same throughout this entire line. Energy moves from the rider's center of gravity through her elbow to the bit as she follows the horse's mouth. The energy only goes in that direction—in the same way that water only goes one way through a hose: The rider can turn the energy off or slow it down, but it never goes from the bit to the elbow.

4.1 The Connecting Powerline—the line from the elbow to the bit—unites horse and rider. The rider's arm feels like it "reaches" for the bit, but the elbow is elastically connected to her Vertical Powerline, including her seat. This supple connection within the rider is responsible for connecting the horse's hindquarters to the bit.

Posture Checklist for Your Connecting Powerline

Elbows

Find your Connecting Powerline by beginning with your *elbows*. Whereas your hands belong to the horse, your supple elbows are elastically connected to your Vertical Powerline through your hips and your seat (fig. 4.1). The elbows connect you and your horse where two spines meet, and the quality of that connection is important. Keep your elbows elastically connected to your back and hips but slightly in front of them. Elbows that are too loose or sticking out fail to connect the rider's seat and back and the horse's hindquarters to the bridle. Elbows that aren't elastic enough cause tension because the contact isn't inviting; this makes the horse reluctant to reach honestly to the bit and it prevents him from using his whole body. Try Exercise 1, "Who's Drawing on Whom," to learn how the connection should feel (p. 49).

4.2 Rider, trainer, and 5* judge Lilo Fore says that riders can align themselves with their horses by imagining their upper arms as pillars that frame and stabilize the rider's core and the horse's forehand. In this photo, Annie's upper arms are firm without being tight, and they channel Dancer's forehand onto her line of travel. Annie's hips move with Dancer's motion; her seat and legs direct the horse's energy through these pillars.

Upper Arms

The rider's elbows work with flexible but stable *upper arms* that frame and channel the horse. FEI 5* judge and top trainer Lilo Fore helps riders align themselves with their horses by asking them to imagine their upper arms as pillars that frame and stabilize the rider's core and the horse's forehand (fig. 4.2). The rider's hips move with the horse's motion toward the contact, directing the horse's energy through these pillars onto the line of travel.

Wrists

When your *wrist* is in a *middle position* (see p. 25), it's as straight as it is when you shake hands, and your energy flows freely through the wrist and hand toward the bit. The back of your hand forms a straight line through the back of your forearm; this is the desired riding position. Your supple wrist asks for flexion by moving your knuckles smoothly from the *middle position* toward your belt buckle. A *hollow* wrist—in which the wrist rotates the knuckles away from the rider's center—is a tense wrist; it's an unnatural position and it blocks the flow of energy (figs. 4.3 A–C).

4.3 A–C (A) The correct position of the wrist is straight, as if you are going to shake hands. In describing this, Ingrid Klimke says the thumb is like a roof on the top of your hand. The rider maintains the right length of rein by holding the thumb against the index finger. The rider's other fingers can then be soft and flexible.

(B) The rein aid for flexion comes from the rider's inside fingers and wrist. Annie's hand stays forward and her wrist bends toward her belt buckle. Many riders make the common mistake of trying to create flexion by pulling the arm back.

(C) Annie demonstrates some common mistakes. First, this hollow wrist is stiff so she can't feel with sensitivity. Second, her thumb is not on the rein as it should be.

Hands

Keep your *hands* in a "work place" that is about the width of the bit, in front of the saddle and close to the withers. The *thumb and index finger* are positioned on top, and they hold the rein, preventing it from slipping and getting too long. Your other *fingers* are soft and are used, when needed, for suppling your horse. Although your fingers shouldn't move unconsciously—or constantly—they move when needed to give an aid.

Many people use the term "fist" when describing the hand, implying that the fingers are closed tight, which should rarely be the case. Closing the fist needs to be reserved for giving an aid. The rider with tight fists has no feeling in her hands, and communication from the horse to the rider is shut down. Energy doesn't flow through. To be "heard," this rider must then resort to being even tighter or pulling.

The line from elbow to bit needs to be flexible—not too loose or too tight. If the rein is too loose, energy can't go through it, and if it is too tight, there can be no feel. When contact is inconsistent, the horse has no way of recognizing a subtle aid. The elastic strength of the rider's torso and elbows allow her hands to be soft, following the horse's mouth.

Making the Connection

When, during the warm-up, you are suppling your horse, the reins might be a bit sloppy, but when you start the work session, your horse should "accept the contact." That's part of the purpose of Training Level dressage tests. "Acceptance of the contact" means that your horse "draws" on the reins—like a little fish on your line—even when you're using them.

Although acceptance of the contact is the horse's responsibility, it's the rider's job to tell him that it's his job. Horses aren't like cars that go into gear and stay in gear. Horses need "reminding" aids. When you close both legs, you can expect to feel your horse inflate ("puff up") in the forehand and come to your hand in a nice way. In horse-rider communication, your leg aids are like a ringing telephone; your horse needs to answer the "phone" by stepping "in front of your leg," through his back, to the bit. This is his way of saying, "Hello!" Be sure your reins are the right length and teach him to answer your ringing phone by reaching for the bit. Effective riders who look like they're doing nothing are actively checking in with their horses with frequent half-halts and transitions. Because of the frequency and the refinement of their communications, there is a measure of balance and ease.

A Well-Executed Half-Halt

The half-halt enables the dynamics of the Circle of Energy and pushing away from the bit. I'll be discussing half-halts frequently throughout these pages, but for now let's look at the three parts of a well-executed half-halt that makes pushing away from the bit possible:

1 The rider gives enough of a driving aid to confirm her horse's forward-thinking, soft commitment to her hand. The horse reaches for the bit. The rider's energy continues flowing forward. Then…

2 …the rider pushes with her deep Vertical Powerline into her fixed hand. She may need to close her fingers. This action closes or gathers the horse's frame from behind as he gracefully steps under his rider's center of gravity and adds a bit of weight to a hind leg. The horse's forehand stays relaxed. This half-halt simply causes the horse to push away from the bit and shift weight back to the hind leg. He lightens in front and improves his self-carriage (fig. 4.4). When the rider makes the common mistake of using her hand against the seat (pulling back), the horse shortens in *front* of the saddle instead of *behind* it, and the hind legs become inaccessible to her.

> The combination of the horse's commitment to the bit and the rider's well-timed half-halts cause the horse to push away from the bit consistently, creating a self-perpetuating ball of energy.

3 When the rider feels her horse add weight to a hind leg, she should soften her hands immediately. This softening invites the horse to stretch into the bit as he connects and collects, and it also gives him immediate reward.

The combination of the horse's commitment to the bit and the rider's well-timed half-halts cause the horse to *push away from the bit* consistently, creating a self-perpetuating ball of energy—the Circle of Energy on which the rider's aids travel with ease.

A PEEK INTO PART II: "How Horses Work"

Pushing Away from the Bit—the Ideal Contact Situation

When your horse reaches for the bit, he "pushes" on it slightly. We sometimes hear riders complain: *My horse is pulling*, but the horse, from his point of view, can't pull on the bit. (The rider sometimes pulls, though.) The horse reaches for the bit and pushes on it slightly. If he pushed on it more than slightly, he might end up "leaning" on the bit and using your hands as a "fifth wheel."

Most riders know how the energy goes from a thrusting hind leg, through the back, and to the bit, but when I ask students in my clinics, "What happens to the energy after it gets to the bit?" most riders don't know. Here's what should happen:

Ideally, instead of leaning on the bit, the horse should yield to it respectfully, "push away" from it, or "bounce off" it. This moment of "pushing away" should happen every stride, and during that moment, the horse shifts weight from the bit back to his hindquarters. In that moment of shifting the weight back, your horse becomes lighter in front and his self-carriage improves.

There's a little "Go" and a little "Whoa" in every stride—just as there is a little "Go" and a little "Whoa" and "Soften" during every half-halt.

Here's how the dynamics of that works:

- During the "Go" moment, your horse thrusts and reaches with a hind leg, and the energy flows through your horse's topline and goes to the bit. Your horse pushes on the bit, and because of your dynamic, connected riding position, he draws on your Connecting Powerline, including your elbow, which engages your Vertical Powerline, including your seat. This connection causes the "Whoa" moment.

- At this "Whoa" moment, your horse pushes away from the bit, shifts weight to the hindquarters so he carries himself better, and becomes instantly lighter in the hand, which invites the next moment.

- This is the moment within the half-halt when you "Soften" all your aids, which invites the next moment, the "Go" moment of the next thrusting stride.

"Pushing away from the bit" should be an ongoing situation that happens within the self-perpetuating rhythm of pure gaits, and it results in the horse's proud self-carriage.

how riders work

4.4 In the half-halt, the reins that normally follow the horse's mouth become stabilized. Mica Mabragana demonstrates on Infanta HFG as she fixes the rein and pushes into it with her Vertical Powerline. As a result of Mica's half-halt, the horse's neck stays long and free as the hindquarters engage.

THE CONNECTING POWERLINE

Use the Hands Last

When you'd like to minimize the need to use your hands, always use them last. That is, always give your horse a chance to respond purely to your other aids—seat (weight) and leg. You can also use your voice. Then your horse always has a chance to respond *before* you use your hands.

Make your seat and leg aids so interesting that he can't help but listen. Make your rein aids boring and "after the fact." With this approach, you'll certainly minimize the need to use your hands. U.S. Olympian, Debbie McDonald, calls this "weaning the horse off the hand." The horse is ridden almost solely from seat and leg aids. However, using your hands last and least doesn't mean your connection can be less than ideal. On the contrary, your horse has to be *reaching to the hand;* he must be *in front of the leg* (see p. 69) and *on the seat*. When he steps under your seat, and he's working "through" his back and respectfully to the hand, we say he's "on the seat" or "under

Weak Hands

Hard hands lack the ability to feel. When German multiple gold medalist Isabell Werth conducted the 2001 United States Dressage Federation (USDF) Symposium in Phoenix, Arizona, she repeatedly told riders, "Make your hands *weak*. Follow the mouth." Her German-to-English translation of her intention enhanced the meaning (fig. 4.5). During that symposium, the riders evolved incredibly as a result of her constant requests to follow their horses' mouth with "weak" hands.

4.5 German Olympian Isabell Werth is one of the greatest horsewomen of all time. Here she is riding her Hanoverian gelding Satchmo at Wiesbaden in 2007. When Isabell gave a USDF-sponsored symposium years ago in Arizona, she counseled riders: "Make your hands weak and follow the mouth." You can see, in this photo, that she follows her own advice. At that symposium she also said, "Inside leg to outside rein" countless times. Later, she told me, "I said it as often as I think it when I'm riding."

the seat" because he responds purely to seat aids and you don't need your reins; he is "weaned off your hand." When your horse steps directly underneath your seat, his "self-carriage" includes carrying you!

Why do riders revert to the hands so easily? There are lots of reasons, and the most obvious is that we spend most of our lives exercising eye-hand coordination. Many riders have no experience influencing anything with the seat and legs. They don't know how it feels to have a horse bend and turn from the placement of the leg and seat, so they give up on that too easily. They don't persist because they have no way of knowing or trusting that leg and seat aids work. The system of Dressage Dynamics works, but only if you use it consistently.

Overuse of the hands is also a result of the horse not reaching honestly to the hand; hands don't work until the horse is stepping to the bit. But, the rider who persists in trying to influence her horse with seat and leg aids encourages the horse to step to the bridle, which is what makes the rein aids effective. Then she can communicate with her hands. To help minimize the use of your hands, try Exercise 2 (p. 50).

It's been said that everything you do on a horse involves some version of go, stop, and steer. If you use your Vertical Powerline for GO and your Connecting Powerline for WHOA, how do you steer? Remember, the Vertical Powerline can spiral to help you make a turn. We'll cover the Spiraling Powerline in the next chapter (see p. 53).

EXERCISES

EXERCISE 1
Who's Drawing on Whom?

Purpose To help you develop the situation in which half-halts work and your horse can push away from the bit.

Directions Within the rein connection, ask yourself: Are you drawing on your horse? Or, are you and your horse drawing on one another? Or, is he drawing on you? You want him to draw on you. The pressure in your hands should not be caused by you "holding" the contact or by pulling.

Step 1 Keep enough contact so the rein isn't loose, and your horse has the opportunity to draw on you.

Step 2 Then, ask him to draw on you by closing your leg.

Step 3 Once he is drawing on the rein, you can follow his mouth in the same way you follow him with your seat and legs—your rein aids will now become audible.

EXERCISE 2
Half-Halts to Minimize the Use of Your Hand

Purpose To practice riding forward in downward transitions in order to minimize the use of your hand.

Directions Before you begin, check these two aspects of your technique:

- Be sure your body is sitting toward the bit, not leaning back against it.

- As you shorten the strides, remember your softening aids after each half-halt—even exaggerate them (fig. 4.6). Feel as if you are "gathering" your horse from behind. Start simply by doing a downward transition from walk to halt.

4.6 Annie is shortening Forte's stride with half-halts, and she exaggerates the softening part of the half-halt. As a result, Forte feels he gets more freedom when he is collected instead of less! If you can do this, it will serve you forever when you ask for collection.

Step 1 First, confirm your horse's commitment to the bit, then…

Step 2 … half-halt by pushing with your seat and leg into your stable, fixed hand to shorten the stride. Don't make the common mistakes of leaning back or bringing your hands back. Ride the half-halt forward in a marching rhythm.

Step 3 When you feel the stride shorten, soften the rein. Exaggerate the softening so your horse's neck can actually become longer as you shorten the stride. He will feel that he gets *more* freedom when he is collected instead of less! This will serve you forever when you ask for collection.

Step 4 Repeat three times, and each time your horse shortens the stride, soften the rein. Half-halt-soften, half-halt-soften, and finally, half-halt-soften. On this third half-halt, immobilize your hips and your horse will close his frame from behind into a square halt.

By doing these transitions several times, you'll need to use less and less hand. Your halts will become more square as your half-halts start to influence each hind leg equally.

Step 5 Practice in both directions, and then practice with downward transitions from trot to walk and from canter to trot.

Essential Information about the Connecting Powerline

- The Connecting Powerline is a straight but supple line from the elbow to the bit. Your Connecting Powerline is attached to your Vertical Powerline when your elbow is elastically connected to your hip and seat. This connection unites and coordinates you and your horse.

- Control of the line from the elbow to the bit is important to the building of trust because it has the potential to be rough on the horse.

- Shared energy goes from your center of gravity through the elbow to the bit.

• This energy only goes in one direction in the same way that water only goes one way through a hose. You can turn the energy off or slow it down, but this energy never goes from the bit back to the elbow.

• Use the Posture Checklist to develop an ideal connection.

• When you offer an inviting hand, the horse must be trained to accept the contact.

• When the hand is passive, it follows the mouth of the horse.

• When you want to influence the horse, you can half-halt by fixing the hands (not following, see p. 74) and pushing with the Vertical Powerline into the contact. In this way, half-halts *connect* and then *collect* the horse from behind.

• Half-halts cause the horse to "push away from the bit." That is, instead of leaning on the bit, the horse yields to it, shifts a bit of weight to his hind legs, and lifts himself proudly into self-carriage. At the same time, he remains committed to reaching politely for the contact.

• When horses listen more and more to the seat and leg, you'll need to use your hands less and less.

CHAPTER FIVE

The Spiraling Powerline
Flexibility to TURN

As you know, your Vertical Powerline makes two walls that prevent your horse from falling left or right. For turning, however, this Vertical Powerline becomes a Spiraling Powerline. Your spine spirals to the right or the left—that is, your hips stay square with the horse's hips, and your spine above it spirals. As it spirals, your rein aids automatically move your horse's shoulders onto your intended line of travel.

Your head will be inclined to lead, but don't let it. Your shoulders, head, and elbows are passengers: They turn only because your spine spirals. If your hips were to turn along with the shoulders, your position wouldn't support the horse's bend and his haunches would swing out. So, to support the horse's bend, your hips stay parallel to the horse's hips, and your shoulders turn to ask the horse's shoulders to turn. Your spiraling spine causes the turning rein aids to come into effect: Your inside leg connects to the outside rein automatically. When the horse is working "through" his back, and you are grounded (because of your Vertical Powerline), your inside-leg-to-outside-rein connection (*diagonal* aid) lightens the horse's forehand and moves his shoulders to the inside.

Remember that your left and right Vertical Powerlines only work when your feet are *grounded* to the earth (see p. 31). If you grip the saddle with your legs, lift your heel, and try to push your horse to the left or right with muscles, the Powerline won't work. And, if you collapse in the ribs or the hips, it won't work. Whereas you must sometimes use active aids (with muscle) to *shape* your horse and show him how to stay within his boundaries (see p. 22) these aids shouldn't be prolonged so you end up "supporting" the horse.

You make a choice: Do I want to ride with muscle or with my weight and Powerlines? Weight and Powerlines are stronger for the rider and nicer for the horse.

Bending and Turning

Use your Spiraling Powerline to support and guide your horse as you channel him on your desired line of travel on straight lines, through bends, and corners (fig. 5.1). Your inside aids, along with your outside leg, shape your horse in bend. Your Powerline spirals ever so slightly on its axis toward the line of travel, which weights the

5.1 As Mica spirals slightly to the inside, Infanta's shoulders turn. Mica's buttons are aligned with her horse's crest. You can see, on both the inside and the outside, how Mica's aids shape her horse in bend.

inside stirrup. (Remember from the beginning of this book how your horse follows your weight—see p. 13.) Then your inside-leg-to-outside-rein connection supports the bend and turns your horse.

This inside-leg-to-outside-rein connection is effective only if you can stay straight and use your inside and outside aids equally. For this, you need to be aligned with your horse. Check to be sure your seat is square and your shoulders are pointed in the same direction as your horse's shoulders.

Keep the buttons or the zipper on your shirt aligned with your horse's crest, and be sure your horse's shoulders are mobile enough to align with your buttons. Keep your hips parallel to your horse's hips. This aligns your spine with that of your horse.

Use Exercise 1 to get the feeling of how to turn (p. 58). I have mentioned the *diagonal* aids—inside leg to outside rein—commonly used as the bending and turning aids. But almost all riders, in an effort to bend and turn the horse, are inclined to misalign their bodies in a way that "abandons" the outside of the horse. The horse's energy can only be channeled "through" his body when the rider is centered.

When my students have this problem, I remind them of the *unilateral aids*—that is, the aids on one side of the body. I call them the "Triangle of Aids" and discuss them next. We have an Inner Triangle of Aids and an Outer Triangle of Aids. It doesn't mean we stop using the diagonal aids, but it helps us remember to stay aligned.

> Almost all riders, in an effort to bend and turn the horse, are inclined to misalign their bodies in a way that "abandons" the outside of the horse.

The Inner and Outer Triangles of Aids

You can coordinate your aids easily by imagining a Triangle of Aids on the *inside* and another triangle on the *outside*. The surface of your triangular influence is wide. On each side, the triangle goes from your elbow to the bit, to your foot, and back to your elbow. Each triangle works like this:

- *The Inner Triangle (using the inside leg to the inside rein)* puts the horse in front of the leg and helps supple and bend him (fig. 5.2 A).

- *The Outer Triangle (using the outside leg to the outside rein)* connects the horse, collects him, improves "throughness," and turns him (fig. 5.2 B).

5.2 A & B (A) Rachel's inner aids make a triangle from her elbow to the inside of the bit to her inside foot and back up to her elbow. This Inner Triangle of Aids is responsible for suppling and bending Mouse and putting him in front of the leg.

(B) Rachel's outer aids also make a triangle. This Outer Triangle of Aids is responsible for Mouse's connection, collection, "throughness," and turning.

Visualizing these triangles helps you think of all the individual aids on the inside as one aid, and all the aids on the outside as one aid, so it is easier to coordinate them. Awareness of both the Inner and the Outer Triangles helps to keep you straight and the horse "through." Try Exercises 1 and 2 (pp. 58 and 59) for help in using your Triangles of Aids to develop "throughness."

When a horse is "through," he is using his entire body because the energy goes through his entire spine from his tail to his poll without interruption. Signs of throughness are: the horse sighs or blows air through his nose and lips, his back swings, and his tail—as a reflection of his whole spine—swings rhythmically. Remember his tail is part of his spine. It swings with his back. (For more about "throughness," see p. 102.)

Posture Checklist for Your Spiraling Powerline

Your Spiraling Powerline is actually the same as your Vertical Powerline, except it spirals to enable you to turn, so review the Posture Checklist for your Vertical Powerline (p. 32). In addition, pay special attention to *how* your body spirals:

Head

The rider's *head* must stay connected to her body with integrity. Many riders disassociate the head by looking too far through the turn or by looking down and to the inside. In the process, the rider becomes misaligned with her horse. Keep your chin in the middle of your chest—aligned with the buttons or zipper of your real or imaginary jacket. And keep your chin and your zipper aligned with your horse's crest.

Shoulders and Hips

The rider's *shoulders* and head turn only because her spine spirals slightly to the inside. The rider's *hips* stay squarely parallel to the horse's hips. This spiraling of the upper body causes the inside seat and foot to be slightly weighted, and it causes the rider's outside Triangle of Aids to turn the horse onto his line of travel. Because the rider's hips stay square, they are pointed in a slightly different direction from the shoulders. This is a very mild version of the sixties dance, "the twist." In fact, certain

German textbooks call this "the twisted seat," but the connotation of that term gives the wrong impression. With great ease, the rider's slight change in position should cause bend in the horse.

EXERCISES

EXERCISE 1
Confirm the Turning Aids

Directions Imagine your ideal turning aid: You spiral very slightly toward your direction of travel (without leaning) and move your hands in the same direction. Your horse's shoulders move easily to the inside and the hind end follows on a bent line. In this exercise, you will achieve this by riding a rectangular figure. Use the short end of your arena and the line between E and B. Concentrate on your four corners.

Step 1 Shape your horse in bend before the corner. Your inside leg will "fill up" the outside rein.

Step 2 Turn your horse with your Outer Triangle of Aids and soften the inside rein during the turn.

Step 3 If you lose the bend when you're using your Outer Triangle, then the bend isn't established well enough. Go back and fix that as you approach the next corner.

Step 4 Ride corners to the right and left in walk, trot, and canter.

The wise rider is always asking her horse if he *could* go, stop, and steer left or right *if she wanted him to.* When the answer is yes, yes, and yes, her horse is balanced so that he is "in front of the leg," "reaching to the hand" and "on the seat." Then, the horse's energy flows freely. Beautiful.

EXERCISE 2
Triangles for "Throughness"

Purpose This exercise helps the rider become aware of her unilateral aids (aids on one side of the body). Use of unilateral aids helps straighten the rider and align her with her horse so diagonal aids become more correct and effective.

Directions Ride on a 20-meter circle.

Step 1 Think about your Inner Triangle for one-quarter of the circle. Your long, inside leg asks the horse to be in front of the leg. This leg aid sends energy through his topline to your inside rein. During the time when you're concentrating on the Inner Triangle, your Outer Triangle automatically softens and becomes invisibly more passive; then the horse naturally goes slightly to the outside rein.

Step 2 For the next quarter-circle, think about your Outer Triangle. As you concentrate on it, your outside connecting aids are effective because the horse has just gone to them (in Step 1). "Snuggle" around him with those outside aids, and encourage him to step from the outside hind through his topline to the outside rein. With this connection, you ask him to wait for you and stay balanced under your seat. During this time, your Inner Triangle automatically becomes invisibly more passive, and the horse feels free and in better self-carriage with the help of the outside balancing rein. The outside aids also turn your horse on the bent line of the circle.

On each quarter-circle, alternate between awareness of the Inner Triangle and the Outer Triangle, and you'll see that your horse's balance and "throughness" are very much improved. The aids alternate. They become passive and then active. The horse comes more and more on the aids.

Step 3 As you become more coordinated, use each triangle "as needed," not just for a prescribed time or specific place on the circle.

Step 4 Make this exercise into a 20-meter figure eight so you can work your horse in both directions and gain control over both sides of him.

The *new* inside leg always says, *Stay in front of me and bend*. The *new* outside aids always say, *Engage your outside hind. Step through your body, but wait for me. Stay under my seat—the place where two spines meet.*

Essential Information about the Spiraling Powerline

- When turning, your spine spirals to the right or the left. The hips stay square with the horse's hips, and the spine above it spirals.

- The spiraling spine causes the turning rein aids to come into effect: The inside leg connects with the outside rein. When the horse is "through" and you are grounded, the inside-leg-to-outside-rein connection lightens the forehand and moves his shoulders to the inside.

- For the Spiraling Powerline to work, you must stay:

    1 Grounded to the earth, not gripping the saddle.

    2 Straight and aligned with your horse.

- Imagining an Inner and an Outer Triangle of Aids helps you stay straight and aligned:

    1 The Inner Triangle goes from your elbow to the bit, to your foot, and back to your elbow on the inside. The Inner Triangle puts the horse in front of the leg and helps to supple and bend him.

    2 The Outer Triangle goes from your elbow to the bit, to your foot, and back to your elbow on the outside. The Outer Triangle connects the horse, collects him, improves "throughness," and turns him.

how riders work

CHAPTER SIX

The Visual Powerline
Connecting to the Outside World

While the two primary Powerlines, Vertical and Connecting, sculpt the horse and stabilize his balance, the trajectory of the rider's eyes is a Powerline that goes out from your body—that is, outside the physical system. It connects you and your horse to the outside world. Your body spirals onto your line of travel, and your eyes focus on a point—a dressage letter, tree, fencepost, or a jump—and use it as a frame of reference so the horse can be directed on a planned course channeled by your grounded, Vertical Powerline.

Your bones are pointed onto the line of travel. With your spine aligned with the horse's crest, your toes, knees, hips, shoulders, knuckles, and nose all point in the same direction as the eyes—onto the line of travel (fig. 6.1).

The rider who is constantly looking at her horse's neck has a problem similar to the one who clutches the saddle with her legs. She will always be in her horse's balance; she uses her horse's balance as a frame of reference because she never looks outside it. The rider who stares at her horse's neck is committed to being "on the forehand" and can't influence her horse otherwise. Some riders have nervous eyes; they furtively glance here and there. The horse might experience this behavior in the same way a rider experiences a horse that is always looking this way and that. Maybe it's distracting; it surely can't help.

6.1 My daughter Jennifer Baumert is riding her favorite Grand Prix horse Weltgraf in half-pass. They are both focused on their precise diagonal line of travel. The precision of this line is important because the basic qualities of suppleness, bend, elasticity, and forward activity can only be retained when horse and rider are true to their line of travel. Thinking of your focus as a Visual Powerline provides a reference point that makes balance in the movement relatively easy.

Posture Checklist for Your Visual Powerline

Find your balance by asking yourself the following questions about your position:

- Do I feel the weight of my head in my seat?

- Do I feel the weight of my head and my seat in my feet? (If so, your legs are supporting your seat and upper body correctly.)

- When I spiral to the left or right, does my seat stay squarely in the saddle?

- Are my shoulders pointed in the same direction as my horse's shoulders?

- Are my hips pointed in the same direction as my horse's hips?

- Are my ribs equally tall, left and right?

- Are my eyes, my knees, toes, knuckles, sternum, and nose pointed on my line of travel?

Influence on the Horse's Longitudinal Balance

The trajectory of the rider's eyes has amazing influence over the horse's balance. It can help put horse and rider in a downhill, horizontal, or uphill balance. (See chapter nine, "How the Horse's Weight Distribution Changes," p. 107, for more information on your horse's balance.)

The angle of the floor of your seat in relation to the ground and your torso's position is determined by the horse's balance, but it is influenced by the trajectory of the rider's eyes. When the trajectory is in a downhill balance, your seat is not only inclined to be downhill, but it actually can't follow the horse's back.

When the trajectory of the eyes is horizontal, the floor of your seat offers the possibility of a horizontal frame for the "downhill" horse. It influences the horse's spine to travel in a horizontal path, thus improving his natural balance.

The horse's horizontal frame puts the floor of the rider's seat in a horizontal position. When the rider is in self-carriage with the trajectory of her eyes on a horizontal line, she can influence the horse to come into an uphill posture (fig. 6.2).

If you have problems with the trajectory of your eyes, imagine half-halting with your head. This encourages you to inhale and shift your head up, which improves your horse's balance both longitudinally and laterally. It puts the trajectory of your eyes on the line that encourages your horse to become better balanced. Your seat can't work when your head isn't balanced over the place where the two spines meet.

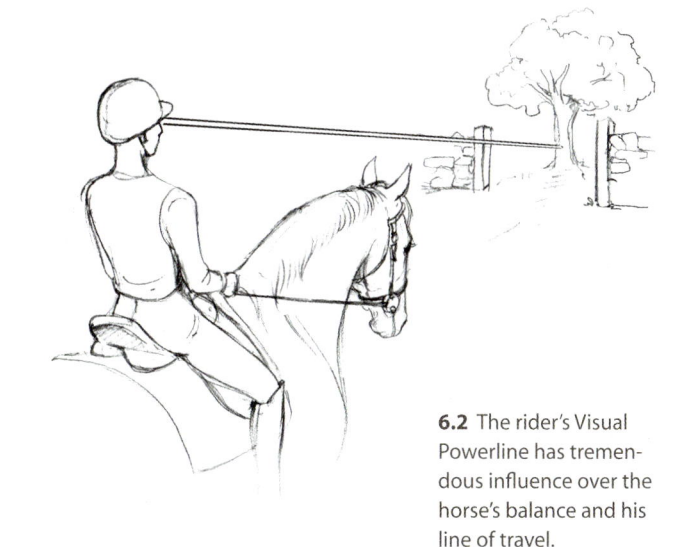

A Half-Halt to Rebalance the Rider

6.2 The rider's Visual Powerline has tremendous influence over the horse's balance and his line of travel.

Experienced riders may not realize it, but they rebalance and realign themselves constantly during a ride. They give themselves many "half-halts" to retain or regain *vertical* and *lateral* alignment. When the horse gets slightly out of balance, it causes the rider to want to hold on to the saddle, but the experienced rider takes her legs invisibly away from the saddle often to keep her position independent and help improve her horse's balance.

When the rider is balanced and aligned, with her joints in a *middle* position (see p. 25), she can be supple and relaxed. The energy from the rider's center oscillates through to the crown of her head and down to the soles of her feet. She absorbs her horse's energy, and the horse absorbs her energy. Energy flows through both as if they were one.

Unless the rider is balanced with the energy flowing "through" her, she can't half-halt to rebalance her horse and ask him to work through his body. The rider half-halt comes first. It all happens at the place where two spines meet.

From that ideal balance, the rider is in the best position to give clear, positive aids (see the next chapter, p. 67). To confirm your Visual Powerline, review Exercise 4 on page 27, then try the exercises that follow.

EXERCISES

EXERCISE 1
Steer with Your Eyes

Purpose To teach you and your horse to communicate with body language.

Directions If your horse is well-behaved, try this exercise at the beginning of your ride when riding "on the buckle."

Step 1 Hold on to just the buckle of your reins with one or both hands, and keep your hands over the pommel of your saddle.

Step 2 Use your eyes to chart your course. Be aware of how your eyes relate to the rest of your body. Your head will want to lead and misalign your body, but don't let it. Be sure your hands, shoulders, knees, and toes also point the way.

Step 3 Track left and spiral onto a diagonal line of travel. Weight your left seat bone slightly and turn with your outside (right) aids. Be aware of how your weight works. You might need to use more outside leg than you expected.

Step 4 As you finish your diagonal line, spiral right to turn right. Weight your right seat bone slightly and turn with your outside (left) aids. Be persistent about your horse following your body.

Step 5 When your horse is able to understand your body language, pick up the reins and begin your warm-up. You'll find that your horse is more in tune with your body language, and you only need very subtle rein aids.

EXERCISE 2
Increase the Power and Focus of Your Eyes

Step 1 Imagine that your eyes have a magnetic quality. Stare at your focal point until your gaze becomes fuzzy. Stay aligned with your horse so he's able to stay squarely under you. Practice straight lines and turns.

Step 2 Be specific. Instead of looking at a tree trunk, look at a specific knot or leaf.

Instead of looking at the letter A, look at the hole in the peak of the A and imagine you can go through it. Instead of looking at a row of cavalletti, look at a specific part of a single pole. Perhaps it is striped and you can look at a color. Then as you approach these objects, find another focal point that's on the horizontal plane farther on.

As you start to use your eyes with more awareness, you'll find that your horse's balance improves and you are better able to follow your line of travel accurately. (Refer to page 211 for the chapter on monitoring and regulating your line of travel.)

Essential Information about the Visual Powerline

- The trajectory of your eyes is a Powerline that goes out from your body. It connects you and your horse to a line of travel in the "outside world."

- When you focus on the horse's neck, you are in your horse's downhill balance and are unable to influence it.

- Use the Posture Checklist to help yourself stay in self-carriage and help your horse balance.

- Be aware of your horse's balance. Is he in a downhill, horizontal, or uphill balance?

- Give yourself many half-halts so you can stay in balance according to the rules of gravity. Use the ground as your reference point. Don't grip the saddle or look down.

- When you and your horse are both in balance, you can give clear aids.

CHAPTER SEVEN

Clear Aids for Communication

Aids for Three Purposes

Normally, we think of the aids as asking the horse for a specific action, but the most successful riders use the aids for three specific purposes:

1 First, they *prepare* the horse for action by shaping him and putting him in front of the leg—the *preparatory aids*.
2 Second, they *listen* to the horse to see if he's ready to respond—the *listening aids*.
3 Finally, when they know the horse is ready, then they *ask for action*—the *action aids*.

Let's look at each kind of aid.

The Preparatory Aids

Most riders have been trained to think of the half-halt as *the* preparatory aid. In every sense, that is true, but the preparatory aids that you'll read about in this chapter are even more basic than that. These preparatory aids make your half-halts effective. They prepare you for the preparatory half-halts by achieving two qualities:

- They shape your horse so he's better connected and more able to be collected.
- They put your horse in front of the leg.

"Shaping" the Horse's Body

The rider's aids prepare the horse for action by *shaping* his body (putting him in the ideal frame and bend). The rider's position and aids sculpt the horse so he is in a balance that maximizes his ability to perform (fig. 7.1). These shaping aids always come first, and they prepare the horse for the *action aids* that follow them. The educated horse knows that the shaping aids mean, *Let's get in a good position to go—or stop—or turn—or just rebalance!*

Riders roughly fall into two categories:

Effective trainers are *leaders* ("shapers") and their riding position and balance control the position and balance of the horse—not the other way around. This requires an educated seat and core strength that maintains positive tension and correct Powerlines.

Some are *followers* ("shapees"). When a horse is out of balance, the rider who is a follower falls into the horse's poor balance and stays there. All riders start out as *followers* because it takes time to develop the strong but supple riding position needed

7.1 Shaping aids: Dutch Olympian Marlies van Baalen rides Kigali here. We can see that Marlies' aids shape Kigali in a prescribed amount of bend—in this case, a 20-meter bend.

to be a leader. "Shapers" make their horses comfortable because they balance them by making them *longitudinally* supple (round through the topline) and *laterally* supple (able to adopt degrees of bend).

When horses become tense or lazy, they invariably lose their bend and "straighten on their own." Note: *Straightness* is normally a positive quality that refers to the horse's correct alignment. However, when a horse "straightens on his own," it means that he loses his bend and suppleness, and he "stiffens." This is a *negative* use of the word "straighten." The horse loses his round topline (longitudinal suppleness) and loses his bendability (lateral suppleness).

When the ability to bend left and right is equal, the horse is "straight" in the positive sense of the word. The rider's seat and legs sculpt and then stabilize the horse in prescribed degrees of bend or straightness. The rider can make her aids in the shape of right or left bend, or in straightness (in shoulder-fore, which still retains the supple ability to bend—see p. 100 for more on shoulder-fore). When the horse is straight (supple and aligned), he retains the ability to bend so it's easy to produce the degree of bend necessary for any movement or figure.

Horse and rider should have a clear understanding of what a 20-meter bend feels like, what a 15-meter bend feels like, and what 10- and 8-meter bends feel like. Once a horse is gymnastically educated, he's far more willing to be shaped and bent, but he would never do it by himself.

When you achieve correct bendability with your horse, you improve relaxation. To help with bending, try Exercise 1 in this chapter (p. 78).

Putting the Horse In Front of the Leg

The second way in which our aids prepare the horse is by putting him "in front of the leg"—that is, he becomes quick or prompt to the aids (review this concept on p. 36). The word "prompt" means "punctual" or "on time." It does not mean "hurried," which would imply a degree of negative tension and disengagement. You don't increase the difficulty of your horse's task by asking him to be "on time."

When you ask for leg-yield, your horse should do it on the *first* stride from a quiet aid—not three strides later. How much of an aid should you use? The answer is always, "As little as possible but as much as necessary."

The whip is commonly considered the aid that puts the horse in front of the leg. By virtue of its length and its proximity to the hindquarters, it can influence the hindquarters more readily than the leg. As a result, responses from the whip are more likely to come from the horse's "hind-pushing" engine instead of his "front-pulling" engine, which sometimes wants to respond instead. (For more information, see "Engines for Pushing and Pulling" on p. 88.)

The whip aids give horse and rider both a feeling for the kind of response you want that goes "through" the horse's body from back to front. The experienced horse responds to the "whispering" whip, which can be extremely effective with movements in high collection such as piaffe, passage, and pirouettes. The whispering whip quietly encourages promptness and engagement from the hindquarters.

You need to teach your horse to respond to a whisper of the whip. If the whisper isn't effective, help the horse understand with escalating reminders—a tap, or if necessary, a stronger tap. Then, repeat the exercise with a whisper, and the horse will be more attentive to the quiet aid. A problem arises when a rider isn't coordinated enough with the use of her whip. In other words, it is easy to whack the horse but extremely difficult to use the whip aid "as little as possible."

Carrying a whip is a responsibility. Exercise 2 on page 79 develops the rider's ability to use the whip with sensitivity. Try it, and when you're satisfied with your progress, try Exercise 3 to make your horse sensitive (p. 79).

When showing in championship dressage classes, whips usually aren't allowed. But your horse should understand how to respond to a leg aid with a clear, prompt step from the hindquarters. There are many other exercises that put the horse in front of the leg without using the whip (such as the turn-on-the-haunches and any exercise that requires changing direction, including the figure eight and serpentines). Then the leg aid, itself, will remind the horse to be prompt, and the whip becomes unnecessary.

Escalating leg aids also put the horse in front of the leg. Like the whip aid, the leg aids should begin with a whisper—with the heels down so you don't lose your grounded Vertical Powerline. If necessary, the leg aid can escalate to a vibrate, a tap, a rat-a-tat, a squeeze, or a kick from the flat of the calf. Be aware that a kick, while sometimes necessary, causes tension. Be sure to allow your horse to go forward, even if he goes forward too much. Soon, he should go quietly to the bit. Repeated "reminders" that don't make the point merely annoy the horse and fail to make your aids effective. Try Exercise 4, "The Prompt Leg-Yield," on page 80, to help put your horse in front of the leg.

The Listening Aids

After you've prepared the horse by shaping him and putting him in front of the leg, your aids *feel* and *listen* to your horse, and *test* to see if it feels like he is ready to go. This is a waiting moment during which you ask, *Are you ready?*

Some riders aren't used to listening with the hands, seat, and legs, so they might need to make a concerted effort to be passive and search for the right feeling to know whether or not the horse is ready to respond to a request for action. If your horse doesn't "hear" your preparatory aids, you don't want to give an action aid.

Ideally, a normal riding session is filled with quiet, interesting conversation between horse and rider. Your ability to listen to your horse depends on your ability to feel and interpret his responses. As you listen, you should automatically think in terms of the Training Scale—the recipe for training horses. This time-tested Training Scale is a left-brained, diagnostic tool, and there are six qualities to check: Rhythm, Suppleness, Contact, Impulsion, Straightness, and Collection (fig. 7.2).

At Training Level, you analyze the horse's *Rhythm* (regularity and tempo); *Suppleness* (roundness and bendability); and the feel of the *Contact* in your hand and your seat. This feel echoes the degree of relaxation or tension in your horse's entire spine. When the horse's back is relaxed, it is swinging, but when the back is stiff, the mouth is hard. These first three training elements provide the foundation for the training of all horses.

At First Level dressage, the horse develops his ability to "thrust" in response to your aids (add *Impulsion*). Your horse should be able to go freely forward and come back from your aids with promptness and elasticity. You also analyze your horse's *Straightness* (alignment), and perhaps the modest degree of *Collection* that is sometimes present at First Level, although it isn't technically required.

At Second Level, the horse should be able to maintain a moderate degree of *Collection* (in addition to demonstrating improvement of all Training and First Level skills). Your "listening skills" determine the training plan every day and every minute of your time in the saddle, and they determine whether the horse is ready for action.

7.2 The Training Scale is the rider's finest diagnostic tool. When the rider listens to the horse, she keeps all these qualities in mind: Rhythm, Suppleness, Contact, Impulsion, Straightness, and Collection. Whatever needs to be improved will most certainly be related to one or more of these Training Scale concepts.

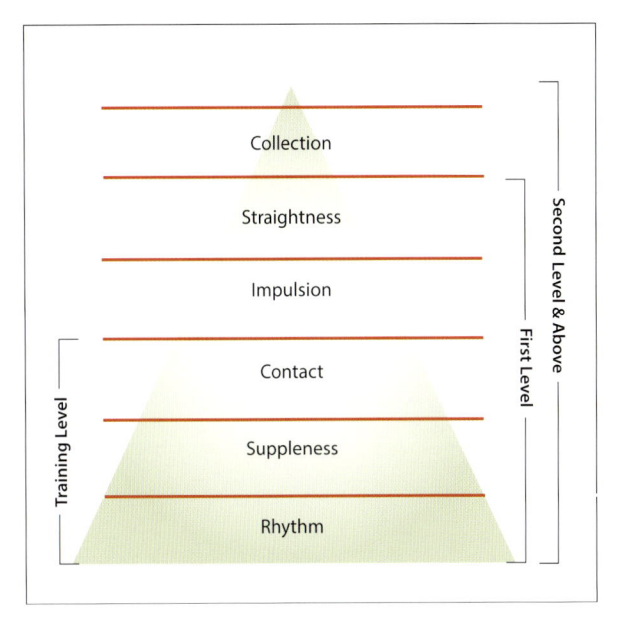

Listening is approximately 50 percent of every conversation! Use all the exercises at the end of this chapter as "exercises in listening."

The Action Aids

Finally, the *action aids* tell the horse what to do—that is, they make a *request for* action. Because of the preparatory aids, the horse isn't surprised by the action aids. He's in a good position to respond promptly and in a coordinated way. Because of the listening aids, the rider is fairly sure the horse will respond.

The preparatory and listening aids are important. Professional riders use them to set up the horse for success and confirm that the horse is ready for action. Then, when the rider asks for action, she's reasonably sure that she will get a correct and prompt response.

Action aids always involve some version of "Go," "Whoa," and "Steer"—and the half-halts that enable them. To be effective, your aids to go, stop and steer need to be audible and well-timed.

To be *audible*, as you know, you must be able to *follow* the horse passively with your seat, hands, and legs. When you are able to follow so much that you are a part of your horse, you can make your aids audible to the horse.

The aids need to speak to the right part of the horse's body. The horse's inside hind leg can only be influenced by your inside leg (or inside whip or spur). The same is true on the outside.

To be *well-timed*, the aids need to be applied at a time when the horse is physically able to answer the question. For example, if you use the aid at the wrong time, the horse may "hear" the aid, but not be in a position to respond. To be able to give well-timed aids, you need to understand the timing of your horse's hind leg.

Within every stride, your horse's hind leg does three things: It *thrusts* off the ground, then it *reaches* to a point under your seat (where two spines meet), and then it lands and carries weight—or *engages* (for more, see p. 89):

- When the hind leg is *thrusting* (pushing off), the horse can respond to your leg aid to go. That's the "Go" moment.

- When the hind leg is *reaching* and making its forward arc, your horse can respond to your directional aids asking that he step under your seat.

- When the hind leg is *landing* on the ground (engaging), he can respond to the part of your half-halt that transfers weight back onto that grounded hind leg. That's the "Whoa" moment.

Things sometimes go wrong. When the rider gives a "Go" aid just as her horse's inside leg is landing on the ground, he's not in a position to go. That's the "Whoa" moment. And, when the rider says "Whoa" just as the hind leg is leaving the ground, it won't work because the horse is already committed to go.

If the rider wants the horse to "reach" more, she can only influence this as the hind leg is reaching.

The aids also need to be given in the right tempo. Some riders are a bit hectic, and give the aids too fast. However, most riders give the aids too slowly. Try riding with a portable metronome. Sing a song or count out loud. Remember that the rhythm is the horse's language. The aids need to be given in the rhythm and tempo of that language.

Your active seat and lower leg aids are primarily in charge of the "Go" command. They have an energizing, activating effect as well as a shaping effect. The lower leg asks the horse to carry the rider forward rather than just propelling forward. The closing of the upper leg and/or lower leg together with the pushing-against-the-fixed-hand aid (p. 74) produces a "Whoa" response and can be used to stabilize the horse's balance or assist in transitions.

There are four rein aids:

- The *following rein*, like the following seat is a "non-message" to be used when all is well.

- The *softening rein* is used to allow the horse space to come into a different gait and/or frame—for example, when going from canter to trot the rein softens to allow the horse into trot. The rein also softens, sometimes invisibly, after half-halts.

- The *fixed rein (primary half-halting rein)* is used for normal half-halts. You push your Vertical Powerline into the fixed hand until the horse connects and/or adds weight to a hind leg. The rider knows when this connecting half-halt has succeeded. She feels it in her seat and back, and her horse becomes light in the front. It's most important that the leg and rein aids soften in this moment.

- The *secondary half-halting rein* is used for a stronger half-halt. When the connection is not made because the primary halt-halt didn't go through, the rider needs to give a stronger half-halt. In this case, she brings her hand back farther and fixes it. Then she pushes into that hand. It's important to note that this hand doesn't pull—it is fixed, and the rider pushes into it. The horse's neck may be shortened for a moment, but as soon as the horse yields, the rider must soften this rein. Strong half-halts shouldn't be necessary very often because they help the horse understand soft half-halts.

Your *seat* and *core* coordinate everything, thus enabling harmony and a whole-body aid.

Using All Three Aids Together

For learning purposes, I talk about aids in an individual way, but they need to work *together* with the timing and skill of an orchestra.

When your aids are well-timed and your horse is prompt to them, he will ultimately be happier in his work because it is easier. Prompt reactions promote efficiency because the horse operates in one piece. You want your horses to be in one piece, and if horses were to think the way we think (which they don't), they would want us to be in one piece too—using whole-body aids. Anytime you want to ask your horse for action, you need to blend your *preparatory* aids, your *listening* aids, and finally, your *action aids.* In competition, the rider needs to ask the horse many questions and get satisfactory answers in rapid succession. However, in everyday training, the discerning rider can be quietly persistent about getting each aspect of the preparatory and listening aids correct before giving the action aid. Then when you give the action aid, you will usually be successful because horses who understand are usually willing.

Whole-Body Riding

Whole-body riding is coordinated by the rider's seat and core and is the epitome of blended aids and harmony. Whole-body riding is heard by the horse in a whole-body way. Many riders have enormous experience with understanding the meaning of each individual aid, but they have trouble putting the aids together in a coordinated way. Whole-body riding is like an orchestra, and each individual aid is a musical instrument. When you put the instruments together, you get music in which each instrument chimes in at the right moment with the right tone, intensity, and intention. Can you imagine an orchestra in which a key instrument—perhaps the oboe—always chimed in late? Not only would it sound bad, but also it would confuse the other musicians, and coordination would be impossible.

The horse certainly can't chime in late. He has an obligation, but as always, it's the rider's job to tell the horse about his responsibilities. He must be:

- *In front of the leg* so he responds to the "Go" aids promptly and appropriately.

- *Under the seat* or *on the seat* so he feels like he is under you and able to listen to and follow your seat. In this situation, he listens to both the "Go" and "Whoa" aids, and he doesn't zoom away from your seat.

- *To the hand* so he feels committed to your hand and is accepting the contact. He's not going either not-quite-up-to your hand or beyond your hand in a disrespectful way. He pushes away from the bit and carries himself—and you!

Teach your horse to be *in front of the leg*, *on the seat,* and *to the hand*, by being sure he responds appropriately to your aids.

Listen to "How" Your Horse Responds

After your aid for action, listen again:

1 Your horse should respond to your seat and leg aids with his back and hindquarters, *not* with his front legs, or by becoming tense in his neck and head. Many horses respond to the leg aid by moving off with the front legs, making themselves long in the frame and becoming tense in the neck. If this is your horse's problem, repeat the "Prompt Leg-Yield" exercise on page 80. Listen! Did he activate the hindquarters in a timely way? Did you receive the energy of the hindquarters through a relaxed forehand into your quiet hands? Be sure your horse responded with his back and hindquarters and not with his forehand and neck, and be sure your hands aren't causing an incorrect response.

2 Your horse should respond to your rein aids by flexing correctly left or right, and he should respond to your half-halts by engaging the hindquarters, *not* by moving his hindquarters left or right. Many horses respond to the flexion aids or the half-halting aids by bending the neck, tilting the head, getting fussy in the contact, or swinging the hindquarters. Some of these problems are caused by a rider overusing her hands or using her arms instead of hands and wrists. If this is your problem, try the exercise on page 179 at a halt.

Sometimes, the horse needs to *learn* to respond to the rein aids correctly. He needs to understand it.

How is your horse's effort? As your horse's training progresses and you increase the sophistication of the questions you ask him, it might be his natural inclination to decrease his output. Your horse might need to be taught that when you increase the question, he must increase his output. Play it like a game, and he'll enjoy his effort.

The "Through" Rider

As I've mentioned, just as the horse's energy ideally goes "through" him, it also goes "through" the rider. The rider absorbs the energy of the horse and vice versa. You can tell when the rider is "through," because the soft, self-perpetuating motion of her seat is echoed quietly in her head and in her feet. This supple rider oscillates up and down in harmonious self-perpetuation. She is like a vertical spring (see fig. 3.1). The motion of her seat and leg meets the automatic swing of the horse's rib cage to cause the "Go" impulse. Then her deep seat combined with the automatic, rhythmic stretch of her frontline causes its own "Whoa" and "Soften" influence.

As a result, the whole-body aids come complete with an "automatic drive" and an "automatic half-halt and soften" within every stride. It's a built-in half-halt. When horse and rider move as one, whole-body aids result in whole-body responses from the horse. That's "throughness" and harmony. In this glorious situation, you and your horse are in a position to develop positively through the levels.

Passive Aids—Freedom for Him and Control for You

Powerlines and Triangles of Aids can actually make your horse feel trapped, and by nature, horses hate to be trapped, so the rider's tools need to be used responsibly by being passive much of the time. *Passive aids* give the horse time when you're not saying anything because you're listening. It's like the quiet time between the notes of your favorite song.

Swedish trainer and FEI judge Bo Jena frequently reminds riders to make "many small givings." The passive aid is the strongest aid because it makes the horse want to be your partner. The passive aids listen. They make the horse a viable partner. The horse feels free, but the rider still has control.

The passive aid is also an invitation. It says, "You can go here!" When, for example, he has too much weight in your left rein and you want him to go more toward the right rein, keep the contact passive and ride to it. It can be so soft that the horse wants to go there: He goes there in a soft way, and then you can give a soft half-halt that will go through because the horse is physically and mentally relaxed about it. And then another invisible soften says, "You're free. I'm not holding you. Carry yourself."

Holding a horse in a specific frame or shape is a common problem. The rider who holds him will always need to do it. This problem indicates a lack of understanding or a lack of trust in the system of Dressage Dynamics. Or it indicates a lack of trust in the horse. The mature rider trusts—even though she knows that sometimes her trust will be betrayed. And then she trusts again.

When the aids are *too* passive, the horse is free in an unbalanced way, and the rider loses control. And, when the aids aren't passive enough, the horse feels uncomfortable and claustrophobic. Your aids need to be effective yet allow the horse to feel free. Freedom is the goal for him. Control is the goal for you. That's the rider's mission, and that mission will be better accomplished when you look at "How Horses Work" in Part II (p. 85).

The Benefits of Traffic Cones

One day my favorite veterinarian walked into my indoor arena, and said, "I see you've been torturing your students!" And she pointed to the cones that were set up to describe 10-, 15-, and 20-meter circles.

Of course, she was only kidding, but this vet was a rider, and it made me realize that she had never ridden with cones. If she had, she would know that they make your riding so much easier! Riders in my arena are relieved to see cones set up because they clearly define the line of travel that channels the horse and keeps him straight.

When the rider isn't very exacting about her line of travel, the horse becomes partially responsible for it, and he invariably misaligns his shoulders and/or his hips (see Sue Blinks' story about how water flows in a stream on p. 185). When your circle lines are precisely defined it becomes relatively easy to align your horse and put him on the outside rein (see p. 189 for the importance of the connection to the outside rein). It's also useful to use cones (or cavalletti poles) to define the diagonal line. Commitment to a very specific diagonal improves every movement on it, and especially those that involve straight flying changes!

> **EXERCISES**

Try these exercises for *shaping your horse*, putting him *in front of the leg*, *listening* to him and asking him for *action*. Make up some exercises of your own that accomplish the same purposes.

EXERCISE 1
Circles for Shaping and Figure Eights to Put Your Horse "In Front of the Leg"

Purpose To help you shape your horse in prescribed degrees of bend and to help your horse step in front of the leg as you change direction.

Directions Practice precision when riding circles (fig. 7.3) If you have trouble with precision, cones help tremendously (see sidebar "The Benefits of Traffic Cones" on p. 77). Start in walk and follow, very specifically, the arc of a circle. "Shape" your horse on 20-, 15-, and 10-meter circles. Be patient but also persistent with your inside-leg-to-outside-rein aids. If you or your horse become misaligned, think about your Triangles of Aids (p. 55).

If you have a horse that's difficult to shape, try just shaping his energy. I am totally unable to say "how" one does this. It's only a thought process. Instead of trying to move your horse's bulky body around, stay in the center and think about moving his energy around. This makes your aids light and clearly directed. You might be surprised at how easily your horse responds. It's better to ride any horse this way. A horse's body always follows his energy.

Make your circles into figure eights. Change direction gradually over a few steps with half-halts in the rhythm of your horse's gait. Each time you start a new circle, give an extra clear aid with the new inside leg to tell your horse, *Now, step in front of this leg!*

7.3 Be persistent about the accuracy of your circles. There are no straight lines or corners in a circle. When every step is the same and the bend is consistent, your horse can establish a comfortable balance on the outside rein. When you change direction in figure eights, give a clear aid with the new inside leg that says, *Now, step in front of this leg!*

EXERCISE 2
Whip Control for the Rider

Purpose To develop your ability to give the minimum aid with your whip so you can use it with sophistication to put your horse in front of the leg.

Directions Consider the carrying of a whip as a responsibility. Minimal use of the whip gives the rider maximum effect.

Step 1 At a halt, hold your whip so it crosses your thigh and points diagonally toward the ground behind your leg. Your thigh is a fulcrum that stabilizes your whip, and you lay the whip gently on the horse by opening the rein against the fulcrum point (fig. 7.4).

Step 2 Your goal is simply to feel the hair on your horse's barrel behind your leg. Peek down to be sure that your whip is steady and feeling the hair at a precise point.

Step 3 Now, move it slightly over a few hairs in a very small area. Be sure you can control the end that is touching the horse.

Step 4 Try it with both hands.

Step 5 Next, do this same exercise at walk, trot and canter.

7.4 Carrying a whip is a responsibility. Annie shows how it should lie on the rider's thigh. To use it, the rider opens the rein. Exercise 2 develops the rider's ability to use the whip with sensitivity.

EXERCISE 3
"In Front of the Leg": A Whip Exercise for the Horse

Purpose When you're able to use the whip "as little as possible" with either hand at walk, trot and canter, you're able to expect the horse to respond to the lightest possible aid. The whip, like all aids, can operate on a wide spectrum of intensities—beginning, of course, with "as little as possible," and ending with "as much as necessary." For simplicity, I'll look at three varieties: the *whisper,* the *light tap,* and the *stronger tap.*

Directions Begin this exercise in the medium walk and prepare to make a transition to trot. For this transition, use your whip instead of your leg—not in addition to it.

7.5 "The Prompt Leg-Yield" is an exercise that tests the horse's reaction to the leg. The reaction should be prompt but not sudden, and the horse's energy should flow through his body smoothly. This exercise also encourages the rider to use her listening aids as she evaluates her horse's performance. If the rider is pleased with her horse's reaction, she should praise him, but if he needs improvement, she can give the test again.

You'll also use your "intent." That is, you must be *thinking* about trot. If you have spent much time with a horse, you probably believe in extrasensory perception. If you don't believe in it, think about trot anyway, and follow these steps:

Step 1 Whisper with your whip, and think, "Trot." At this point, your horse probably won't understand, but listen to his response. If he trots from behind, pat him. The exercise is over for him! He should now be prompt to the leg aid, making the whip unnecessary. The whip should never become the primary aid. It is only there to support the leg aid.

Step 2 If your horse does not trot, tap him with your whip and think, "Trot." If he trots from the tap, pat him and return to a whispering aid for the next transition. When he listens to the whispering whip, the exercise is over for him.

Step 3 If your horse has not trotted from the whisper or the tap, give him a stronger tap with the whip until he trots. Be sure to go with him even if he bolts off. Then pat him. If he overreacts, that's okay. He needs to have a clear understanding of "Go" from behind. Repeat until your horse trots from a whisper.

The most important step is returning to the whisper, and repeating the process. After this exercise, your horse will understand and respond to that smaller aid more promptly.

EXERCISE 4
Listening and Action Aids: The Prompt Leg-Yield

Purpose To help the rider use her listening aids and ask for action.

Directions Track right and go down the long side slightly off the track in a comfortably connected medium walk. Carry your whip in your left hand so it is able to support your left leg aid.

Step 1 Prepare to leg-yield a few steps, keeping the front legs on the track. Flex your horse to the left—toward the outside—and ask for leg-yield along the track with your left leg. Use your listening aids to learn his response in the *first* step after your request (fig. 7.5).

Here's what should happen in the first step: The hindquarters move rhythmically to the inside track. He crosses his left legs over the right legs; you feel the result in your seat as your horse steps through his back. Then you get visual feedback as the energy goes through his neck. He looks and feels "inflated" in front of you: His neck puffs up all the way to the bit, especially on the right. His energy lands comfortably in your hands with perhaps slightly more in the right hand.

Step 2 Listen: Did you feel that? Did that happen in the *first* step? If not, use an encouraging whisper, tap, or rat-a-tat with the whip or leg to explain the rules of the game. This isn't a matter of getting tough or emotional, but of encouraging him to follow the rules. The rule is that he *does* leg-yield—he doesn't *develop* leg-yield. He *does* it in the *first* step. You're the leader. After three or four steps of leg-yield, pat him, straighten and prepare to repeat the exercise. Your listening aids determine whether you need to repeat the exercise.

EXERCISE 5
The Square Serpentine

Purpose To help you blend all your aids and shape your horse, put him in front of the leg, listen to him, and ask for action.

The Square Serpentine works like magic to shape your horse and put him in front of the leg. It also encourages you to listen to your horse and it encourages him to *act*. This is such an effective exercise because it combines many exercises in one: half-halts, turns, straightening, and changing direction.

I call the Square Serpentine the "RSVP" exercise because it uses those dressage letters in the arena as points for making the turns of the serpentine, but it doesn't need to be ridden in a dressage arena. It can be done anywhere you can find or create corners and reference points such as fence posts and trees. You'll be even more successful if you're a bit neurotic about your line of travel.

Directions Start tracking right in walk from the letter C, or the middle of the short side of your riding area, and prepare for the corner coming up.

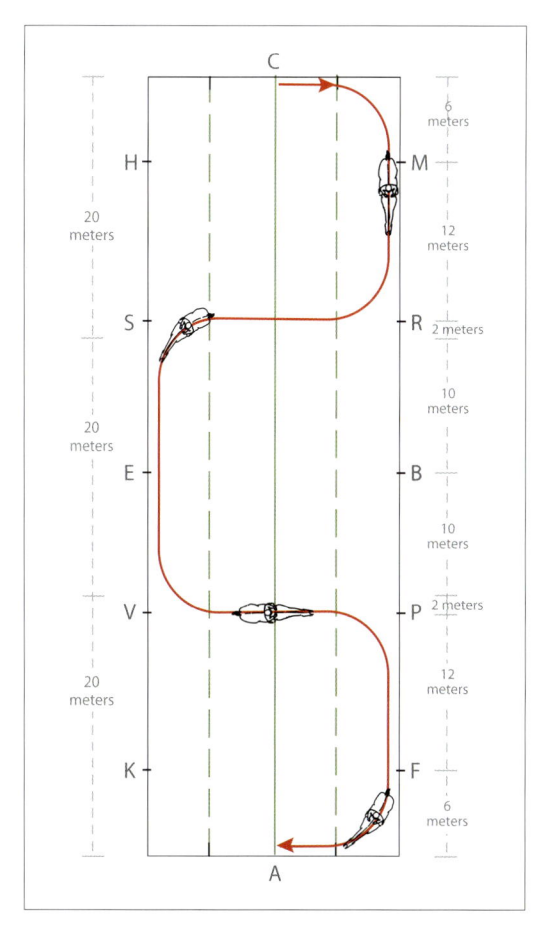

7.6 "The Square Serpentine" is my favorite exercise for shaping your horse and putting him in front of the leg. It also encourages you to listen to your horse, and it encourages him to act. This is so useful because it combines many exercises in one: half-halts, turns, straightening, and changing direction.

Step 1 Before the corner, half-halt with your aids in the shape of right bend. The half-halt asks the horse's spine to balance under your spine. If he doesn't respond to your half-halt before the corner, come to a quiet halt. Then proceed in walk again.

Step 2 Prepare to turn by spiraling slightly to the right and putting a little more weight in your inside right foot and using your bending aids. When he feels the weight in your right foot, he should *surge* in front of your leg and step into the outside rein.

Step 3 Using primarily your outside aids, guide and turn your horse through the corner, retaining the bend. You're finished with the turn when he is straight in shoulder-fore on your next line of travel. If you have a mirror you can check to see if he is straight.

Step 4 Listen. Your horse's response in the corner is a moment of truth. Did he step in front of that inside leg, surge forward, and go to the outside rein? If not, he'll need a little tap from your inside leg. Did he fall in and lose the bend? If so, he might need another tap from the inside leg. Did he fail to turn? If so, he might need a tap from your outside leg. Did he do it really well? Be sure to praise him.

Step 5 Now, at R, prepare to turn again to face the opposite side of the arena, the letter S. Use the same aids that you used in the corner.

Step 6 Listen again: How did he turn? As he approaches the centerline, is he marching and eager? If so, he will be easy to shape in left bend, and he will surge in front of your left leg before S.

Step 7 As you cross the centerline, change the flexion and bend to the left in preparation for your left turn at S. This is the time to notice if he is easier in front of the right leg or the left. Continue by turning left at V and right at P.

Step 8 When you have your coordination during the walk, and your horse understands your aids, do the exercise at trot. Do it in both directions.

Step 9 Try the exercise in canter with flying changes (or changes through the trot or walk) on the centerline.

Essential Information about the Clear Aids

- Aids communicate with the horse in three different ways:

    1 They *prepare* the horse for action by "shaping" him and putting him in front of the leg.

    2 They *listen* to the horse to see if he's ready to respond.

    3 When they know the horse is ready, they *ask for action*.

- The skilled rider gives these aids so they are audible and well-timed. They are *audible* when they come from a place that is generally quiet and harmonious with the horse. They are *well-timed* when they are given at a moment when the horse is best able to hear them.

- The trained horse responds to the leg and seat aids with his back and hindquarters. He responds to the rein aids by flexing correctly. When used in combination, the seat, leg, and rein aids connect the horse and develop "throughness."

- In harmony, the energy flows through you as it flows through the horse.

- In harmony, the horse feels free and balanced. You have control.

PART II · DRESSAGE DYNAMICS
How Horses Work

"How Horses Work," explains the mechanics of how horses balance, and gives you, the rider, ideas for how you can positively influence his balance. Horses have a few innate challenges—even without the added weight of a rider. When the rider understands those issues, she's in a good position to help her horse balance.

When the horse is balanced, he can carry more weight with the hindquarters, which naturally lightens the front end. That's exactly what makes the horse feel free. It's a freedom that can only be attained with the rider's help.

In Part II, I explore the horse's balance issues and the simple tools you can use to help him become supple and balanced.

how horses work

CHAPTER EIGHT

Balance Issues

Understanding Balance Improves It

All horses, despite their seemingly effortless beauty in motion, have some inherent balance problems that are both longitudinal and lateral in nature.

Longitudinally, or from back to front, the horse has a natural balance problem simply because his neck protrudes from his otherwise table-like structure; his balance is innately on the forehand. To counter this issue, you need to help the horse build topline muscles so he can carry himself well and move more easily. The horse's second longitudinal balance issue exists because he is a four-legged creature: When left to his own devices, he's always eager to use his front legs and is somewhat "unconscious" about his hindquarters (fig. 8.1). This also puts the horse out of balance and onto the forehand. Riding half-halts and transitions can help both situations.

Laterally, or from left to right, the horse isn't straight by nature. Because his hindquarters are wider than his shoulders, his natural balance is, once again, on the forehand (see fig. 8.6, p. 100).

Straightening the horse is easy in theory but sometimes difficult in practice. For now, let's look at the longitudinal issues. Think of your horse's hindquarters and his forehand as his two engines—one for pushing and the other for pulling.

8.1 By nature, the horse's forelegs are more eager than his hind legs. Under saddle, the rider does half-halts and asks for transitions that encourage the hind legs to be more responsive and they encourage the forehand to wait.

BALANCE ISSUES 87

Longitudinal Balance

Engines for Pushing and Pulling

Your horse's forehand engine wants to *pull* your horse along. It's the *pulling engine*. This engine is important, but when it does too much pulling, the hind end becomes like a wagon trailing along behind a tow vehicle (fig. 8.2 A). Because your horse naturally wants freedom of the forehand, he prefers to use this front-end engine more than his hind engine. He doesn't realize that overusing his forehand puts too much weight on it, which actually reduces his freedom. As soon as the horse takes a step with the front end, without bringing his hindquarters along the same amount, he becomes a bit long in his frame, hollow in the back, and unpleasant in the hand. The horse needs his rider to explain that *real* freedom from improved balance comes when he uses his hind end more and his forehand less.

You want your horse's hind-end engine to *push* your horse along, which creates a connection from his hindquarters to the bit (fig. 8.2 B). The *pushing engine* has to create enough energy to make that connection. The energy has to get *all the way* from the horse's thrusting hind leg, through the horse's topline, to his reaching poll, and to the bit. Then it can lift and free the front end—your ultimate goal.

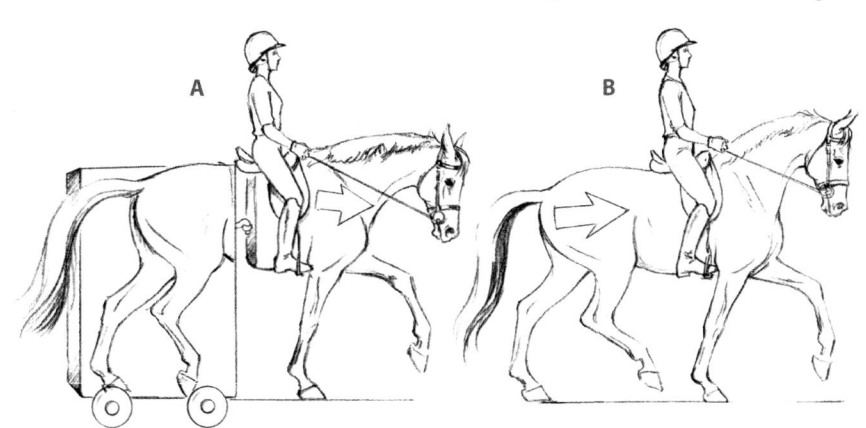

8.2 A & B (A) The hindquarters, when left to their own devices, sometimes act like a trailer being dragged by the forehand.

(B) When the hindquarters are the driving force causing the horse to cover ground, it has the effect of lifting the forehand.

The "Faux" Runaway

As you know, horses don't inherently know that the way to gain freedom is by energizing the hindquarters, rather than the forehand. Fresh young horses or hot older horses are a tough test for the rider's balance as their enthusiastic front legs want to carry the forehand away from the lazy hindquarters. They pull the center of balance forward and away from the rider's seat—the seat that connects the rider to her horse's hindquarters.

The rider feels that her horse is running away, so she's amazed when her trainer says her horse's hindquarters look lazy. The feeling is misleading because the surge of energy is actually very real, but it's caused by the front end that's running away from the snoozing hind end. It's often even an experienced rider's tendency to use prolonged restraining aids with this horse, but that never works.

Years ago at the Aachen Horse Show, one of the American riders was in this situation. Her horse was very hot, and she was persistently trying to quiet and relax him. Her German trainer came along and told her to go for a gallop. Although the rider was horrified at the prospect, that was just the answer to her problem. It got the horse's hind end in gear so the energy that reached her hand came from the hindquarters instead of the forehand. As a result, the horse was very successful in the competition. The American rider retained her horse's enthusiasm for working, but gained control over the whole horse from behind.

When your horse is too strong and you can't (or don't dare to) gallop, do movements in which your leg is required to activate the hindquarters. Find a way to ride your horse from *back to front*. Make turns-on-the-forehand and do leg-yield. If you and your horse know how, do movements such as turn-on-the-haunches, shoulder-in, travers (haunches-in), renvers (haunches-out), and half-pass. Also do transitions between these movements. Do things that require you to use your seat and leg, and use your hands last—and only when you need to. Each time you communicate with your seat and leg more, you need your hands less. Then he will listen to your seat and legs more, and work more from his hind-end pushing engine. To get your horse's hindquarters in gear, do Exercise 1 at the end of this chapter (p. 102).

Thrust, Reach, and Engagement

When you ask your horse to use his hindquarters more, what exactly do you want him to do? When that's clear to you, it can be clear to your horse too. The horse's hind leg sequentially does three things:

- It *thrusts* off the ground…
- then it *reaches* under his body…
- then it *engages* or carries weight when the hoof is flat on the ground.

Thrust is pushing power. Reach is the direction and amount (left, right, and forward) of extension. The reach determines where the hind leg lands—ideally, under your center of gravity, which should be directly over your horse's center of gravity—

where two spines meet. Then your horse's hind foot is in a position to engage (carry weight) and support you both perfectly. In this situation, the rider feels she's being carried, and her seat can be very influential.

When the rider understands and can utilize the dynamics of *thrust, reach,* and *engagement,* it makes the difference between good and great because it clarifies, in your mind, what exactly you want the horse to do with his hindquarters. You don't blindly want "more." You want something specific: thrust, reach, or engagement. Sometimes you want more than one of these qualities, but you should know what you want and why. Let's look at each closely.

Thrust

The energy from each *thrusting* hind leg follows pathways that arc with positive (supple) tension from each thrusting hind leg to the bit (fig. 8.3 A). The horse steps:

- From his left hind leg through the left side of his body, through the poll to the bit in your left hand; this is one unilateral pathway.

- From the right hind leg through the right side of his body, through the poll to the bit in your right hand; this is the other unilateral pathway.

These are two pathways of "throughness." They go all the way through the horse's body, to the bit. To work, there must be enough energy thrusting from each hind leg to reach the bit. "The bit" is, in fact, a very small place, but ideally, the rider should feel the result of a forward seat/leg aid land softly in her receiving hand. It feels like a commitment. It's not easy to send just the right amount of energy through a specific path

8.3 A–C The horse's hind leg does three things: (A) It thrusts, sending energy through the topline to the bit. (B) It reaches, ideally to a place directly under the rider's center of gravity where two spines meet. (C) Finally, it engages or bends and carries weight. Then it thrusts again.

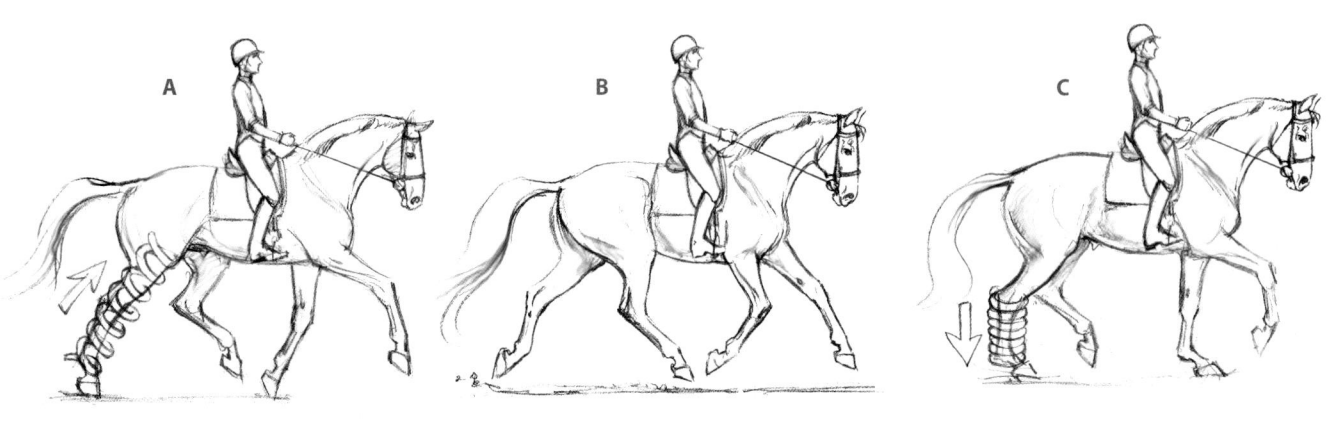

to such a small place, but transitions help the horse to remember to push away from the bit and make a circle of energy.

The rider shows her horse exactly where the pathway of energy should go as she plays with the horse between the forward aids or upward transitions, and half-halt aids or downward transitions. These transitions and half-halts balance the horse from back to front and front to back between the "Go" aid and the "Whoa" aid. As the rider improves her responses to the "Whoa" button and the "Go" button, she improves her horse's longitudinal balance in the process.

When the energy from each hind leg is equal and directed properly, the horse is straight. The energy going through the horse's body builds a bridge of muscle that carries the rider.

This topline bridge is further strengthened and straightened by the horse's sending energy on a very slight diagonal line. When the rider uses her inside leg toward the outside rein (diagonal aids), the energy from the horse's thrust travels diagonally and goes:

- From the left hind toward the right side of the bit on a diagonal pathway or…
- from the right hind toward the left side of the bit on the other diagonal pathway.

In summary, there are four forward-moving pathways of "throughness":

1 Left hind to left bit.
2 Right hind to right bit.
3 Left hind to right bit.
4 Right hind to left bit.

What does the hind leg do after it thrusts? It *reaches*.

Reach

You want your horse to *reach* with his hind legs so he steps directly under your center of gravity—under the place where two spines meet (fig. 8.3 B). Then he carries you in a balanced way. When you're able to influence your horse's direction with your weight and leg aids as described in Exercise 1 (p. 102), you can influence the direction of your horse's reach. When the horse reaches so that he steps *outside* (to the left or right) and/or *short* of the ideal point, the rider will feel as if her horse is pushing himself away from her seat. The rider needs control over how far forward the hind legs step, and whether he steps to the left or the right, or is straight.

How does the rider get that control? On a front-to-back plane, she balances her horse between the "Go" aids and the "Whoa" aids. With the "Go" aids, she asks for more reach, and with the "Whoa" aids, she asks for less. Exercises to help the rider gain control over the amount of forward reach include stretching in different frames (see "Elastic Frames" on p. 109), transitioning within or between gaits, and using half-halts. These exercises give the rider control over the reach of the hind legs from back to front.

But, what about left to right?

Most horses carry at least one hind leg *outside* the center of gravity—too much to the left, or more commonly, too much to the right. Exercises using movements such as shoulder-in, travers (haunches-in), renvers (haunches-out), and half-pass increase the rider's ability to position the horse's hind feet more to the left or more to the right. Shoulder-fore (see p. 100) asks the horse to step directly under the horse's center of gravity. Experienced riders try to achieve this all the time, so for that reason, it's not really an exercise: You want to ride your horse in shoulder-fore all the time.

To position the hind feet precisely, the rider must have extreme control over the line of travel. In a benign way, your horse always does his job in the easiest way, and it's easiest for him to misalign his shoulders or hips and avoid reaching to the place where he carries the most weight. The exact placement of a hind foot in shoulder-fore isn't easy, but once your horse understands, he'll be very willing because he loves feeling balanced (see Exercise 2, "Connect Your Horse in Shoulder Fore"—p. 104).

After your horse's hind leg reaches, it lands, and it carries weight or *engages*.

Engagement

When your horse steps directly under the place where two spines meet, he *engages* in an ideal way—that is, he places his foot in a place where he can most easily carry his weight and yours: under your center of gravity (8.3 C). In the beginning of the horse's training, or during the warm-up of an educated horse's ride, this "engaging moment" causes a connection. The rider can feel this connection in her seat and back. When a horse is fit, strong, and educated enough to be collected, even more weight is transferred to the hindquarters from the forehand, and the rider can feel the horse get lighter in the hand. But how does the rider connect the horse and transfer weight back? Half-halts and downward transitions cause the horse to "push away from the bit," transferring weight to the hindquarters. I discussed this earlier in the sidebar on page 46, but here is more information about this important concept.

Pushing Away from the Bit

In the *thrusting* and *reaching* moments, the horse's energy flows through his topline. When that wave of energy reaches the bit, instead of "leaning" on it, your horse should yield to the contact by "pushing away" from (or "bouncing off") the bit, shifting weight to the hind legs so that he comes into self-carriage and becomes light in your hand as a positive result (fig. 8.4).

Pushing away from the bit happens every stride as a natural result of good riding. It recycles the energy making the work easier for both horse and rider. Although pushing away from the bit is nearly imperceptible to the spectator, the rider can feel it. Search for that feeling and you'll find it. It's the ultimate in correct connection, as the horse remains totally committed to the bit but light in the hand.

When the horse pushes away from the bit, his throatlatch is soft and open. The attitude of his poll is reaching. This flexible and reaching attitude of the mouth and poll is a requirement. When the horse doesn't compromise this flexible reaching attitude of the forehand in motion, half-halts influence the hindquarters. However, if the horse compromises his reaching-to-the-bit attitude when the rider half-halts, his frame will shorten in front instead of closing from behind. It should be noted that there are times when the horse doesn't respond to the half-halt, and the rider needs to use a stronger half-halt. This stronger half-halt will shorten the neck briefly, but once the connection is made and the half-halt goes through, the rider softens and the neck reaches again.

Ultimately, at the highest level, a dressage horse should be able to go from extended trot to piaffe without many rein aids. The jumper needs to cover ground at high speed and then gather himself in a forward way to jump a high fence. In both cases, the rider makes a downward transition from extension to collection in an *upward* way; the rider collects her horse in a *forward* way. That's not possible when the horse doesn't push away from the bit and there isn't a circle of energy. One of

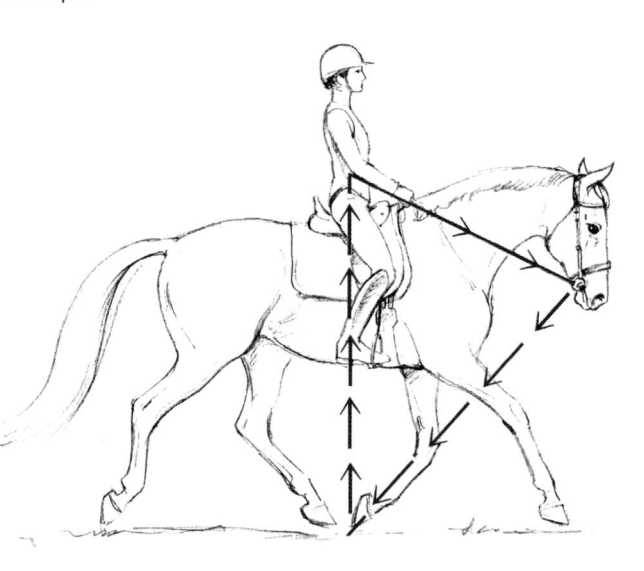

8.4 When the horse is accepting the contact in an ideal way, he "pushes away from the bit." Follow the arrows to see how the energy recycles: First, at the moment of thrust, the energy goes from the horse's pushing hindquarters up through the rider's Vertical Powerline. Second, as the horse's hind leg reaches forward, the energy goes forward through the Connecting Powerline—that is, from the rider's elbow to the bit. Third, when the energy reaches the bit, the horse pushes away from it and transfers weight from the bit to his grounded, engaging hind leg, which improves his self-carriage. Then the horse thrusts off that grounded hind leg again, sending the energy back up through the rider's Vertical Powerline. In this ideal balance, the energy continues recycling.

the greatest keys to learning to ride at the highest level is in developing the ability—in rider and horse—to use the circle of energy to do half-halts and downward transitions with this "upward attitude" because the horse pushes away from the bit. Later I'll talk in detail about transitions and half-halts, but let's look at that briefly now, because it's what makes pushing away from the bit possible.

Half-Halts and Transitions for Coordinating and Connecting

Half-halts and transitions are the rider's primary tools to balance the horse. They coordinate the front-pulling engine and the hind-pushing engine by *connecting* the two engines, and when half-halts and transitions transfer weight to a hind leg, they *collect* the horse. As you work on making your half-halts effective, remember to use your Powerlines. They enable the aids and they make soft aids effective.

Half-Halts

Trainers have always had trouble explaining how to do a half-halt because "half-halt" can mean so many different things. The complicating factor is that half-halts come in all sizes and shapes. For example, the half-halt can mean:

- *Balance under me in shoulder-fore left (or right).*

- *Balance under me so I can shorten the stride in preparation for a transition from trot to walk.*

- *Balance under me and gather yourself in preparation for an extended trot.*

- *Balance under me to half-pass right—and stay in front of my inside leg so you don't make the common mistake of losing balance and going onto the forehand.*

- *Balance under me in preparation to jump this fence.*

Are you getting the idea? The half-halt can mean hundreds of things, but it always means, *Balance under me—where two spines meet.* And there's a recipe for that. The generic half-halt recipe is always, **"Go"**, "Whoa," "Soften." Your aids say:

- *Go* to the pushing engine that often wants to snooze. Your Vertical Powerline asks the energy from the hindquarters to connect to the bit.

- *Whoa, stay under me* to the pulling engine that is often too eager. Your Vertical Powerline pushes against or sits against your fixed hand (you may also need to close you fingers) to achieve this. As you know from Part I, your hand rarely comes back and shortens the neck. Rather, your Vertical Powerline pushes into and *connects* to the hand that stays forward.

- *Balance on your own*. You soften the aids. The rein aids don't give the horse anything to lean on or brace against, and he's free to balance and carry himself. The leg aids also soften. You should never be holding on to your horse or gripping his rib cage. Otherwise, your horse would experience your leg in the same way that he experiences the girth—certainly not something to respond to!

The rhythm of the half-halts is the same as the clock-like rhythm of your horse's gait. When the energy from your horse's hindquarters goes "through" his whole body, very small aids influence the entire horse in his rhythm.

An adequate pushing engine together with connecting half-halts prevent the front end from running away and help the hindquarters balance and carry as much weight as is appropriate for the horse's level of training.

Transitions

Transitions do exactly the same thing. Upward transitions ask the pushing engine to *thrust* and *reach*, sending energy through the horse's back to the bit. Downward transitions ask the horse to push away from the bit and engage or add weight to one hind leg or the other. Transitions and connecting half-halts coordinate your horse's two engines in a circle of recycling energy.

The Circle of Energy and the Circle of Aids

As you connect your horse's two engines, you're sometimes asking for forward energy and sometimes bringing your horse back. These aids are usually very small and come close together in the rhythm of your horse's gait. Feel for the self-perpetuating *circle of energy* that builds your horse's bridge of muscle over his topline (see pp. 90–91). As you know, the energy goes from the horse's thrusting hind foot, through the topline to the bit. Then the horse pushes away from the bit and that energy returns in the form of weight to an engaged hind leg—ideally, under the place where two spines meet.

The rider's aids "ride" on this perpetual circle of energy, making a "circle of aids" or a "circle of influence." Try to feel it ongoing, like a song in the rhythm of your horse's gait. Every stride there's a tiny encouragement to the hindquarters, a tiny shaping aspect to the aid, a tiny confirmation of the balance, and a tiny soften. It's invisible to all but the very educated onlooker.

When the horse is connected from back to front and from front to back, the energy goes around and around ("through"). As you go from canter to trot to walk and back to trot and canter, you change the rhythm, but the circle of energy stays the same. You don't want your horse to stop and then start all over again in the new gait. You want to feel that he uses the same energy for walk as for trot and for canter, which makes the transitions seamless. When the energy returns to the hindquarters, his engine still turns at the same speed—like the wheel on a paddleboat keeps going.

For the circle of aids to work effectively and efficiently, the "Go" and the "Whoa" need to work equally. The horse "thrusts forward" and "balances back" every stride in repetitive motion like the predictable rock of a rocking chair.

Try This

Imagine an empty rocking chair. With your hand, set your imaginary rocking chair in motion. It rocks forward and back equally in a self-perpetuating way, *until* you need to remind it with another push from your hand. Your horse is the same. The forward-thrusting motions and the engaging-back motions of your horse balance him when they are equal. This recycled energy is self-perpetuating, but like the rocking chair, you need to remind your horse to keep it going. If you ride in a clock-like way with this in mind, you'll immediately know which is weaker: the forward or the back. When you're able to monitor your horse's longitudinal balance in this very fine way, you need frequent but very small aids.

Many horses have some degree of engagement avoidance and some degree of forward avoidance. When the rider is able to recycle the horse's energy and has the feeling of the rocking chair going back and forth, she can usually feel the moment when the horse avoids either engagement or thrusting, and she can usually prevent that from happening.

Engagement Avoidance

In a benign way, horses would rather work without working too hard. Here's how they avoid engagement:

- *Laterally*, they swing the hindquarters or shoulders in or out (fig. 8.5 A). Riders who work on keeping the horse's body parts aligned on the line of travel get improved engagement and collection from their horses because they're straight (aligned).

- *Longitudinally*, some horses leave the hind leg on the ground too long, and these horses are in a "sprawled" position by the time they thrust off the ground with it (fig. 8.5 B). In this case, it helps for the rider to encourage the horse's hind leg to pop off the ground sooner by giving a quicker aid.

- *Longitudinally*, some horses pop off the ground with the hind leg too quickly, which puts weight onto the forehand (8.5 C). These horses are croup high. In this case, the rider needs to prolong the weight-bearing moment of engagement with half-halt aids.

Forward Avoidance

Some horses lose the forward flow. An honest connection between the rider's seat, leg, and hand is crucial. When the rider uses the seat and leg, the horse must step toward the hand and accept contact with the bit. That's the rule for riding horses. The leg is like a ringing telephone: The horse must respond by stepping toward the bit in the same way that we would pick up a ringing phone and say hello.

Riders would do well to realize that the word "forward" can have various meanings that are actually quite different. When a trainer says, "Go more forward!" does she mean:

- Take longer strides?
- Take quicker strides?
- Add energy?

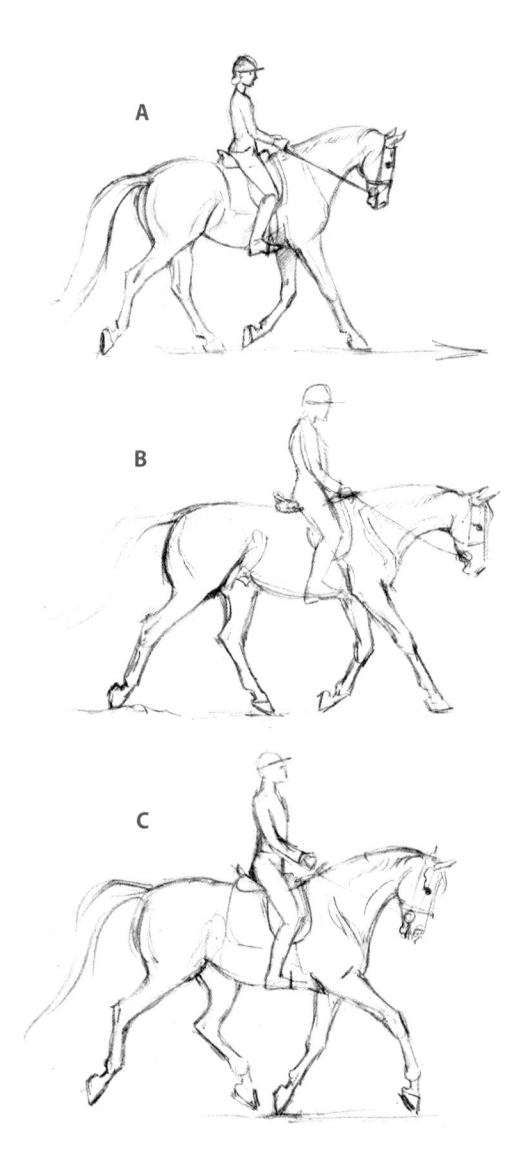

8.5 A–C The horse can avoid engaging and carrying weight in three different ways: (A) He can swing his hindquarters in or out; in this case, he stops stepping under his center of gravity and puts his weight on the forehand.

(B) He can leave his hind legs on the ground too long, which makes his frame long and, again, puts his weight on the forehand.

(C) He can pop his hind legs off the ground too quickly, making his croup high and, again, putting weight on the forehand.

Know what you want from your horse, and as you read further, you'll know how to ask for what you want.

Establishing workmanlike gaits is the purpose of the Training Level dressage tests and is a goal in the basic training of every horse in every discipline. The horse should go "forward in a clear and steady rhythm." The rider's *shaping, listening,* and *action aids* need to blend within this clock-like, reliable, rhythmic forwardness. When the rider's body absorbs the motion of her horse, and she is consistent in the tempo of her aids, the horse's body is encouraged to sing the same song and harmonize with his rider. (For more about the tempo of the aids, see p. 165.)

Activating the Hindquarters

An *activating* aid mobilizes and quickens the hindquarters with a little rat-a-tat from the calf or the whip. It's different from a *driving* aid that can have the effect of sending the horse forward and flat. It is used to enliven and quicken the hindquarters. It eagerly speaks to those hind legs and says, *Come on, come on! Are you ready? We're going to do something fun!* It's often necessary to activate and quicken the hind quarters at times when they are inclined to get slower, such as in corners or on small circles. Activating the hindquarters helps to change their mechanics from "pushing" off the ground to "carrying" the weight with a higher, more active step. It causes a change in the angle of the horse's pelvis, changing his shape longitudinally. At the same time, if the horse is aligned, the mechanics of the forehand changes, too. The front legs change their mechanics from "pulling" to "lifting" the forehand.

Normal riding accomplishes this changing of the mechanics of the forehand and hindquarters too, but the activating aid specifically encourages the horse to carry more promptly so the front-pulling engine starts to lift the torso. This activation of the hindquarters greatly assists in encouraging a horse to collection. Sometimes, when the rider activates the hindquarters, the horse initially becomes croup high, but in time, he learns to respond by lowering the hindquarters because the hind legs bend, which directly makes the croup lower. Turns-on-the-forehand and turns-on-the-haunches are exercises that directly help the rider to activate the hindquarters and encourage prompt responses from the hindquarters without covering more ground. Your horse will be in front of the leg and ready for action.

The Predictability Factor

When your horse's rhythm is reliable, there is no avoidance. The rhythm and tempo (speed of rhythm) are as predictable as the rhythm of a song. Be sure that *your* rhythm is just as reliable as his so your aids happen in the right tempo. Some riders ride too fast, but many ride too slowly. The clear and steady rhythm is self-perpetuating, and this predictability factor builds relaxation and mental confidence for both horse and rider.

There's something great about knowing what's going to happen next. So, I'm not simply talking about balancing your horse physically. *Mental* balance goes hand in hand with *physical* balance. When you and your horse both know what's going to happen next, you have mental and emotional peace of mind. When your body knows what's going to happen next, it can become even more metronome-like. That's Dressage Dynamics: the horse-and-rider working machinery that recycles energy automatically. In this state of "throughness" and harmony, the rhythm improves, your horse's back swings and he builds strong back muscles—a requirement for longitudinal balance and correct collection.

Now let's look at your horse's lateral balance issues. As you know, he isn't innately straight and this makes him unbalanced. He'll never solve this alignment problem on his own, but you can help him solve it (see p. 69).

Lateral Balance

When the horse is unbalanced *laterally*, he can fall left or fall right. When on a circle, or a bent line, we say the horse "falls in" or he "falls out." However, if he's balanced left to right and right to left, he can follow your very specific line of travel through straight lines and perfectly accurate bent lines. To follow a normal line of travel that's straight in some places and curved right or left in others, success is all about "bendability." Even when the horse isn't traveling on a bent line, his body should always have the ability (be ready) to bend and the ability to turn. Horses learn to balance laterally (from inside-leg-to-outside-rein aids) on a circle, and then when you go straight, the horse retains that bendability, balanced on the outside rein.

The Straightness Issue

When the horse can bend equally left and right, he's supple and straight. But, remember, horses are born challenged in the straightness department. Your training goal is to straighten him so that each hind leg carries an equal amount of weight and sends an equal amount of energy straight through the body. That sounds easy, but the plot thickens for two reasons:

- The horse's hips are wider than his shoulders (fig. 8.6). As a result of these wide hips, when left to his own devices, the horse will go down the track with his haunches "in," and his shoulders in the unfavorable position of "out."

- Horses are one-sided like people. The one-sided horse is physically crooked, which prevents the energy from flowing equally from the hind legs to the bit. Most horses have a left hind that carries more weight than the right. The right hind leg is inclined to step slightly to the right instead of narrowing to step underneath his weight—the place where two spines meet. As a result, the thrust of that right hind foot sends the horse's left shoulder out, causing him to lean on the left rein and take too little contact with the right rein. Some horses are one-sided in the other direction, but either way, a "crooked" horse can't step straight forward through the back to the bit longitudinally without guidance from his rider.

8.6 By nature, the horse is wider in his hips than he is in the shoulders. Left to his own devices, the horse's wide thrust from behind is inclined to throw his weight onto the forehand. Under saddle, the rider can help her horse step under his center of gravity by narrowing the hind legs in shoulder-fore.

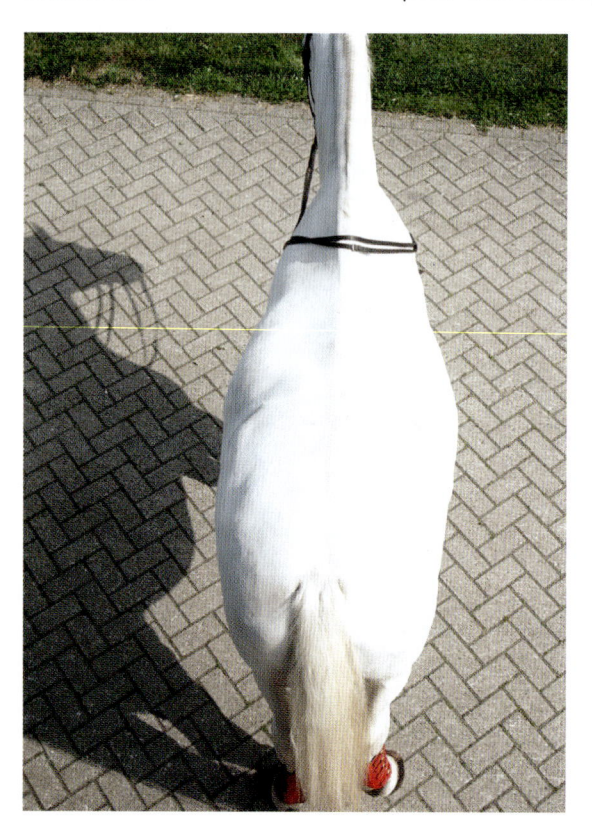

The Shoulder-Fore Solution

The problem is solved when the hind leg that is thrusting in the wrong direction can be narrowed to step under the center of gravity and bear weight (fig. 8.7). The rider narrows the inside hind leg (with her inside leg) so it steps in the track between the two front feet, and the outside hind aligns with and steps in the same track as the outside fore. The primary diagonal aids are inside leg to outside rein. The opposite diagonal aids are active only when needed: The inside rein asks for a little inside flexion and the guarding, outside leg prevents the outside hind from going out.

The discerning rider rides her horse in shoulder-fore all the time so he's straight and bendable to either left or right. When

how horses work

8.7 Mica works to narrow the footfall of Infanta's hind legs by doing shoulder-fore. The mare is slightly flexed left here, which identifies the left as the "inside." Mica rides from the inside leg to the outside rein, and she asks the inside (left) hind foot to step directly between the forefeet and under the place where two spines meet—under her center of gravity. Infanta's outside (right) hind needs to stay aligned with the outside fore.

BALANCE ISSUES 101

the bridge of muscle is strengthened equally to the left and the right, it is straight and strong. That's the perfect situation for developing collection.

Avoid these common problems with shoulder-fore:

- Some riders ask the horse to go sideways. Remember that shoulder-fore is a straightening exercise without lateral tendencies.

- Some riders *bend* the horse's neck. There should be slight *flexion to the inside* at the poll so the horse is *bendable,* but the neck should be almost straight.

To balance your horse in shoulder-fore, do Exercise 2 on page 104. You'll find a steady, self-perpetuating rhythm and relaxation with a nice feel in your hand.

"Throughness"

When the horse is longitudinally and laterally balanced, his energy goes through his entire spine freely and it recycles; then we say the horse is "through." The USDF definition of "throughness" tells us that the energy flows not only back to front but also front to back in a complete circle of energy, so the rein aids influence the hind legs. Do Exercise 3 on page 104 to help develop "throughness."

USDF Definition of "Throughness"

"Throughness" is the supple, elastic, unblocked, connected state of the horse's musculature that permits an unrestricted flow of energy from back to front and front to back, which allows the aids/influences to freely go through to all parts of the horse (e.g., the rein aids go through to reach and influence the hind legs.) "Throughness" is synonymous with the German term "*Durchlaessigkeit,*" or in English, "throughlettingness."

EXERCISES

EXERCISE 1
Get Your Horse's Pushing Engine in Gear

Directions To get your horse's pushing engine in gear, start from the moment you walk out of the barn with your horse in hand. Do you have to pull him out by his face, or does he step smartly from his hind legs and walk next to your shoulder? He might need to be asked with a cluck or a tap from your whip.

Step 1: Walk in Hand Ask your horse to give you the same walk that you will expect when you're sitting on him (fig. 8.8 A). While walking in hand, his only restrictions are the weight of the saddle and bridle. (When you mount, no matter how skilled you are, your weight is an additional restriction.

how horses work

8.8 A & B (A) Before Annie mounts, she hand walks Forte to warm up his hindquarters and get him moving from behind.

(B) Annie mounts and rides in a fairly free walk. She waits for the hindquarters to work in a self-perpetuating way.

Ideally, you want the energy stepping through his back and to your hand before he has this restriction.) Your horse's walk should convey a quiet workmanlike attitude. When you have a self-perpetuating, relaxed walk, get on. Many top riders hand walk their horses for 10 or 15 minutes before mounting.

Step 2: Mount and Walk on a Long Rein Walk on a long rein (if it feels safe). Be sure the pushing engine is still in gear given the added restriction of your weight (fig. 8.8 B). Carry your own weight in a balanced way so your horse's body won't be inclined to become like a hammock. If you have a mirror in your arena, walk parallel to it and ask yourself: *Why are we covering ground? Is it because of the front-end pulling engine or the hind-end pushing engine?*

Listen to the rhythm of the four-beat walk. When he's balanced, your horse takes energetic steps from behind that are deliberate and self-perpetuating, but not hectic. Feel the energy flowing under your seat. When he's stepping "through" his body, you can steer him easily with your body. Give yourself a steering test by riding simple figures and diagonal lines without rein contact. (Repeat Exercise 1 on page 64.) Leave your hands on the withers and point him on your line of travel with your eyes, shoulders, hips, knees, and toes, and step in the direction you want to go. He'll follow your weight and reach in that direction.

BALANCE ISSUES

EXERCISE 2
Connect Your Horse in Shoulder-Fore

Directions If you were successful with Exercise 1, you got your horse's pushing engine in gear and were able to steer without reins. This next exercise helps you connect your horse's engines by doing upward and downward transitions with half-halts in shoulder-fore.

Step 1 Shorten the stride and put your horse on the aids. Half-halt to rebalance him from behind into a shorter frame. This shorter frame invites you to shorten your reins. Channel your horse in the shape of shoulder-fore: The inside hind steps into the space between the two front legs (fig. 8.9 A). Keep the outside hind in alignment with the outside fore. Ride straight toward a mirror if possible so you can monitor your horse's shape. This is difficult, so be quietly persistent.

Step 2 Do forward-and-back transitions in the walk: Go from a free walk on the diagonal, back to a medium walk before the corner and through the short side and the next corner. Then do a free walk on the diagonal again. These transitions show your horse exactly how to respond. Ride from inside leg to outside rein in shoulder-fore, which balances him on the outside rein and helps him relax.

8.9 A & B (A) Annie asks for walk in shoulder-fore to help Forte balance.

(B) In the working trot, Annie tries to maintain the balance in shoulder-fore.

Step 3 Do shoulder-fore in trot and in canter (fig. 8.9 B). Shoulder-fore is difficult but persist quietly. When you're successful, your horse will give it to you more readily, because he likes to be balanced too!

EXERCISE 3
Transitions for "Throughness"

Directions Everyone knows how important it is to balance the horse on the outside rein, but very few riders are persistent enough about it to actually achieve the goal of "throughness." If you don't have a dressage arena, map out a 20-meter circle in your riding area. Although it's not important that the circle be exactly 20 meters, it *is* important that it be an exact circle because you want every stride to be the same.

how horses work

Find the center of your circle, and pace off 10 giant steps in four opposing directions. Mark these points with cones. This gives you an exact circular pathway that gives your horse a cylindrical shape to his body that balances him on the outside rein (fig. 8.10).

Step 1 Point your horse's nose exactly on the line of travel. Then, with your seat and legs, shape your horse's body like a banana on the arc of your circle. Do a working trot three-quarters of the way around, then walk one-quarter. Repeat while you help your horse find a consistent, balanced rhythm and frame in shoulder-fore. Try to keep the same feel in your hand. To ask for walk, keep your hands steady and push quietly against them. Your horse should keep reaching for the hand that stays forward. That will cause him to close his frame a little from behind while keeping the neck long. If the connection is lacking:

- Try using your inside leg with more ambition than you think you need. This helps position his inside leg under the center of gravity and it commits him to the outside rein.

- If the contact is too light or noncommittal, use your upward transitions to push him more forward.

- If he's too forward for the balance, use your half-halts and downward transitions to ask him to stabilize the balance. Sometimes make a transition to halt, or to halt and turn-on-the-forehand, so he learns to stay under your seat and carry more weight with the hindquarters.

Step 2 When he's balanced under your seat, where two spines meet, he'll feel nice in the hand. Repeat the exercise in the other direction: Trot three-quarters and walk one-quarter.

Step 3 Then do it with canter-trot transitions, too. Retain the shoulder-fore position at all times. Canter for three-quarters and trot for one quarter. Do straight lines sometimes, as well.

8.10 Mica rides Infanta from the inside leg to the outside rein on a precise circle to develop "throughness." The cylindrical shape of the outside of the horse's body is a sign of "throughness."

BALANCE ISSUES 105

Step 4 Mark off a precise 15-meter circle somewhere else and incorporate that into your riding. Change directions often. Soon you'll refine the invisible "Go" and "Whoa" aids until you know exactly how much you need to help your horse stay connected and balanced. He'll give you a steady, self-perpetuating rhythm in relaxation and with a nice feeling in your hands.

Essential Information about the Horse's Balance Issues

• When left to his own devices, the horse is always eager to use his front legs and somewhat unconscious about his hindquarters. This puts the horse out of balance and on the forehand.

• The rider can help by thinking of the horse's hindquarters and his forehand as his two engines—the hindquarters are for pushing and the forehand is for pulling.

• The rider can help her horse coordinate his two engines for a better balance with half-halts and transitions that slow down the forehand and encourage the hindquarters.

• The horse isn't "straight" by nature. And, because his hindquarters are wider than his shoulders, his balance is, once again, naturally on the forehand.

• The rider can help her horse's balance with shoulder-fore, which narrows the wide hindquarters and helps the horse step under the center of gravity.

CHAPTER NINE

How the Horse's Weight Distribution Changes

Improve Balance by Suppling and Strengthening

The word *balance* means *stability*. The rider who can monitor and regulate her horse's longitudinal (front-to-back) and lateral (left-to-right) balance has a stable, relaxed, sensitive horse. Then she can start to influence her horse's weight distribution—the amount of weight the horse carries with his front end in relation to his hind end. That's a different kind of balance.

When you see the horse in profile, his frame from tail to poll reveals his weight distribution. We refer to this weight distribution as his *longitudinal balance*. This use of the term "balance" refers to the location of the horse's center of gravity. We often say a horse is in a *downhill* balance, a *horizontal* balance, or an *uphill* balance.

Normally, throughout training, the horse's longitudinal balance develops and changes. It also changes during every ride. The center of gravity of a young horse is farther forward than the center of gravity of a trained horse. Likewise, the horse's center of gravity during his warm up is usually farther forward than it is at the end of his ride. As the horse's hind pushing engine becomes an engine that carries more weight, his center of gravity moves back. The horse's front-pulling engine, with the help of his abdominal muscles, starts to elevate the forehand. As a result of these changing forces, the horse develops longitudinally from a downhill, crooked animal to an uphill, straight, magnificent animal. But it all starts with downhill balance.

9.1 A By nature, the horse is in a downhill frame with most of his weight on the forehand. He starts his warm-up in this frame that he was born in. This balance isn't wrong, but the rider can improve it.

9.1 B As the horse warms up, the rider's shaping aids help him come to better balance in a more horizontal frame. He carries about 50 percent of his weight with the forehand and 50 percent with the hindquarters.

9.1 C In collection, the horse develops an uphill frame as he starts to take significant weight with the hindquarters. The forehand is visibly light and free.

Downhill Balance

When you first get on your horse, he's on the forehand (fig. 9.1 A). That means he has more than 50 percent of his weight on the shoulders. This balance isn't wrong: Horses are born on the forehand because the neck and head are attached to the front of an otherwise table-like structure.

This is his natural balance, and he starts every ride like this, where he's comfortable—as he is in the field, in his stall, or on cross-ties. If he's like 99 percent of horses, he's a bit crooked as well as being on the forehand. This on-the-forehand, crooked situation isn't a problem as long as you understand it and know the path to a better balance. As he develops over time, he spends less time in this frame because he understands the aids that improve his balance, and he becomes physically adept at carrying himself straighter and in a better balance. Normally, the horse's on-the-forehand balance improves quickly. During warm-up, the horse develops a physical connection with his rider in shoulder-fore. He becomes straighter and as a result, his weight is automatically distributed so he is in a horizontal frame.

Horizontal Balance

When your horse is horizontally balanced, he has approximately 50 percent of his weight on the front end and 50 percent on the hind end (fig. 9.1 B). It feels like he's carrying the same amount of weight on all four feet. Some of the well-bred horses of today are already close to this balance when they are born. The mature, well-schooled, and well-muscled horse also may start out in a horizontal balance. In the 50/50 balance, the horse no longer needs his neck to keep his balance, so it—along with the rest of his spine—can be relaxed and free. This is your first goal for all horses.

Uphill Balance

The end goal for dressage horses and jumpers is to develop an uphill balance in which the horse carries more weight with his hind end than with the front end—in a state of collection (fig. 9.1 C). Competitive dressage horses start elementary collection at Second Level. Consistent collection is a long-term goal. The average horse can't sustain a collected balance for long without a few years of bodybuilding. Further degrees of collection at the higher levels take even more bodybuilding.

High Collection

The highly trained horse demonstrates high collection by carrying an enormous amount of weight with the hindquarters when he is jumping high fences or doing the highly collected dressage movements—piaffe, passage, and pirouette (fig. 9.1 D). In the pirouette, the horse briefly carries 100 percent of his weight—and the rider's weight—on one hind leg. He only spends short periods of time in this high collection, no matter how strong or well-trained he is.

Assess your horse's longitudinal balance with Exercise 4 on page 115.

9.1 D In high collection, the equine athlete can carry a great deal of weight on the hindquarters for short periods of time. This includes the jumper at a high fence and the dressage horse in piaffe, passage, and pirouette.

Elastic Frames

The rider develops her horse's balance by suppling him. When she can create and be a part of the recycled, rhythmic energy, her aids ride on the energy that goes from the hind legs to the bit and back to the hind legs. Then the horse will follow the rider's hand to whatever frame she desires. The rider's seat and leg send energy to the hand at whatever length of stride and height of neck she desires, and then the horse pushes away from the bit and the energy is recycled back to the hindquarters.

Working Frame

The horse's working frame reflects his natural balance and conformation. It's the frame in which he does the working trot and working canter (fig. 9.2). In this frame, he can most easily be "connected" from back to front because it's the same as, or slightly shorter than, his frame in nature—

9.2 The Working Trot. Horses develop a connection with the rider in the working gaits as you see here. Infanta reaches through her neck for the bit as her hind leg "tracks up" or steps to the place where her forefoot is leaving the ground. Her frame is slightly shorter than it is naturally, for instance, when she is standing in her stall or on the cross-ties, so that she can be elastic and athletic. The other paces are all developed from the working paces.

9.3 The Lengthened Stride. The horse reaches throughout his topline, lengthening both the stride and the frame. The lengthened stride is first required at First Level and is a reflection of the horse's impulsion.

when in the pasture, the stall, or the aisle. When the frame is very slightly shorter than it is naturally, it allows the horse to be elastic and athletic. His topline "bridges" like a strung bow, and his energy can be recycled with half-halts, so his gaits become self-perpetuating and develop into a 50/50 balance. The horse is in complete comfort in this working frame. Unless the horse has a fleshy crest, the poll is the highest point of his topline.

Lengthened Frame

The horse covers more ground with longer strides while keeping the same rhythm and tempo (speed of the rhythm). The rhythm doesn't quicken as it is usually inclined to do; it stays clocklike (fig. 9.3). The frame lengthens as the stride does, and the energy circles through horse and rider with the aids riding on longer, not faster, waves of energy. Lengthenings are first required in First Level to test the horse's impulsion. They develop the horse's ability to reach for the bit, so it's critical that he is on, or in front of, the vertical with his poll the highest point.

Collected Frame

This is first required at Second Level where we find collected trot and collected canter (figs. 9.4 A & B). It is shorter than the working frame because the joints of the hindquarters bend and carry more weight (engage). As the joints of the hind legs bend, the

9.4 A & B (A) The Collected Trot. In collection, the horse retains the rhythm, activity, and energy of the working gait, but he shifts more weight to the hindquarters and the hind legs bend a bit more; the center of gravity shifts back. As a result, the horse takes higher, bouncier strides and he is freer in front. Mica and Infanta demonstrate this very well.

(B) The Collected Canter. The effect of Mica's half-halts is clear. Infanta's hindquarters step under the center of gravity and the forehand is light and free. The horse is clearly in an uphill, collected balance.

9.5 The Medium Trot. In the medium gaits, the horse retains the lift of collection and the reach of the lengthened stride. The result is a lofty, ground-covering stride and a longer frame.

croup lowers, and the front end lifts and lightens. The steps are lofty and energetic. The horse's neck falls down from the withers but is actually high because the shoulders are high. The horse's neck doesn't lift without his shoulders lifting. The horse lifts and carries the rider with expression. The waves of energy recycle in a shorter, higher circle, and the aids ride on the collected circle of energy. Unless the horse has a fleshy crest, the poll is the highest point.

Medium Frame

This frame combines lengthening *and* lifting (fig. 9.5). Medium paces are first required at Second Level. The horse retains his ability to thrust as he does in lengthenings, and he couples it with increased ability to lift his body as he does in collection. The waves of energy are both longer and loftier. The horse is more expressive than in the working frame. The energy continues to recycle in the same way. Unless the horse has a fleshy crest, the poll is the highest point.

9.6 The Extended Canter. In the extended gaits, the collected horse reaches to his maximum ability. We see the result in Infanta's uphill posture as she gives Mica the most ground coverage possible.

9.7 The Stretch. The horse should always be willing and able to follow the contact when the rider gives the reins forward. Infanta reaches forward and downward toward the bit and lifts her back. In this photo you can see the bulging of the topline muscles both in front of and behind the saddle. Mica feels it under the saddle, too. It feels good.

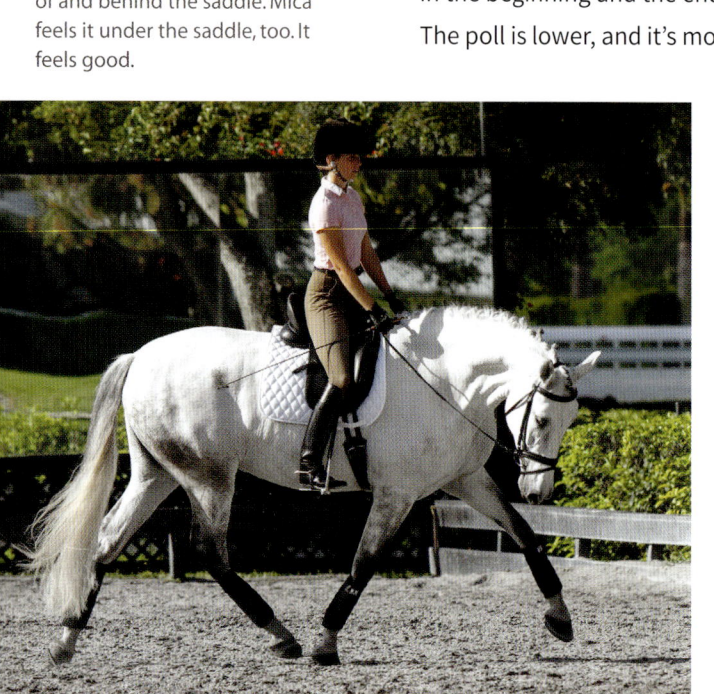

Extended Frame

This frame is the one in which the horse covers as much ground as possible (fig. 9.6). Think of a speedboat taking off. The horse's nose should reach to the place where the front foot is destined to land. The waves of energy are maximized. The poll is the highest point.

Stretching Frame

This refers to the frame in which the horse gradually "chews the reins" from the rider's hands and follows the bit by reaching in a forward-downward direction (fig. 9.7). The "chewing" (as opposed to distressed "chomping") is a sign of relaxation and acceptance of the bit. Stretching encourages relaxation of the entire topline. The neck "falls down" from the withers as it does in nature. This posture directly causes the back to lift, giving the topline a round, swinging action. It encourages reaching toward the contact through the base of the neck and the entire topline. Stretching is appropriate in the beginning and the end of the ride as well as during breaks throughout the ride. The poll is lower, and it's most important that the neck is evenly arched.

Sometimes riders make the mistake of allowing the stretching horse to be too long, disconnected, and on the forehand. The stretching frame—with connection—is used frequently for a high-headed horse that isn't naturally inclined to use his back well and might be difficult to connect. As the horse's neck is lowered and is carried by the upper muscles of the neck, it pulls the horse's back up (see fig. 19.2, p. 202).

Assess your horse's frame and self-carriage by doing Exercises 1 through 3 (pp. 113–115). As you make transitions and teach your horse how to use his body in different frames and balances, you'll benefit from being aware of timing and how to develop impulsion without speed. I cover this subject in the next chapter (p. 117).

EXERCISES

EXERCISE 1
Ask Yourself: How Is My Horse's Weight Distributed?

Directions Do you feel there is more weight on the horse's front legs? Is there equal weight on all four legs? Or, do you think he is collected and carrying more weight on the hindquarters? When he is on the forehand, don't focus on getting your horse collected. Focus on the next step, which is getting a balanced, horizontal frame with equal weight on all four legs, and a relaxed neck. Here's how:

Step 1 In shoulder-fore, do upward and downward transitions on an accurate 20-meter circle. Trot-walk-trot. Canter-trot-canter.

Step 2 On the circle, invite him to balance on your outside rein, and change directions often, using figure eights or serpentines. Lengthen and shorten the frame. Look for relaxation and a perfect rhythm. As he builds muscle, he'll become horizontal in his balance and, finally, he will collect. You'll know when he's strong enough to collect because the horizontal frame will be easy, and he'll offer strides of collection during your transitions.

EXERCISE 2
Ask Yourself: How Round Is My Horse?

Directions If you'd like your horse to be rounder, ask yourself *where* you would like him to be rounder. Riders are often preoccupied with the horse's head, and they try to make the horse rounder at the poll when the horse may, in fact, have the common problem of being *too* round there and not round enough through the rest of the back—that is, at the base of the neck in front of the withers, under the saddle, and in the loin area behind the saddle.

While many judges and trainers complain about horses that are too low in the poll (also behind the vertical), some riders are unwittingly asking their horses to be lower there. Often, riders need to be more sensitive with the poll, and instead, make their horses rounder *at the base of the neck*.

Step 1 If your horse is too round at the poll, go straight down the long side of your arena like a hunter. Let your horse reach out to the bit in a relaxed, rhythmic way.

Step 2 In shoulder-fore, circle 20 meters on the short side. Look down and visually check to see if your horse is wide at the base of the neck—in front of the withers. Roundness and fullness at the base of the neck is a visual indication that the horse's entire back is round. Still in shoulder-fore and on your circle, direct more energy with your seat and legs through the base of his neck. The outside of your horse's neck should puff up.

Step 3 To make your horse rounder at the base of the neck, be sure he is balanced on the outside rein, and then push the outside hand forward or lengthen the rein the amount that the horse will still take the bit. Don't throw the connection away (see "The Cue to Lower the Neck," p. 201).

Step 4 Go straight down the next long side in shoulder-fore to confirm your horse's reach to the bit.

Step 5 Transition to walk and check out your horse's neck as he moves naturally. Is the accent of his neck motion on the up and back? Or is it on the forward and downward? If the accent is on the up and back, he isn't reaching through his back. Put your horse on a large circle again, and repeat what you did in Step 3 to help him reach forward-downward so the energy flows through the base of the neck.

EXERCISE 3
Ask Yourself: Is My Horse Heavy in My Hands?

Directions The rein aids aren't for your horse to lean on or brace against. If your horse is leaning on you or you're inadvertently holding him, your horse isn't pushing away from the bit. (Review this concept on page 46 if you need to.) When horses are used to leaning, they start to hold their bodies tightly to accommodate. The energy doesn't recycle, so to get the circle of energy going, you'll need to do effective transitions both forward and back.

It's similar to when your car gets stuck in the mud and you need to rock it forward and back to get it out. Your transitions will gently rock the balance forward and back. Show him what you want and explain that your hands aren't a fifth wheel. Here's how you can "wean him off the hand":

Step 1 From a working trot, ride straight lines and accurate circles.

Step 2 Do a downward transition and see if he takes some of that weight back onto the hind legs. Then release the rein a little to tell him that you're not going to hold him up.

Step 3 With a light contact, go forward again, then repeat the downward transition.

Step 4 Pat him often on the inside neck to see if he relaxes his neck, carries it, and retains the bend.

Step 5 Do turns-on-the-forehand or turns-on-the-haunches to get him thinking about his hind legs; the more he thinks about them, the less he'll depend on your hands.

Step 6 If your horse is heavy on only one rein (for example, the left rein), shape him like a banana in shoulder-fore left. Half-halt with the left seat, leg, and rein, and concentrate on filling up the right rein that he doesn't want to accept. This will put his shoulders in the middle. Release and pat him often with the rein that your horse wants to depend on. Then, soften both reins until the horse stretches through the base of the neck and carries his own neck.

Step 7 Do these exercises in both directions in walk, trot, and canter.

EXERCISE 4
Ask Yourself: How Long Should My Horse Be?

Directions Whereas we often hear about horses that are too short, some are too long. Some riders, in an effort to avoid restricting the horse, ride the horse in a frame so long that he can't be athletically connected from back to front in a supple way. Imagine your horse when he is standing in the field. Imagine him in his stall or on the cross-ties. Then, as you ride him in the walk, trot, and canter, look at his profile in the arena mirror or in a video. He should be the same or slightly shorter than he is by nature, so he can be elastically connected. If he is longer than he is by nature, he'll be flat and unathletic in his frame; if he's much shorter than he is innately, he'll be too tight to be athletic.

Step 1 When your horse is *too long*, do a working trot on a 20-meter circle. Then make a downward transition to walk that you feel will close your horse's frame. Push against your fixed hand to close your horse from behind. Don't use your hand against your seat, which would just shorten his neck. Do a turn-on-the-forehand or a turn-on-the-haunches to communicate with your horse's hindquarters. Then make an immediate upward transition that will invigorate the hindquarters and increase the activity. Repeat these transitions and turns on the circle until your horse feels better connected and more "closed" in the frame. As he offers this shorter frame, you can shorten your reins. Do these transitions on straight lines, too.

Step 2 If your horse has become *too short*, do the same exercise and invite him to stretch on the circles. After you use your leg, do a mini rein release by touching the withers, and he'll relax and adopt a more comfortable frame. Adjust your reins to accommodate his new frame.

You can assess the correctness of your horse's frame by the relaxation of his neck, the feel in your hand, and the swing in his back.

Essential Information about Weight Distribution

- The horse's balance develops and changes. As the horse's pushing engine becomes an engine that carries more, the horse's center of gravity moves back. The front-pulling engine, with the help of the abdominal muscles, elevates the forehand.

- As a result of these changing forces, the horse develops longitudinally from having a downhill, crooked frame, to a horizontal frame, and finally to becoming an uphill, straight, magnificent animal.

- The rider develops her horse's balance by suppling him.

- The aids ride on the circle of energy that goes from the hind legs to the bit and back to the hind legs. The horse follows the rider's hand to whatever frame she desires.

- This suppling and strengthening work helps the horse balance.

how horses work

CHAPTER TEN

Impulsion and Engagement

Timing the Aids to Maximize Freedom

Have you ever taken the tiny spring out of a ballpoint pen? If so, you probably have compressed it, let it go and watched it sail effortlessly across the room (fig. 10.1). The science of springs is all about releasing stored energy. When the horse's hind leg *bends* and *carries weight* (engages), it stores energy, and when it *thrusts* and *reaches*, it releases that energy. The released energy that results in suspension (when all four legs are off the ground) is impulsion.

It only occurs in trot and canter, because walk doesn't have a moment of suspension. In the trot and canter, some degree of impulsion should always be present, but in dressage tests, judges begin to pay special attention to it at First Level when horses are required to lengthen the stride. It's worth noting that the German word for impulsion is *Schwung,* which has greater meaning. *Schwung* implies not only power and connection but also swing in the back, which is a prerequisite for collection (see p. 125).

Skilled riders know how to use this principle to create effortless "boing" (spring) from their horse. These are often the same riders who win at horse shows. They effortlessly and invisibly maximize the horse's impulsion without losing balance because they have timing.

10.1 Have you ever taken the tiny spring from a ballpoint pen, compressed it and sent it flying effortlessly through the air? The horse's hind legs act the same way. When the hind leg is engaged, it is compressed and carrying weight. When it thrusts, the horse "springs" off the ground.

Timing the Aids for Thrust, Reach, and Engagement

Whereas it's the horse that has impulsion and engagement, the rider has to be a partner for it to actually work. Well-timed aids are impulses that occur in the tempo and rhythm of the horse's gait. When the rider increases her horse's engagement, she feels for that "Whoa" moment when the hind leg lands and she sits a little heavier in a half-halt that leverages weight back to the hindquarters. When the horse's hind foot is on the ground, bent and carrying weight, it's like a coiled spring. Then, when the spring releases in the next moment of thrust, the rider gets free "boing." Suddenly, the horse has more power and self-carriage.

To master the timing of the aids, know that only your inside leg (and inside spur or whip) can influence your horse's inside hind leg. The same principle is, of course, true on the outside. When you learn to feel the moments when the hind leg carries, thrusts, and then reaches, you can help the horse at each moment.

- There is only one moment when your leg can influence your horse's inside hind leg to *thrust*: the moment when it thrusts off the ground. The rider sends an impulse in the thrusting moment (see 8.3 A, p. 90).

- The aids that influence your horse's ability to *reach* are an extension of and follow the aids that influence thrust (see fig. 8.3 B). The rider rides the wave of energy during suspension and guides the hind leg to the right point—to shoulder-fore.

- There is only one moment when your half-halt can add weight to your horse's hind leg: the moment when it is coming flat onto the ground and coiling (*engaging*). At this moment, the rider adds weight to coil the spring of the hind leg (see fig. 8.3 C).

Can you feel these moments? Some people feel them automatically. For obvious reasons, we say those riders "have feel." Almost all riders have to learn it by using a mirror or with the help of an eye on the ground. Here's how you can identify the moment of *thrust* in walk:

USDF Definition of Impulsion

Impulsion is thrust and the releasing of the energy stored by engagement. The energy is transmitted through a back that is free from negative tension and is manifested in the horse's elastic, whole-body movement. (Note: Impulsion is associated with a phase of suspension such as exists in trot and canter, but which does not exist in walk or piaffe. Therefore, impulsion is not applicable to the walk or the piaffe, even though both have energy.)

In *walk*, the inside hind leg is leaving the ground—or thrusting—at the same moment that:

1 Your horse's rib cage is swinging to the outside.

2 Your inside knee is inclined to fall down.

3 Your horse's inside foreleg is farthest back.

Feel for the moment of thrust in the walk by using Method 1 or 2. If you can't feel it, use your eyes and look down at your horse's inside fore to use Method 3. In time, you'll learn to feel it, and then your aid will become automatic.

In *trot*, the inside hind leg is thrusting off the ground as you are rising out of the saddle—or the would-be rising moment when you are sitting. From this, we know that the moment of engagement of the inside hind is the sitting moment—as it should be, because the rider can best add weight when she is sitting.

When the aids are used at the wrong moment, they are not only ineffective, they also make the horse dull to the aids because the horse isn't in a position to respond. For example, many riders in rising trot are inclined to squeeze their legs with the intent of driving the horse at the sitting moment, which as just explained, isn't effective and makes the driving aid less meaningful to the horse.

Learn to feel the correct moments, so you can use your driving and half-halt aids at the right time. The horse's movement is rhythmic and ongoing, like a song. Your body has to sing the song. There is a self-perpetuating little "Go" and "Whoa" within every stride. Feel for this rhythmic pattern. Make your aids in the same tempo as you want your horse's rhythm to be (fig. 10.2). This is homework for many months or years. Later you will be able to say that you have "feel." To help the timing of your aids, do Exercise 1 on page 120.

10.2 The rider is the metronome for her horse. The aids should be given in the right tempo—not too fast and not too slow.

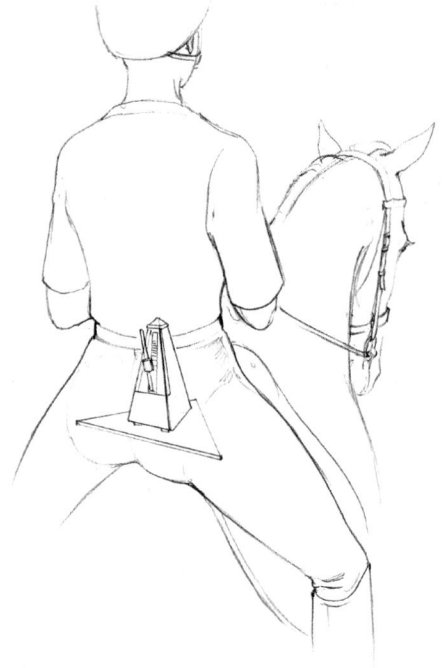

The Tempo of the Aids

Impulsion dissipates when the tempo is either too fast or too slow. You want to find a tempo that maximizes your ability to connect your horse in a self-perpetuating way. The timing of your aids must be correct (that is, your aid to "Go" or "Whoa" needs to be given at a time within your horse's stride when he is able to respond), and the tempo (or the speed of the aids) needs to be ideal. Some riders give the aids too fast, but most give the aids too slowly. If you need to increase the tempo of your aids, it doesn't mean the aids get louder. Think of the tick-tock of a clock. It's useful to be aware that horses are inclined to slow down in corners and circles, and they're inclined to speed up on straight lines. If your horse speeds up or slows down on his own, he'll lose engagement, thrust, and reach. He'll lose impulsion.

To confirm the consistency of the tempo of your aids, ride with a metronome or ride to music that has the correct timing for your horse's gaits. The walk tempo is usually about 100 beats per minute. Trot varies from horse to horse but is often between 138 and 154 beats per minute. Canter is usually 96 beats per minute.

10.3 When the rider understands the timing of the aids in leg-yield as Mica does, she has taken a giant step in understanding the moments when she is able to influence her horse.

EXERCISES

EXERCISE 1
Timing and Free "Boing"

Directions The rider who has mastered the timing of the aids for leg-yield has taken a giant leap in her ability to coordinate the aids (fig. 10.3). There is a little "Go" and a little "Whoa" in the leg-yield aids. The rider's leg and seat aids say, *Go forward and sideways,* to influence the thrust and reach phases of the inside hind leg.

In the "Whoa" or "Wait" moment, the rider snuggles with the outside aids into the engagement phase. Get the feel of this by trying the following leg-yield exercise:

Step 1 Begin by choosing a line of travel. Commit to a specific line for the forehand during your leg-yield. For example, you might track left, go down the centerline at A, and leg-yield to R. Ride the line straight with no leg-yield first. Your horse's shoulders need to stay on the one-and-only line of travel to R.

Step 2 Next, leg-yield in walk on this line of travel. Flex left and use your left leg rhythmically at each moment of reach. In a normal, not-too-steep leg-yield like this one, you ask your horse's inside hind leg to reach toward his outside foreleg. Be aware of your influence over his reach.

Step 3 Sit square and receive the forward-sideways energy with your right aids at each moment of engagement. Your outside aids keep the angle of his body parallel to the long side by preventing him from falling right. Left-right-left-right. Ask-receive-ask-receive. Be sure your receiving aids aren't too active. Receiving is a passive activity.

Step 4 When your horse understands, he should maintain this forward-sideways movement on his own with very few reminding aids, but those reminding aids should be made at the right moment. Be sure he feels eager and is responding promptly to your aids with an active rhythm. Check out the tempo of your aids.

Step 5 Next, do this leg-yield in trot. When you get to R, do a half 20-meter circle lengthening the stride. Then repeat the exercise.

Check to feel that the leg-yield has improved the lengthening by making it lofty. The lengthening should improve the leg-yield by making it more active. Be sure to do this exercise in both directions.

EXERCISE 2
Building Impulsion in the Trot

Directions This exercise utilizes *counter-canter* to develop power and straightness in the trot (fig. 10.4). The nice thing about the exercise is that you can use it with a relatively green horse because the counter-canter is only done on a straight line, so technically, it's only psychologically difficult rather than physically hard.

Step 1 At the beginning of the long side, pick up the counter lead. This may be counterintuitive for your horse because he might feel he should pick up the true lead. If he has trouble, start on the quarterline (at Point Q on the drawing) so your horse feels he can legitimately pick up a lead that allows him to turn toward the wall. In time, you'll be able to pick up either lead from anywhere you want.

10.4 In this exercise, the rider does transitions between counter-canter and trot. It is an easy exercise because the counter-canter is done on a straight line, so it is really only psychological counter-canter. It works to develop straightness and expression in the trot. When the rider takes the natural impulsion and straightness from the counter-canter and is able to infuse these qualities in the trot, the horse does a much more expressive trot.

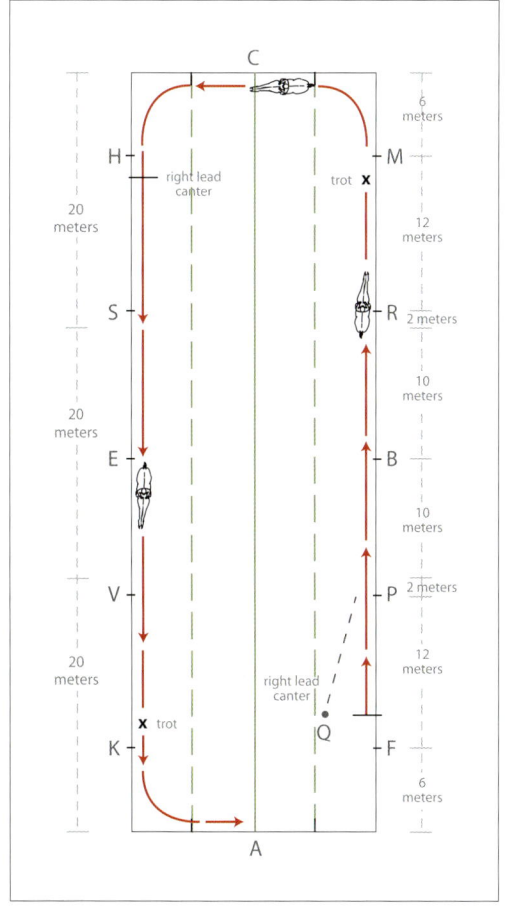

Step 2 On the long side, keep your horse straight in shoulder-fore right. Keep the neck straight and push the shoulders toward the wall. Be sure the hindquarters don't go in or out; keep them on the track.

Step 3 Before the corner letter (at Point X on the drawing), ask for trot. Trot through the corner, the short side, and the next corner.

Step 4 At the beginning of the next long side, repeat.

Step 5 Do this in both directions.

Because canter is a "jumping" gait, it has more natural impulsion than the trot. Counter-canter is the ultimate exercise in straightening. By combining both, this counter-canter exercise will add power, straightness, and swing to your trot.

EXERCISE 3
Feeling the Moment of Engagement

Directions Preparing for the turn-on-the-haunches is good preparation for anything because the rider has to search for that moment when the inside hind leg is bearing

10.5 Dutch Olympian Marlies van Baalen rides Rodrigo in turn-on-the-haunches with a nice connection between the inside leg and the outside rein in left bend. Marlies is getting a clear feeling of engagement when the hind legs step under her seat and engage. Preparing for turn-on-the-haunches is good preparation for anything because it helps the horse engage, and it helps the rider connect to that engagement.

weight, and she also has to search for the feeling that her horse steps right underneath her seat—the place where two spines meet (fig. 10.5).

1 Shape your horse in bend.

2 Feel the connection between your inside leg and outside rein.

3 Retain the bend, and step by step ask him to turn with a little leading inside rein and your outside aids.

Get the feeling of turn-on-the-haunches often. It is preparation for anything.

Essential Information about Impulsion and Engagement

- When the horse's hind leg bends and carries weight (engages), it stores energy, and when it thrusts and reaches, it releases that energy. The released energy that results in suspension is impulsion.

- Well-timed aids are impulses that occur in the rhythm and tempo of the horse's gait.

- When the rider increases her horse's engagement, she feels for that "Whoa" moment when the hind leg lands, and she sits a little heavier in a half-halt that leverages weight back to the hindquarters.

- When the horse's hind foot is on the ground, bent, and carrying weight, it's like a coiled spring. Then, when the spring releases in the next moment of thrust, the rider gets free "boing." She absorbs her horse's energy so she and her horse are connected in the circle of energy. She rides the wave of free energy and can add reach by driving at that moment. Suddenly, the horse has more power and self-carriage.

- Not only must the timing of the rider's aids be correct, but the tempo of the aids needs to be ideal. Some riders give the aids too fast, but most give the aids too slowly.

how horses work

CHAPTER ELEVEN

Leverage for Collection

When the horse's energy is going through the horse in a way that is rhythmic, supple, energetic, and straight, the back swings and it gets strong. Even if you've never felt a horse's back swing, look for that feeling anyway.

Collection happens within this self-perpetuating, swinging situation because of the principle of leverage. Leverage makes difficult work exponentially easier for the horse. It's easier for the rider too—starting with the shoulder-in at Second Level and developing to the highly collected Grand Prix movements of piaffe, passage, and pirouettes. You can make the science of Mother Nature work for you!

The Science of Leverage

The French word "*lever*" means "to raise." The English version of the word "lever" refers to a long, solid object such as a seesaw (or your horse's strong, swinging back) in which one end rises easily when you push the other end down. When engagement increases, the hindquarters lower because the joints bend more, so the forehand naturally becomes light and maneuverable (fig. 11.1). Work becomes easy for both horse and rider. It works in dynamic, rhythmic motion because the horse's back is strong, supple and swinging. Leverage overcomes the resistance of the weight of the forehand, causing it to rise with ease. The forehand becomes light and free. Leverage and collection cannot occur without the supple, strong, swinging back.

As the horse develops collection, the wise rider asks for only a little at a time so the hindquarters have a chance to become strong slowly. Frequent stretching and walk breaks rejuvenate the horse's muscles and relax him.

11.1 Collection can happen when the horse's strong back is swinging in a self-perpetuating way. Then when the hind legs bend, the hindquarters lower and the horse's back becomes like a lever that lifts the front end with ease. This principle of leverage is a law of nature, and when we use it, we make difficult work easy.

LEVERAGE FOR COLLECTION   125

Collection

Collection is a state of improvement in the horse's natural balance in which the horse carries more weight with his hindquarters as a result of correct, horse-friendly mechanics. He takes shorter strides without losing impulsion, causing the hind legs to bend more. As a result, the hindquarters lower and carry more weight, giving the horse an uphill frame with an arched, upward-reaching neck.

False Leverage

True leverage occurs when weight is transferred straight from front to back. It also occurs between inside leg and outside rein to straighten the horse and lighten the front end. *False leverage* occurs when the rider uses the inside rein to gain control, and the horse's weight goes on the forehand. Note that in a dangerous situation, it's not wrong to use the inside rein like this and put the horse on the forehand.

This was the case for Samantha one day when she and Igor were hacking in the field. Just as she was admiring how Igor's back felt, he adopted a giraffe-like pose and turned to stone. Igor was studying what was perhaps a crouched cougar at the edge of the wood. Even though Igor had been domesticated and never encountered life-threatening dangers in real life, his instinct to "revert to alert" persisted.

Igor was utterly unconscious about the speck of humanity on his back. Samantha knew that the best way to Igor's mind was through his body. Think "bend," she said of the neck and back that felt like a telephone pole. Samantha used *inside*-leg-to-*inside*-rein aids.

These *unilateral* aids (aids on the same side) are the *primary* bending aids. Even though most of us have been taught to use *diagonal* aids (inside leg to outside rein), sometimes we need unilateral aids. When it comes to safety, we just want the horse to go forward to the hand—any hand.

In many emergencies, these inside aids are the only ones that break up the horse's counterproductive rigidity. Samantha directed Igor's energy so his neck could be lower and looser. It was a start—a beginning that directed the energy in a way that would encourage looseness and relaxation.

Igor appreciated his rider's intervention. He soon sighed in relief and forgot the cougar. Once the neck was relaxed, Samantha gained control over Igor's whole body in bend. Then, she could balance him with *inside*-leg-to-*outside*-rein aids. Dangerous moments arise for every rider. Unilateral aids help, and there are no rules against half-halting with the *inside* Triangle of Aids. Half-halting with the inside aids also helps when the horse isn't yielding correctly to the inside rein. The horse can't go on the outside aids until he is accepting the inside aids.

Relative and Absolute Elevation

When the horse is straight, connected, and collected, the height of the withers and the shoulders is determined by the degree of engagement of the hindquarters. That is, the height of the horse's neck is "relative" to the engagement of the hindquarters, so this situation is called *relative elevation.* The horse's neck rises because the withers rise, and the rider can ride the forehand up or down by engaging the hindquarters more or less. For example, a Prix St. Georges dressage horse should, ideally, be able to demonstrate any level frame, from First Level up to his level of Prix St. Georges training.

When the horse is in relative elevation, he's working in a gymnastically sound way. The bridge of muscle is strong and the joints of the hindquarters bend and engage; the croup lowers so the forehand is naturally higher, lighter, and freer.

When the neck is falsely high because of the rider's hands, it's called *absolute elevation* and is gymnastically unsound. The horse's neck is up, but the shoulders are down. The uninformed observer might not know the difference between false and true collection, but in absolute elevation, the horse is in an impossible situation. Here's why:

When the shoulders are down and the neck is high, imagine what the horse must do to "reach" for the bit. In this position, he cannot reach for the bit without bringing his poll back and hollowing his neck in an upward, star-gazing way.

Be sure your horse's energy comes through the base of the neck in such a way that the withers can come up. Many riders have difficulties with channeling the energy through the base of the neck. If you are one of them, skip forward to Exercise 5 on page 160.

Finding Collection

Invariably when the rider thinks about increasing collection directly, something goes wrong. Often the neck shortens, and the horse gets tight and unhappy. That's why most experienced trainers don't directly ask their students for more collection. They ask for the underlying qualities that will give them collection—more impulsion or maybe more straightness. Maybe the neck is too high, and the horse isn't supple enough. They ask for something that gives the horse the ability to collect, and then it happens easily. Here are some exercises the rider can do that develop collection:

11.2 A & B Shoulder-in is the "mother exercise" of collection and the basis for all other lateral exercises. It sets the stage for the other lateral movements: travers (haunches-in), renvers (haunches-out), half-pass, and pirouette. First required at Second Level, shoulder-in leverages the inside leg and outside rein to mobilize and lighten the forehand. All lateral exercises directly develop collection. (A) Marlies demonstrates with Phoebe.

(B) Coby van Baalen rides shoulder-in with Kigali in a high degree of collection. The horse is in a clear uphill balance with great freedom of the forehand.

- Lateral movements, such as shoulder-in, haunches-in, and half-pass
- Rein-back
- Transitions that skip a gait (trot-halt-trot or canter-walk-canter)
- Half-halts

Shoulder-In

Shoulder-in, first required at Second Level dressage, is the "mother exercise" of collection, and it embodies the basics for all further lateral movements. In shoulder-in, the hind legs remain on the line of travel as they do in *shoulder-fore*, but the shoulders are brought to the inside until the outside fore steps in front of the inside hind (figs. 11.2 A & B). When standing behind or in front, you can see the horse steps on three tracks. It's critical that the three tracks not be obtained by moving the hindquarters out. That would put the weight on the shoulders instead of lightening them. When you move the shoulders, you displace weight to the hindquarters, which is your goal.

There is no value to the shoulder-in when riders make any of these common mistakes:

- Bringing the inside leg too far back swings the haunches out, causing loss of bend and putting the horse on the forehand. The angle of shoulder-in to the wall must be achieved by mobilizing the shoulders—not by pushing the hindquarters outside the line of travel.

- Overusing the inside rein makes a "neck-in" and prevents correct bend.

- Lifting the outside seat bone and leaning to the inside causes the rider to lose the pathway of "throughness" from the outside hind leg to the outside rein. Connection, "throughness," and self-carriage are impossible.

Test with *Überstreichen* to see if your collection is true.

Überstreichen

When the rider gives her horse the *Überstreichen* test, she releases one or both reins for several seconds (fig. 11.3). Ideally, the horse should retain his posture during this release. This test specifically asks the horse: *Are you in balance? Can you carry yourself without my aids holding you?* Some riders are unaware that they hold. The aids should balance your horse, not hold him up, and the horse shouldn't brace against the aids or lean on them.

11.3 The late, legendary German master, Dr. Reiner Klimke, frequently asked his students to pat the horse on the inside neck. The release of the rein rewards the horse and promotes relaxation. When the horse retains his balance, it is proof of self-carriage.

The late, legendary German master, Dr. Reiner Klimke, frequently asked his students to pat the horse on the inside of the neck. This required the rider to release the inside rein completely for several seconds—and reward the horse in the process. The release of the inside rein clearly gave the horse a little breathing room and promoted relaxation. It was also a test. It was proof that the horse was in self-carriage—or not. It was proof that he was balanced between the inside leg and the outside rein. The ideal result during the release of the inside rein is a horse that carries on happily without changing his rhythm, his bend, or his balance. It's proof that the horse is in relative elevation.

Try the shoulder-in and the rein-back exercises that follow to help you develop collection. Chapters Twelve and Thirteen will help with transitions and half-halts. Then, always test the quality of your collection with *Überstreichen*.

EXERCISES

EXERCISE 1
Shoulder-In for Collection

Directions In shoulder-in, you'll need to retain the 10-meter bend while going on a straight line (fig. 11.4).

Step 1 Confirm your horse's bend by doing a 10-meter circle in walk at the corner letter. When your circle is correct, every step will be the same. If retaining the bend is difficult on a circle, you won't be able to retain it while going straight in shoulder-in, so spend time with this if you need to. Before you make yourself and your horse dizzy or tired, make some straight lines and repeat your circles in different places and in different directions. When you can walk the circle comfortably, do it in trot. Then go on to Step 2.

Step 2 Before going straight in shoulder-in, do a half-halt in the shape of 10-meter bend with a deep inside seat and leg and an outside guarding leg. This half-halt says, *Wait a second. Pay attention to these bending aids. Here's what we're going to do now.*

Step 3 Now go straight down the long side retaining the 10-meter bend. The inside rein leads the shoulders to the inside, and the outside rein allows the shoulders to go in. The hindquarters follow the track in straightness as they always do. You should feel the connection between your inside leg and outside rein.

Step 4 Go only 12 meters and then straighten. You should feel a better trot (fig. 11.4 B).

Step 5 Then circle 10 meters again to reconfirm the bend and repeat the shoulder-in.

Step 6 Do this exercise in both directions.

EXERCISE 2
Rein-Back

Directions Rein-back directly engages each hind leg under the horse's center of gravity (fig. 11.5).

Step 1 From trot, do a square halt at A.

11.4 A & B (A) In shoulder-in, the horse retains the 10-meter bend throughout his body but travels on a straight line.

(B) After you have done shoulder-in in trot, straighten on the long side. You should feel a better trot. Shoulder-in improves the quality of the collected trot.

11.5 The rein-back directly creates engagement. As the horse steps straight back in diagonal pairs, one hind leg is engaged and then the other. Carl Hester and Uthopia gave the judge a remarkable demonstration at the European Championships in 2011 in Rotterdam, the Netherlands. Notice that Carl rides the rein-back in a very forward way. Uti keeps reaching for the bit, and Carl's hands are channeling him with forward expression.

Step 2 Lighten your seat and ask for only one or two steps of rein-back. It's not necessary to do more to achieve this goal of engagement.

Step 3 As you ride out of the rein-back, be sure you retain the engagement. You'll find that your trot is greatly improved.

Step 4 Do transitions at B, C, and E also, and repeat the exercise.

Step 5 Do this exercise in both directions.

EXERCISE 3
Überstreichen Asks: *Are You in Balance?*

Directions Try Dr. Klimke's exercise (see p. 129). On straight lines and large accurate circles, pat your horse on the inside neck. Two things can go wrong during the release:

1 If the horse looks to the outside when the rider gives the inside rein, it's a sign that the horse wasn't bent through the body from the inside leg and balanced on the outside rein. Rather, the rider's inside hand was unwittingly holding the "bend." No problem. Just re-explain the bending aids, and try again. And again.

2 If the horse drops his head or raises it when both reins are given, it's a sign that the rider was holding the horse's head and neck with her hands.

If your horse doesn't pass the test, he will, with that bit of freedom, put his neck in its natural position, based on what the rest of his body is doing. The horse always goes to the balance he has earned based on his engagement and balance. The rider can learn what she needs to do from this. Listen. Reapply the aids that help your horse balance and then release again.

There is more than one way the rider can release. *Überstreichen* can be toward the horse's ears or toward the bit. The rider can touch the withers often, which helps keep the energy flowing from the elbow to the bit, and it instantly makes the horse feel comfortable and centered. A mini-*Überstreichen* is invisible and just softens within the contact without making a loop in the rein. Regardless of how you release, do it frequently to encourage self-carriage and give your horse a feeling of freedom. This softening of the aids represents trust in the horse and trust in the system. The mature rider trusts, knowing that her trust will sometimes be betrayed. But when she continues to trust in the system and trust her horse, the ultimate reward is hers. In the next chapters, I'll look at two methods of developing collection: the use of *transitions* and *halt-halts*.

Essential Information about Collection

- Leverage makes difficult work exponentially easier for the horse.

- Because the horse's back is supple and strong, the forehand of the horse rises easily as the hindquarters lower in engagement. The forehand naturally becomes light and maneuverable.

- True leverage that creates collection is caused by the connection between the inside leg and the outside rein (diagonal aids). However, it isn't always wrong to use inside leg to inside rein (unilateral aids). Especially when safety is concerned, unilateral aids can be useful.

- *Relative elevation* is gymnastically correct and describes the situation in which the neck of the horse rises because the hindquarters engage, making the forehand light and free. *Absolute elevation* describes the incorrect situation in which the neck is elevated but the withers remain down.

- When the neck is high and the withers are down, the horse is in a hopeless situation.

- When riders want more collection, they do well to concentrate on qualities such as alignment, impulsion, and engagement. Exercises that develop collection include lateral exercises, rein-back, halt-halts, and transitions that skip a gait.

- *Überstreichen* encourages collection and tests it. By releasing the rein, the rider says, *Can you carry yourself?*

how horses work

CHAPTER TWELVE

Transitions

Connecting and Collecting Your Horse

If riding were just transportation, it would be about getting to your destination in the allotted time and then having enough skill to stop so you could get off. Some riders still seem satisfied to merely go from here to there in their gait of choice, but more discerning riders are sometimes dissatisfied with the quality of their transitions between and within gaits.

The purpose isn't to get into or out of the gait of choice, but rather to do it with grace, in a way that improves the horse. When riding reaches a fine sport and art form, transitions are about their effect on the horse's shape, balance, and self-carriage. It's not enough that the canter depart happened.

An "engaged" transition is one in which the horse's hind foot steps to the ideal point of engagement—under the center of gravity. Then the energy—and the rider's aids—are more likely to "go through" the horse's body.

The more thoughtful rider has evaluative questions running through her mind after each transition. She asks: *Did my horse stay straight in the canter depart, or did the haunches go in or out? Did the shoulders stay in front of the hindquarters? Did he step honestly under the center of gravity and bear weight? Did the energy go through the back to the bit? Did the neck stay relaxed? Did the canter depart happen at the moment when I asked for it or a stride later? Was the transition "clear" or was it prefaced by a shuffling little gait that doesn't have a name?* The answers to these questions form your training strategy as you try to explain to your horse what you want the next time.

Becoming the Leader of the Dance

Any transition is a *change*. You say to your horse, *Let's do this now.* When transitions are fairly frequent, they improve communication by keeping both parties tuned in to each other. These transitions not only make life fun and interesting for the horse, but they also put the rider in the position of leader because she is the one asking the questions, *Can you do this? How about this? Can you do that?*

This is one of the tremendous side effects of purposefully training with transitions. The rider becomes the friendly leader, and the horse listens because the work is interesting. Even when the transitions aren't totally successful, you'll notice that the gaits improve anyway—and that's the point.

When horse and rider are physically and mentally balanced, and the horse is frequently asked transition questions, the horse is, in fact, "always prepared"—physically and mentally.

Connecting and Collecting Transitions

12.1 Mica and Infanta demonstrate a consistent working trot in which every stride is the same. This consistency within any gait is the basis for good transitions.

The terms "connecting" and "collecting" refer to the rider's reason for doing the transitions. Correct connection always comes before collection. To begin, the horse should be able to do a consistent working trot or canter—one in which he is exactly the same every stride (fig. 12.1). The horse shouldn't increase (or decrease) the tempo, length of stride, or energy without the rider's permission. He shouldn't change his flexion or lose straightness. This consistency requires balance and speed control, and it's not always easy to achieve.

When every stride is the same, the horse feels "connected." This connected harmony can be achieved and confirmed with *connecting transitions,* which are *transitions between two adjacent gaits*. For example: Walk-halt-walk. Trot-walk-trot. Canter-trot-canter. *Connecting transitions* can also be *within* gaits. For example, working trot-lengthened stride in trot-working trot. Medium walk-free walk-medium walk. Working canter-lengthened stride in canter-working canter. These transitions balance the horse between the "Go" aids and the "Whoa" aids. As the balance develops, the downhill horse starts to become connected in a horizontal frame (see p. 108).

136 WHEN TWO SPINES ALIGN: DRESSAGE DYNAMICS

how horses work

12.2 A–D Trot-halt-trot transitions develop collection because they skip a gait. That is, there are no walk steps between the trot and the halt. The horse goes clearly from trot to halt and back to trot. These transitions require that Infanta engage behind in the downward transition and lift the forehand into the upward transition. Canter-walk-canter transitions also develop collection because they skip a gait. There should be no trot steps.

Collecting transitions skip a gait. For example: Trot-halt-trot—with no walk steps (figs. 12.2 A–D). Transitions that skip a gait require the horse to lift his torso in the upward transition. This changes the mechanics of how the horse works because the front legs stop pulling and start lifting the torso, which allows more space for the hindquarters to step under. Collection, and the transitions that create collection, are not possible if the connecting transitions aren't going through. If you try to collect a horse that isn't properly connected, he'll become hollow, crooked, and/or he will stop working with his hindquarters. Even top riders on Grand Prix horses are constantly thinking about the quality of the connection, which makes collection easy. Try Exercise 1 on page 144 to develop clean transitions that connect and collect the horse.

Training-Level Transitions

When a horse enters the competition arena at a working trot in a Training Level dressage test, he is not required to make any transitions that skip a gait. Even though the test says to enter the arena at trot and do a transition to halt at X, the rider can, and probably should, walk a few steps before the transition to halt. He is also encouraged to walk (briefly) before the next transition to trot after his salute. Transitions such as these between adjacent gaits serve to improve the connection, which is one of the goals of Training Level.

At First Level, the horse is required to do his first transition at X without walk strides. He goes from trot to halt—and back to trot—in a balance that requires a degree of collection.

At Second Level, he's asked to do the more difficult transitions that skip a gait, like walk-canter-walk.

TRANSITIONS

Upward and Downward Transitions

Some horses have trouble with upward transitions and some with downward transitions. Some have trouble with both, but as one improves the other generally improves, too, since they set one another up for success. The engaged upward transition makes the downward transition much easier, and vice versa. Here's how:

- *Upward transitions* are all about the *thrust* and the *reach*—the timing of them and the power of them. Upward transitions reinforce the "Go" aid. When the hind foot steps under the horse's center of gravity, carries weight, and thrusts reliably toward the hand, we say the transition is *engaged*. A surge of energy goes through the horse's topline, through the poll, and lands nicely in the rider's hand. When upward transitions are not engaged, the energy doesn't reach the bit, or it goes beyond the bit, or it's not straight, sending it out a shoulder. The rider can use the upward transitions to get a more solid feel in the hand. For example, a lengthened stride can invite more energy and contact.

- *Downward transitions* are all about the engagement. They reinforce the "Whoa" aid. Downward transitions are the result of half-halts that bring the horse back, make his body rounder, and the strides shorter but not less active. It feels as if the transition touches one grounded hind foot or the other—that is, the half-halt that creates this transition connects the rider to whichever hind foot is grounded. The rider feels the grounded hind foot in her seat, her elbows, and in her hand where it "connects" the bit to the horse's hind end—from front to back. But the energy, at the same time, keeps rolling forward from back to front. Engaged downward transitions ideally recycle the energy, returning it to a hind foot during the moment of engagement. The horse's neck stays relaxed and free; he "closes" his frame from behind as he steps to the ideal point of thrust. Then the horse is set up for a good upward transition.

Bit by bit, muscular changes in your horse's body occur that prepare him for collection. These are physical changes that eventually make collection easy for him. The horse needs to be prepared for collection mentally, too. Some people feel that dressage is a bit of a claustrophobic situation for horses. There is a bit of truth to that, but when done well, the horse should feel free in collection rather than trapped. The body parts that the rider asks the horse to compress are behind the saddle, and he's not emotionally averse to compressing his hindquarters. He is, however, emotionally averse to having a tight neck and being held behind the vertical. In normal training, that may happen briefly, but should never be a posture that is maintained.

Once the horse is in a horizontal balance, he might offer strides of collection. He carries a little more weight behind and his gaits become springier. He presents himself in a more uphill frame with a lighter forehand. That's a sign that the horse is ready to collect.

Tips for Good Transitions

Make Only One Change at a Time

For example, don't change flexion during a transition between or within gaits. In a transition from a four-beat walk to a two-beat trot or a three-beat canter, the rhythm changes—but the energy, frame, bend, and line of travel all stay the same. In a transition from working trot to a lengthened stride in trot, the frame changes but the rhythm, bend, energy, and line of travel all stay the same. Of course, upward transitions can be used to increase the energy, but only when the rider consciously wants or needs more energy or a more solid contact. Then she can—by choice—increase the energy in an upward transition to improve the contact.

Energy Conversion

Transitions are about energy conversion. There is not, necessarily, more energy in the upward transition than in the downward transition. The rider takes the energy of walk and turns this same energy into trot or canter. She takes the trot energy and converts it to walk energy or canter energy. Transitions are easier when the energy level stays the same. The horse doesn't "burst" into canter from trot or "burst" into a medium trot from the collected trot in a way that leaves the hind legs trailing behind him where they can't carry much weight. He doesn't "fade" to collection from the medium paces. In fact, because these inclinations are so pervasive, it is helpful to imagine the reverse: Softly fade into your medium paces (so you don't lose the hindquarters) and burst forward into your collection. That will help the energy stay consistent. When the energy varies within the transitions, it makes smooth transitions difficult.

When the energy stays the same during up and down transitions, it goes to the rider's hand in the downward transitions in the same way it goes to the hand in upward transitions. This isn't always possible, but it's always the goal. Remember the Circle of Energy. The energy never goes backward through the reins (pulling) from the bit to the rider's elbow. It's similar to how water flows from the hydrant in the barn, through the hose to the water bucket: Water never goes from the bucket through the hose to the hydrant. It always goes from the hydrant to the bucket. You can, however, slow the amount of water or turn it off. Your rein aid can slow the energy or shut it off or recycle it—but it can't make it go against the current.

As you decrease the length of stride while keeping the energy the same, the height of the stride naturally increases. What you lose in length, you gain in height, so these transitions help develop collection. When the energy stays the same, the horse learns that big strides don't become small strides. Rather, big strides become short, high strides. The energy of a big stride becomes compressed into a smaller circle of energy and within a rounder, shorter-framed physical body—making the stride and the frame higher and more expressive. The rider takes the same amount of energy, shapes it, and moves it around. You can do transitions between lengthening and working paces or between medium and collected paces. Do Exercise 2 on page 145 to help you monitor the energy.

Monitor the Frame

In transitions *between* gaits, many horses want to become longer in the frame. For example, in the transition from trot to canter, the horse might be inclined to get longer in the frame because he keeps his hind legs on the ground too long and disengages during the transition.

In transitions *within* the gaits, the frame should change as much as the length of the stride changes.

Relax the Neck

When the horse's neck stays relaxed during a transition, it's a very positive sign because the state of the neck is a reflection of the entire spine. The horse can't have a relaxed back if he has a tense neck. A transition that is accomplished with a relaxed neck is the direct result of a rider who has learned how to influence the horse with very little hand. Her horse has learned the body language of half-halts: The horse engages when he responds to half-halts by shortening his frame from behind instead of shortening and tensing the neck.

When the rider *does* need to use her hands, she brings her hips toward her fixed hand instead of pulling her hands back. As a result, the horse's hind legs follow the rider's hips forward to engagement. They step under and carry more weight.

how horses work

Monitor the Bend

Your "shaping" aids need to prevail during your transition. As you know, horses are inclined to take the bend away and straighten (in an incorrect way by losing alignment and stiffening) on their own whenever they have an opportunity (see p. 100). Pay attention to how much bend your horse has. If he has 15-meter bend before your transition, he should have 15-meter bend during and after his transition. Anytime you do a transition, you are increasing your request; if he negotiates by decreasing or losing the bend—or getting crooked—your horse hasn't improved.

Monitor the Rhythm

The rhythm is the beat or footfall that is characteristic of walk, trot, or canter. "Tempo" is included in this definition, because it is the speed of the rhythm. To make a "clear transition" from one gait to another, you go from one characteristic footfall to the next without any muddled, shuffling or undefined steps. You go, for example, from a four-beat walk to a two-beat trot clearly.

When the transition is within a gait, for example, from working trot to a lengthened stride, the rhythm and the tempo of the rhythm stay the same—like a ticking clock or metronome with a steady beat that never changes. Do Exercise 3 on page 146 to help you monitor the rhythm and energy.

Monitor the Speed

Downward transitions will be smooth if you're able to monitor the miles per hour. For example, decrease the length of stride in trot until your horse is momentarily going the same miles per hour as walk; then walk. Decrease the length of stride in canter until you're going the same miles per hour as trot; then ask for trot. If there is too big a discrepancy between the speed of each gait, the transition will be abrupt and awkward.

Look for the Possibility

Doing transitions that are engaged is like creating anything else you want in life: You look for the possibility and then arrange for it. In the canter-trot transition, looking for the possibility of trot is the best kind of preparation you can do. Wait until a half-halt touches a hind leg—until you feel it is engaged—and the inside hind foot is stepping directly under you, so you can gain access to it. As your half-halts give you access, you know the transition will probably be smooth. Feel for the *possibility* of trot in the walk, the possibility of walk in the trot, the possibility of canter in the trot or in the walk. Ideally, anything should be possible. Think that way. To help you look for the possibility, try Exercise 4 on page 147.

Have a Clear Idea

We've all ridden the horse that is like a wind-down toy. You ask your horse to go, and he may be quite obliging at first, but then you notice that he is going a little less…and less…until you're finally sure that the pace is lacking. Or, he may be accelerating bit by bit. This is a situation in which the rider's mind needs to be the leader. You need to have a fixed idea of what, for example, a working trot is. That's the only trot that you do, and every step is the same—exactly the same—until you decide to do something else. If you want him to lengthen the stride on the diagonal but he fades and loses energy on the final quarterline, you can't do a good transition at the end of the diagonal. You will have lost the engagement of the hind legs, along with the solid back-to-front connection and the "swing" in the back. Have a clear idea of what you want, ask for it, and expect your horse to continue until you ask him to do something else. This is the mark of a well-trained horse (fig. 12.3).

Teaching Your Horse with Clarity

At our farm, we've had some memorable horses, and one of the first ones was Chablis who was trained to Grand Prix by Robert Dover many years ago. Chablis taught me what Robert Dover taught him. One of those lessons was that every step of extended trot was the same. When he did an extended trot on the diagonal, every step was exactly the same: M-X-K, H-X-F. He always gave us the same number of strides before and after X, the same length of stride, the same balance, and the same energy. Chablis had a very clear idea of what an extended trot was, and I'm sure he got that idea from Robert Dover. In turn, Chablis gave *me* that understanding. His extended trot was absolutely the best he could do, and he did it consistently from start to finish.

This clarity regarding the paces needs to be in the rider's mind first, and it is what makes good transitions possible. You need to know what you want. If you're not sure, try something, but make it specific and consistent. Down the road, a trainer might tell you that your idea of the pace needs to be more or less, or maybe he will say it's just right. Transitions are best done from a very defined, distinct pace. In Chablis' case, he gave us a clear idea of what, exactly, an extended trot was, and what a collected trot was. We were never going from something fuzzy to something else fuzzy. With Chablis, the task of doing a transition at the letter was easy because he had such a specific definition of each of the paces.

how horses work

12.3 Well-trained horses have a clear, very specific idea of what each movement is. They get this clarity from their rider. Robert Dover and Kennedy are clearly in agreement during this extended canter in San Juan Capistrano, California, in 2004.

Always Do Something That Has a Name

Sometimes riders—especially when they're taking a break—wander aimlessly and use their aids unconsciously. This teaches the horse that there is more than one set of rules. Later, at a horse show or a clinic, how should the horse know that the rules are different? Consistency gives horses confidence. For taking breaks, we have the free walk and stretching. Ride them as if you were being judged. These defined paces maximize the potential of the horse by making him free in front and controlled by the rider behind.

Always do something that has a name. That doesn't mean you can't take a break, but your horse must not turn into a "hammock" when you do. And you can't turn into

12.4 A & B (A) Mica and Infanta demonstrate an exemplary free walk. The horse retains the basics of rhythm, suppleness in the back, and reach through the topline. It's evident that this walk has enough energy and overstride. It would get a very high mark if it were being judged. More important, it maximizes the scope of Infanta's movement.

(B) In the transition to medium walk, Mica keeps the rhythm and activity and channels Infanta into shorter strides in shoulder-fore.

a slouch. Give your horse the longest rein possible so he can stretch and relax in the walk while retaining the bridge of muscle that he has built to carry you. Always do something that has a name. Then your horse will understand clearly (figs. 12.4 A & B).

EXERCISES

EXERCISE 1
Clean Transitions That Are Connecting Then Collecting

Directions To improve your connection, go for a playful, organized game of "Go and Whoa" that involves up and down transitions between adjacent gaits—that is, walk-halt-walk, walk-trot-walk, trot-canter-trot.
Try these pointers:

• Make the transitions at predictable places so your horse starts to cooperate, and you can wean him off your hand. You can make your transitions at the middle of each long and short side, or you can make them at the letters R, S, V, and P. It doesn't matter, but in the transitions, use your hands last, and you'll need less and less hand. Your horse will learn to listen to your body language and anticipate where your transitions will come.

• Pay special attention to the first step in the new gait—your horse shouldn't fall or collapse into the slower gait—and burst into the faster gait. The balance should stay the same, and the transitions should be clean—that is, you go from a four-beat walk to a two-beat trot with no shuffling steps; you go from a two-beat trot to a three-beat canter cleanly. Clean transitions help connect the horse in a balance that makes his back swing. You'll find the swinging back when you have those two qualities:

1 He steps rhythmically forward from the leg to the hand in a clean upward transition.

2 He is always willing to come back and step under your seat from a light seat-against-rein aid.

In the process, you build the basic qualities of Training Level: Your horse's muscles are supple and loose, and he moves freely forward in a self-perpetuating rhythm, accepting contact with the bit.

When your horse's connecting transitions are easy, and your horse is fit enough, try collecting transitions that skip a gait: Trot-halt-trot. Canter-walk-canter. Follow these pointers:

- Do them at the same predictable places as you did before.

- Make the transitions easier by doing a 10-meter circle at a letter. Then do the downward transition in the last stride of the circle as you approach the track. When these transitions are clean and easy, your horse's ability to engage and collect becomes greatly enhanced.

EXERCISE 2
Energy Conversion

Step 1 Go from working trot to walk, and back to trot several times. Concentrate only on the energy and the feel in your hand. Try to keep the feel in your hand the same in the walk, the trot, and the transitions between them. Feel that you use your seat to convert the trot energy to walk energy, and the walk energy to trot energy. Keep the same energy all the time. Recycle it with transitions.

Step 2 Now try this: Do a downward transition from walk or trot to a halt. This is not the same as a stop. When you stop your car, you put it in "park" and turn off the key. When you bring your horse to a halt, you leave his engine idling, and go forward again soon. The energy needs to keep rolling through your horse as you halt. When the horse learns to keep the energy running in the halt—like a car that is idling—his transitions improve because he is ready to go!

EXERCISE 3
Retaining the Rhythm

Directions In trot, lengthen for only a few strides, and then come back. It doesn't matter if you only lengthen slightly, but aim for that elastic-band feeling in which the rhythm always stays the same and the circle of energy isn't interrupted. Perhaps your horse only over-strides a few inches. The point is that you retain the same rhythm, energy, and relaxation of the neck. You've probably noticed how horses naturally want to increase the tempo when they do upward transitions, and decrease the tempo when they do downward transitions. Both of these problems allow the horse to disengage.

If it helps, put a metronome in your pocket. When you retain the same tempo, he won't hurry onto the forehand in the lengthening.

Anytime the stride lengthens and quickens at the same time, the horse goes more on the forehand. In the following exercise, you avoid that by combining the lengthened stride and the leg-yield. The leg-yield requires that the rider use her inside-leg-to-outside-rein half-halts to ask the horse to reach with his inside hind leg toward his outside foreleg. This helps the horse engage to the ideal point and puts him in an advantageous position to push off into a "scopey" lengthening that doesn't get faster.

The following exercise takes your horse's natural inclinations and helps him overcome them. It not only helps you bring more suppleness to the lengthening, but it also adds more power to the leg-yield (which is inclined to become less energetic). When you decrease the length of the stride but keep the energy the same, the *height* of the stride increases. What you lose in length, you gain in height. This is how collection develops.

Step 1 Your goal is to keep the rhythm, so have a song in your head, or carry a metronome as you ride. Begin by tracking right in trot.

Step 2 Turn down the centerline.

Step 3 From your right leg, leg-yield left two or three steps toward the long side. Keep your horse parallel to the long side, and keep that song in your head. Make the music crescendo a bit during the leg-yield.

Step 4 Then, with your outside (left) Triangle of Aids, straighten from the leg-yield, ride a line parallel to the long side, and lengthen the stride. Maybe the music gets softer during your lengthening, and the tempo stays the same.

Step 5 Then make the motion of the floor of your seat and your circle of aids smaller, push against your hand to half-halt, and bring your horse to smaller strides. Then ask for leg-yield to stronger music again.

Step 6 Straighten and lengthen again to a soft beat.

Step 7 Repeat in the other direction.

Step 8 If your horse stiffens too much in the lengthening, do that part of the exercise on a large circle.

Try This

- Try switching the times when you're inclined to sit or rise to the trot. Sit to the lengthening. Rise to the leg-yield, and feel your horse's back come up. This will set you up well for the next lengthening.

- Ask for more contact in the lengthening and a lighter contact in the downward transition to your working gait. Your horse will get used to gathering himself and engaging the hind legs with minimal use of your hands.

EXERCISE 4
Looking for the Possibility

Directions Looking for the possibility of a transition is all about gaining access to the hindquarters and keeping connected to them.

Step 1 Do a trot-walk transition and immediately do a leg-yield or shoulder-fore. Then trot off again.

Step 2 Next, halt briefly and do a turn-on-the-forehand or a turn-on-the-haunches. Then trot off again. The turn or movement teaches him that he needs to stay connected and listening with his hindquarters in the walk. Even if the turn or the movement isn't perfect, it improves him anyway and makes the next upward transition more supple, engaged, and obedient. It makes the next transition more *possible*.

Step 3 Do variations of the same theme: Leg-yield or confirm your shoulder-fore before the transition to canter. These transitions help you retain the ability to "Go" in downward transitions, and they help you retain the ability to "Whoa" in the forward work. When the circle of aids is working you can easily adjust your horse within that circle, making anything possible. You want to be in the "land of all possibilities."

Essential Information about Transitions

- The purpose of transitions isn't to get into the gait of choice, but rather to do it with grace, in a way that improves the horse. Transitions can improve the connection and then collect him.

- Transitions not only make life fun and interesting for the horse, they also put the rider in the position of leader.

- Transitions between two adjacent gaits connect the horse. For example, trot-walk-halt-walk-trot.

- Transitions that skip a gait require the horse to lift his torso and engage his hindquarters. For example, trot-halt-trot, canter-walk-canter.

- Upward transitions are all about the thrust and the reach. They reinforce the "Go."

- Downward transitions are all about engagement. They reinforce the "Whoa."

- Use the following tips for good transitions:

    1 Make one change at a time.
    2 Convert the energy.
    3 Monitor the frame.
    4 Relax the neck.
    5 Monitor the bend.
    6 Monitor the rhythm.
    7 Monitor the speed.
    8 Look for the possibility. (Feel for the right moment to make the transition.)

- Have a clear idea of what you want, and *always do something that has a name* (see p. 143).

CHAPTER THIRTEEN

Half-Halts

Connecting and Collecting Your Horse

Half-halts influence your horse in the same way as transitions. They improve your horse's gaits because they improve his balance by "engaging" him, so he can carry himself better. Half-halts, like transitions, can have a *connecting* effect or a *collecting* effect. When you're successful, you get a cascade of positive events: The hindquarters come through in a more supple, elastic way, the back swings, and bit by bit, your horse carries more weight with the hind legs and is freer in the front.

What the Heck Is a Half-Halt?

From earlier (p. 94), you might remember that half-halts can mean many different things, and they, literally, come in all sizes and shapes. Remember that a half-halt can mean:

- *Balance under me in left bend so you can prepare to do a left shoulder-in.*

- *Balance under me with shorter, more active strides to prepare for a transition from trot to walk.*

- *Balance under me and gather yourself in preparation to thrust into an extended trot.*

The half-halt can have countless meanings, but it always means, *Balance under me—where two spines meet*. The generic half-halt recipe is, "*Go,*" "*Whoa,*" "*Soften.*" These three parts of the half-halt are equally important for the hot horse and for the lazy horse.

- Riders of *forward-thinking* or *hot horses* often forget the *forward* part of the half-halt. They think they only need to come back, because, mistakenly, they think they already have "Go." Remember the *faux runaway* on page 88? That horse is going, but not from behind.

- Riders of *lazy horses* often forget the "Whoa" part of the half-halt. They think they only need *forwardness* because, mistakenly, they think they already have "Whoa."

The fact is, the hot horse might need more "Whoa" and the lazy horse might need more "Go," but all half-halts need some version *of both* because the rider has to be able to *participate* to be able to adjust her horse. Here's a closer look at the three parts of the half-halt.

"Go": Part 1 of the Half-Halt

The seat and leg aids—and the entire Vertical Powerline—send a message to the pushing engine: *Step up to my hand.* The rider sits *toward* a receiving, soft hand that follows the mouth. Judge and trainer Janet Foy likens the horse's back-to-front connection to an electrical connection (fig. 13.1). If there were a light bulb at the horse's poll, it would light up when the energy gets all the way to the poll. When the horse is honest to the bit, the light is always on. However, in some cases, that light bulb is just flickering and threatening to go out. When that's the case, you need to push and ask him to step more honestly through his body, through the poll, to the bit.

When you're successful, the horse draws, not so much on your hands, but on your elbows, lower back, and seat—that is, on your Vertical Powerline. The hands are just a conduit. That's the connection within you that creates the connection within him. The horse feels "puffed up" or inflated in front of you—like a cushion that you can half-halt against. If you don't have that, the half-halt won't work and you need to go back and achieve that connection. Many riders make the unconscious mistake of sitting against the motion in this phase.

13.1 Judge and trainer Janet Foy says the energy flowing through the horse's topline should reach the poll and "turn on the light." When the horse is in front of the leg, this light won't flicker and threaten to go out during half-halts.

how horses work

13.2 Mica and Infanta demonstrate the "Whoa" moment of the half-halt; Mica pushes against a low, fixed hand to gather her horse from behind. Infanta's right hind leg is about to engage.

"Whoa": Part 2 of the Half-Halt

During the "Whoa" moment, the horse's hind leg finishes its flight pattern and comes under the center of gravity of both horse and rider to engage and carry weight. At this moment, the "light" is still on at the horse's poll, and the rider sits against or pushes against a fixed hand instead of a following hand (fig. 13.2). In so doing, the rider transfers some of that weight in the front to an engaged hind leg. The horse pushes away from the bit and gets lighter in the hand.

Sometimes, the horse doesn't respond to the ideal half-halt, in which case, the rider needs to give a stronger half-halt. The rider brings the hand back, fixes it, and then pushes against it. This isn't a pulling hand because the rider is still pushing to a fixed hand. Part 3 of the half-halt must follow immediately.

"Soften": Part 3 of the Half-Halt

When the rider feels the hindquarters "connect" to the front, the softening aid happens immediately, which invites the horse to step "through" and confirm his commitment to the bit (fig. 13.3). The softening of your hands and other aids encourages and allows freedom and self-carriage. You don't throw away the contact, but rather the softening occurs within the contact. This is the reward for the horse. Remember "many small givings." It's the most important part of riding because it constantly invites self-carriage in whatever frame the horse's body is honestly earning from behind. Try Exercise 1 on page 156 for details on how to do a half-halt.

13.3 Mica softens the inside rein to keep the "front door" open for the horse. This moment allows the horse to carry himself and feel free.

Automatic Half-Halts

In the automatic half-halt, the rider's seat, leg, and hand aids work every stride in a self-perpetuating, flowing circle of "Go," "Whoa," and "Soften" aids. When the horse has a swinging back and the rider has swinging hips and rhythmic aids, the horse can work in rhythm, with small "Go" and "Whoa" aids that provide boundaries and balance him automatically every stride. Communication is very quiet but very constant, like the rock of a rocking chair or the pendulum of a clock. The rider's aids "ride" on this circular flow of energy through the horse, and they serve to improve, stabilize, and confirm the forward balance of the horse. They shape him and position him so the work is as easy as possible.

When automatic half-halts occur every stride, the horse never gets too far out of balance and very tiny aids are effective. He can collect easily and assume an uphill frame suitable to his strength and training.

Imagine This

Remember your empty rocking chair from page 96? You set it in motion by pushing it either forward or back. Of course, it continues rocking forward and back in perpetual motion until you need to give it a reminder to keep going. It's the same with your horse. Every balanced stride has a *thrusting-reaching* moment and a *carrying* moment, which represents, respectively, a little "Go" and an equal "Whoa."

Visualize the rocking chair as you ride. At the rising trot, think of the rising moment as the "Go," and the sitting moment as the "Whoa." You'll notice that your horse might need a little more "Go" or a little more "Whoa" to stay in a balanced rhythm. If he is hurried, he might need a little more "Whoa," and if he's lazy, he might need a little more "Go," but he will definitely need both. The chair can never rock forward but not back, or vice versa.

The pendulum on your clock has to tick and tock, too. Think of the rocking chair or the clock while you walk and canter, and you'll learn to feel what your horse needs to stay balanced. This requires frequent small aids instead of infrequent, large aids. Most riders don't realize it, but they don't *ride* all the time. They do a lot of riding some of the time instead of a little bit of riding a lot of the time.

When you do a little bit of riding a lot of the time, you're able to use small half-halts to tell the horse what to do. These are *positive* half-halts because they tell the horse what to do. When you forget to ride all the time, you end up in a position of needing strong half-halts to tell the horse what *not* to do. You might think of these are *negative* half-halts. Sometimes negative half-halts are necessary, but when they are, try to follow up with a positive one. Transitions tell your horse what *to* do so they are always positive. When your half-halts aren't working well, transitions will help make your communications positive, and they will improve your half-halts. Try Exercise 2 on page 157 to help you use half-halts for transitions.

Half-Halt Problems

Here are some common half-halt problems. Some of them are different versions of the same problem, but it helps to look at the problems in different ways.

Problem 1—Incorrect Aids

The most common rider problem occurs when the rider—unknowingly—sits against the movement all the time. Then she needs to use too much aid and will get too little of a result. The balance goes downhill, the neck yields and shortens, while the hind legs remain inaccessible to the rider because they go out behind her. Try to ride the energy of your seat and leg toward your forward hand. Be sure not to lean against the hand. Your energy—as well as the horse's energy—should keep going forward in a circular way. Check your riding position.

Problem 2—The Horse That Doesn't Wait

Many horses are anxious to end the moment of engagement when they're carrying weight. When the horse avoids the engaging moment, it's impossible for the rider to drive and ask the horse to thrust in the next moment. Prolonging the moment of engagement develops the horse's strength and improves the thrust that always follows engagement. The great German jumper trainer Franke Sloothaak makes a point of training his horses to wait for him. He says, "Only when the horse waits can you add impulsion." Try Exercise 3 on page 158 to help you use half-halts to make your horse wait for you.

Problem 3—The Horse Loses Balance in the Corner

This problem is related to not waiting. In anticipation of the corner, the horse leans to the inside. As a result, his hind feet are no longer balanced under him, and he is unable to bend properly around your inside leg. Try Exercise 4 at the end of this chapter to help your horse understand how to balance through corners (p. 159).

Problem 4—Half-Halts That Don't Go "Through"

Sometimes horses feel too eager or too lazy, and the half-halts don't go through. They don't influence a hind leg. The horse might be just plain inattentive or too far out of balance to feel a subtle half-halt. The rider needs to do a transition or a stronger half-halt that may, in fact, be quite visible. If the rider pushes against a fixed hand without results, she may need to bring the hand back until a connection is made, and then push against that hand (review the stronger half-halt on pp. 151–152).

Strong half-halts should make soft ones work. If you remember to release and return to a light aid, you will train your horse to respond to light aids. Too many strong half-halts make the gaits smaller instead of grander, and they make the rhythm choppy instead of cadenced. If strong half-halts don't lead to soft ones, you need to go back to the drawing board and improve the balance by riding transitions in shoulder-fore.

When the rider doesn't use enough half-halts, the horse becomes tense from lack of balance. The rhythm becomes hurried or inconsistent instead of cadenced. Only time and experience with your horse can tell you how many half-halts to make, when to make them, and how strong they need to be, but one thing is for sure: The more frequently you "converse" with your horse, the better he will understand quiet aids.

Problem 5—Half-Halts That Lose Energy or Engagement

Your horse shouldn't lose his rhythm or energy as you half-halt. Your seat and leg pushing against the hand should enhance, not interrupt, the rhythm and swing of the horse's back. Be sure to keep the engine running. If your half-halts interrupt the rhythm, experiment with weaker ones, or put more "Go" and less "Whoa" in your half-halts, until you get the effect you want in a more forward way. You should be able to do a rebalancing half-halt or two *without* doing a transition as described in Exercise 3 (p. 158).

Problem 6—Half-Halts That Align the Horse Correctly

Be aware of the degree of your bend—or straightness. The half-halt shouldn't change this, but many horses are inclined to put one or both hind legs out when the rider half-halts. In so doing, they disengage and stiffen. (Review page 69 for more about straightening in a negative sense.)

The *sophisticated* half-halt straightens the horse in a positive sense by aligning him in shoulder-fore. The half-halt only helps your horse when he keeps his "shape." As you come through a corner, your horse should know, from how you prepare him, what you are asking for on the long side or the diagonal. When you half-halt in bend, he needs to retain that bend, and he may expect a circle, a shoulder-in, or a half-pass. When you come through the corner in shoulder-fore with half-halts that coil up the energy, you may be going to ask for an extension on the diagonal. He's not allowed to disengage by widening the hind legs or swinging them in or out (which would put him on the forehand). To help your horse become more supple and "through" in the half-halts, try Exercise 5 (p. 160).

Square Half-Halts with a Relaxed Neck

The horse that does a square halt probably does square half-halts too, which means the half-halts influence the engagement of each hind leg equally. As a result, the horse is straight and collectible. Remember, you're in charge of the alignment: The hindquarters stay straight, and the horse steps equally, left and right, toward the bridle.

This situation works most easily when the neck is free. Try Exercise 5 (p. 160) to learn how to do half-halts that make the neck longer. Then the half-halts can align and shape him, put him on his line of travel, add or subtract energy, and maintain or enhance the rhythm and length of stride. But most of all, they do the generic thing: They say, *Balance under me so we're ready to do anything*!

EXERCISES

EXERCISE 1
How to Do a Half-Halt

Directions Before beginning this exercise, be sure that the "Go" portion of your half-halt is working. Keep the "light on" at your horse's poll (p. 150). In working trot, ride with your energy going *toward* your hand; your horse draws on your hands. In so

13.4 In this half-halt, Annie has stopped following with her hands, and she pushes into them with her whole Vertical Powerline. Telurico, her Lusitano stallion, has responded by bringing his hind legs under, and he keeps his neck long.

doing, he will draw on your elbows, lower back, seat, and your entire Vertical Powerline. Feel this connection because the connection within you is what makes the connection within your horse. Be sure you're tall, from the crown of your head to your seat, to the soles of your feet. Be sure your leg supports your seat.

When your horse's commitment to the bit is confirmed, try these three ways of doing the "Whoa" portion of your half-halt, and you will see which one works best.

Step 1 Intentionally, do it wrong—just once. Your horse will forgive you. Half-halt by bringing your hands back toward your seat. Observe the result and then ride forward, once again, with your energy toward your following hands. Find the connection again.

Step 2 Next time, half-halt by bringing your hands and your seat closer to one another. Observe the result and then ride forward, once again, with your energy toward your hands, feeling the connection.

Step 3 Finally, half-halt correctly. Stop following with your hands but keep them forward (within, perhaps, the space of a dinner plate over the withers) and then push against them with your leg, seat, and vertical body (fig. 13.4). The horse will interpret these aids by bringing the hind end under and keeping the neck long and free.

If you have a problem keeping your hands forward:

- Touch the withers frequently with both hands as you see in the photo of Annie on page 160 (see fig. 13.5).

- Imagine that you're riding with a neck strap. Half-halt against the neck strap or against your horse's withers so his neck stays relaxed and his torso will be encouraged to come up.

EXERCISE 2
Half-Halts for Smooth Transitions

Directions In the Training Level tests, horses are allowed to do their transitions between two letters, but later, you'll need to make transitions at a specific letter. Make a clear system of half-halts that you and your horse can rely on for getting the transition exactly when and where you want it. Begin in working trot. Count three half-halts in the rhythm of your horse's trot stride:

Step 1 Halt-Halt Number 1 rebalances your horse in the trot.

Step 2 Half-Halt Number 2 tells him he's going to do something. (He's not allowed to do the transition on half-halt number 1 or 2, because you want to be able to do balancing, engaging half-halts *without* a transition.)

Step 3 Finally, on Half-Halt Number 3, ask for your transition to walk by prolonging the weight-bearing moment of engagement then making your seat and upper body move as they do in walk.

Make it your goal to do your transition on the third half-halt, but if you don't succeed, use a stronger half-halt. Remember, a strong half-halt is only used so the horse responds to a quiet half-halt later.

EXERCISE 3
Asking Your Horse to Wait for You

Directions Many horses run through the rider's aids. If this is your problem:

Step 1 Start in the working trot and prepare to walk. Pretend you're going to do a transition to walk. Prepare to walk with half-halts, but *don't* walk. Your horse will probably try to quit initially, because he'll be expecting a slower, easier situation, but if your seat doesn't create the transition, he shouldn't do a transition.

Step 2 Find that moment when he was going to quit, and go forward in trot again. If he "bursts" forward, his hind legs are probably pushing out behind him. Instead, go softly forward in a more elegant trot. Repeat that several times.

Step 3 Soon, instead of preparing to quit, he'll gather himself in preparation for whatever you decide to do next. He'll be in a better balance. You want to feel your horse gather underneath you. Ask him to go forward in a more expressive, but not faster trot.

Step 4 Next, when your horse is waiting for you, actually do the transition to walk, and immediately do an exercise. You might do a turn-on-the-forehand or a turn-on-the-haunches, a leg-yield, or a shoulder-in. Or, you might immediately go back to trot. This helps you and your horse learn to develop a walk that is rideable. Then, be sure to ride it. Transitions improve the paces only when they are ridden, rather than just allowed to happen. Educate your horse by playing with many half-halts—with and without transitions.

Step 5 Do the exercise in canter, too. From the canter, prepare to trot but don't trot. Feel the hindquarters engage and then ride quietly forward in an improved canter. This exercise in canter can be especially difficult for young horses that are very forward in the canter. Your goal is to be able to rebalance your horse with half-halts in the canter before asking for trot. He will, no doubt, break into trot because he honestly misunderstands. You'll need to teach him this new level of sophistication. You'll teach him that you can half-halt with or without transitions. When you finally do a transition to trot, immediately do something such as leg-yield or shoulder-in—either to the left or the right. The exercise helps him stay balanced.

EXERCISE 4
Using Halts to Improve Your Half-Halts before Corners

Directions Corners are one of those places where your horse is inclined to lose his balance. Right before the corner he tends to lose his alignment and stop stepping under the center of gravity. The classical "half-halt before the corner" doesn't always work because he doesn't "wait" for you. If Exercise 3 (for the horse who doesn't wait) didn't work, try this:

Step 1 Ride down the long side tracking right in shoulder-fore. Think inside leg to outside rein.

Step 2 Before the corner, do a quiet transition to halt, facing the wall.

Step 3 From the halt, step to the right and turn the corner, again using inside leg to outside rein.

Step 4 You are not finished with the corner until you're in shoulder-fore on the short side.

Step 5 Do this in both directions.

Soon your horse will start to anticipate your downward transition and will stay more balanced and organized when approaching the corner. Then you'll be able to do the "almost transitions" as you did in Exercise 3. And finally, you'll only need to do

13.5 Annie demonstrates how half-halts can be done with an invitation to stretch. Telurico is beautifully engaged and is very round in his topline. Even in this still photo, we can somehow see how relaxed he is!

a half-halt before the corner. Return to the halts in the corner whenever your horse starts to forget this lesson.

EXERCISE 5
Half-Halts That Make the Neck Long and the Back "Through"

Directions A half-halt goes "through" when it adds a bit of weight to a hind leg. As you know, the moment after that connection is made, the rider softens the hand. Then, the horse continues to seek the bit. Concentrating on this little softening causes the horse to seek the bit in a deeper, rounder place (fig. 13.5). There's a window of time during each stride in which the rider can soften like this, and the horse comes more and more "through" his back and stretches. Soon the downward transitions can be done with little or no hand because the horse needs the hand less, and he listens to your seat and body language more. In this way, you wean the horse off the hand.

Try this exercise on large circles with downward transitions at predictable places, so your horse will start to anticipate the downward transition, the hindquarters will engage easily, and he will reach toward your hand.

Step 1 From working trot on a 20-meter circle, do half-halts to shorten the stride without losing activity. Shorten and shorten until your horse is covering the same amount of ground as he would in walk. Stretch him as the strides shorten and engagement increases.

Step 2 At this point, your horse will be asking if he can walk. Say, *Not yet,* and then say, *Okay, let's do it now.* Concentrate on your softening rein in the first step of walk so he stretches into the walk strides.

Step 3 From collected trot, you can shorten the stride until you're in half-steps or even piaffe, if your horse can do it. If not, you can play with shortening the strides in a stretch—but never with pressure.

Step 4 Be sure your fingers stay relaxed, and your horse's neck and back will probably stay relaxed, too. Do this in canter also.

Essential Information about Half-Halts

• Half-halts influence your horse in the same way as transitions do.

• Half-halts improve your horse's gaits because they improve his balance by engaging him so he carries himself better.

• The half-halt can have countless meanings, but it always means, *Balance under me—where two spines meet.*

• The half-halt recipe has three parts: "Go," "Whoa," and "Soften."

• In the automatic half-halt, your aids work every stride in a self-perpetuating, flowing circle of "Go," Whoa," and "Soften" aids.

• Common half-halt problems include these situations:

   1 The rider who is behind the motion all the time is always saying "Whoa," so her half-halt aids are muted.

   2 Some horses need to be encouraged to "wait" for the rider. If the horse doesn't respond to the half-halt, the rider needs to use a stronger one. Then she can

return to a quieter one. Some riders need strong half-halts because they don't half-halt often enough to keep the horse balanced. Frequent small half-halts are more effective than a few big ones.

3 Some horses lose energy and engagement in the half-halt.

4 Some horses stiffen in the half-halt. The rider can use half-halts in bend and in stretch to help.

Conclusion

As you can see, to understand "How Horses Work" is to know that it's all about physics. It's scientific, and if you can ride your horse with the science of equitation in mind, you'll be harmonizing with him in the most natural way possible—according to the rules of Mother Nature. For this, the rider is further rewarded by gaining the horse's love, respect, and ultimate cooperation.

The rider who learns to follow her horse and respect his natural strengths and weaknesses becomes the alpha figure and the leader that the horse ultimately wants to follow. The rider becomes the leader.

In Part III, I'll explore ways in which you can maximize your ability to stay in control. You won't be in control of the horse directly, but you will control qualities of the ride that keep you at the helm without the horse losing his feeling of freedom.

PART III • DRESSAGE DYNAMICS

How Two Spines Meet in Balance

In Part III, "How Two Spines Meet in Balance," you can use what you know about "How Riders Work" and "How Horses Work" to gain control of the balance. You monitor and regulate aspects of the horse's shape and movement to improve the balance. Notice that you are not controlling "the horse." Instead, you're monitoring and regulating aspects of your ride.

I chose the terms "monitor" and "regulate" with care. When the rider "monitors," she listens to the horse. When she "regulates" aspects of the ride, she leads him and guides him. In the process, the rider has control, but in a respectful way. As you know, most horses are natural followers, so if the ride is well balanced, the horse will be happy to follow his leader. The qualities that you will monitor and regulate include:

- The *rhythm*. You want to ride in rhythm because it's the horse's language.

- The *energy*. You want to monitor and regulate the amount of his energy, which will give you a balance between suppleness and brilliance.

- The *flexion*. The old masters of dressage said that a supple poll was the first key to the horse's back. They were right. You want to monitor and regulate the flexion of the poll.

- The *alignment*. The horse needs to be aligned within his own body; the rider needs to help her horse straighten because he can't do it on his own. The harmonious horse and rider are also aligned with each other—where two spines meet.

- The *bend*. It's been said that "bend control" is horse control in the friendliest sense. That's true.

- The *height of the neck*. You want to monitor and regulate the height of the neck because that's the second key to a supple back. The energy needs to flow through the back as well as the neck, both of which make up the spine.

- The *length of the stride*. You want to regulate the length of the horse's stride—it's the key to longitudinal suppleness and elasticity.

- The *line of travel*. The ability to control your horse's line of travel is critical to being able to monitor and regulate all the other qualities. If he falls off your line of travel, he loses the other qualities. With the ability to control the line of travel, you can achieve the next quality…

- …the shape of *figures and movements*. Precision and crispness here is the crowning achievement that will build your horse into an athlete.

Use these balancing tools as a checklist every time you ride. They help your horse balance so he can be free to perform to the best of his ability. And you become the leader of the dance!

how two spines
meet in balance

CHAPTER FOURTEEN

Rhythm

Speaking Your Horse's Language

Rhythm is your horse's language in motion. The rider can only communicate with her horse in the predictable rhythm of his motion—in the four-beat rhythm of walk, the two-beat rhythm of trot and the three-beat rhythm of canter (including periods of suspension in trot and canter). Whenever the horse loses his balance, the quality of his gaits suffers because the rhythm becomes unclear. The best riders help their horses balance by maintaining the rhythm and giving their aids in the rhythm of the horse's gaits.

That rhythm is what gives each gait its distinguishing qualities. The four-beat *walk* is a marching gait in which there is always a foot on the ground. Five-star judge and trainer Anne Gribbons once quipped that it's a sign of old age when the walk is as thrilling to watch as the trot and canter. But, in fact, the walk can be elegant. The two-beat *trot* is a swinging gait. Developing the trot is about developing swing. Without swing, collection is impossible (see p. 125). The three-beat *canter* is a bounding gait with a significant period of suspension. Each of the gaits has its own unique beauty.

The term *rhythm* refers not only to the regularity of the footfall but also to the tempo of it. The *regularity* is the correct sequence of the footfall (in walk, trot, or canter), and *tempo* is the speed of the rhythm. (Note the difference between the *tempo* and *speed*. Tempo refers to beats per minute. Speed refers to miles per hour.) The predictability factor that is inherent in rhythm builds

14.1 Because of the self-perpetuating nature of the treadmill, people and horses using them work in rhythm and in balance. Each stride has a moment of flexion and a moment of relaxation. Horses on a treadmill don't make rhythm mistakes in the walk.

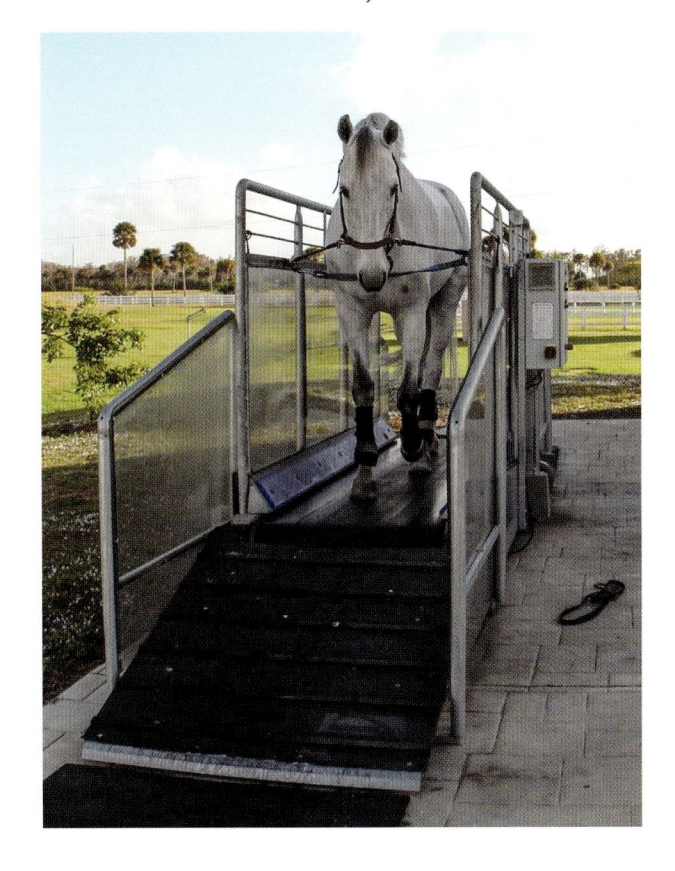

physical looseness and mental confidence for both horse and rider. Here's how:

Physically, the horse's muscles flex and relax every stride in the rhythm of song. He works in rhythm like pumping iron at the gym: "Flex-*relax*-flex-*relax*." It's worth noting that a horse's walk rhythm is always perfect on a treadmill (fig. 14.1). The treadmill persistently keeps the consistency of speed stride after stride. Riding with a metronome can help those who have trouble with this consistency. (See page 169 to learn the specifics of riding with a metronome.)

When the integrity of the rhythm is retained, the horse always gets these moments of relaxation. The rhythm should be self-perpetuating, which makes work easy. These

Cavalletti

One of the best ways to develop rhythmic relaxation with the right amount of energy is to use cavalletti (fig. 14.2). Some horses are initially quite spastic over cavalletti but learn to negotiate them with ease. Cavalletti almost always improve the horse's gaits. Correctly spaced, they set the horse up for success. The ideal spacing varies from horse to horse and should be carefully determined by the trainer.

- For walk, approximately .8 meter apart (2 feet, 7 inches).
- For trot, approximately 1.3 meters apart (4 feet, 3 inches).
- For canter, approximately 3 meters apart (9 feet, 10 inches).

Try This

Start in walk or trot by going over one cavalletti. Then, when your horse is comfortable, add more. When he is confident going through cavalletti, you have the correct working tempo. Imagine that your horse always felt as he did through the cavalletti. When his rhythm is perfect:

- The movement becomes self-perpetuating.
- The back swings in trot.

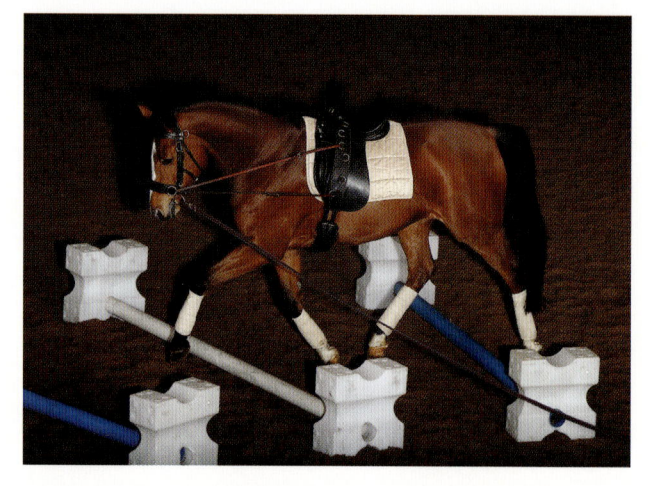

14.2 Notice how beautifully this horse is using his body. Even in a still photo, you get a sense for his clock-like rhythm. Longeing or riding your horse over cavalletti develops the gaits by improving the integrity of the movement, including its rhythm and its quality of self-perpetuation.

These same principles apply to jumping. The horse needs to move in the ideal rhythm and tempo before, during, and after the fence. The speed—as determined by the length of stride—is determined by the rider. The horse shouldn't vary the rhythm and tempo on his own by speeding up on straight lines and slowing down on bent lines. If the rider can manage this, her horse will be working in balance and with confidence.

reliable moments of relaxation are what give the horse his beauty and grace in the short run, but they give him longevity over time. That's why well-ridden horses often work well into their twenties.

Mentally, the predictable rhythm of walk, trot, or canter brings peace of mind for both horse and rider. It's always comforting to know what's going to happen next.

A dressage horse's gaits are judged on their freedom and regularity. When the horse is free in the pasture, he has no obstacles and usually demonstrates regularity in the rhythm of all three gaits.

Training systematically adds obstacles that can potentially challenge the horse's balance, causing the rhythm to deteriorate. First, the trainer adds the obstacles of a saddle and bridle, then a rider. When the rider takes the reins and asks for contact, there is another obstacle. Next, the horse needs to learn to accept the rider's seat and sympathetic hands. The rider can help the horse accept the seat by rising to the trot until the horse is warmed up, then sitting for only short periods of time. As soon as the horse—or rider—loses the rhythm or becomes stiff in the sitting trot, the rider can rise again. Soon, the horse will accept the sitting trot for longer periods of time. Then he will accept the half-halt. With the help of the rider, the horse keeps his balance and maintains his metronome-like rhythm—even with the addition of obstacles.

> Mentally, the predictable rhythm of walk, trot, or canter brings peace of mind for both horse and rider. It's always comforting to know what's going to happen next.

Later, more interesting obstacles are added: small jumps or simple figures and movements such as leg-yield or shoulder-in. Even later, the horse may be required to jump large fences or do high-level movements such as piaffe, passage, and pirouettes. Regardless of your horse's specialty, exercises become more difficult as his training progresses, and maintenance or improvement of the rhythm is a major measure of his progress.

As the exercises require more power, they're only gymnastically beneficial for the horse when he can do them with a rhythmic, swinging back. Great riders consciously try to increase the horse's power for more difficult exercises while maintaining the rhythm, the relaxation of the neck, and the swinging back. Then the power creates *cadence*—an accentuated rhythm that is elastic and expressive.

The USDF definition of *cadence* is: "The marked accentuation of the tempo and (musical) beat arising from springiness and elasticity. Expression."

Remember what you read in "Impulsion and Engagement" (p. 117) about the

14.3 Top dressage riders are ultimately able to increase the influence of their half-halts until the horse reaches the highest degree of collection without losing the rhythm. Carl Hester and Uthopia demonstrate a piaffe that is cadenced and energetic, but relaxed.

science of springs: Half-halts create a "boing-boing-boing" effect with springing, swinging gaits. Dressage riders are ultimately able to increase the influence of half-halts until the horse can trot or canter in lightness nearly on the spot without losing rhythm or energy (fig. 14.3).

When the rider concentrates on maintaining the metronome-like rhythm, she and her horse become coordinated. The swinging back is the key to an enhanced sense of feel and timing. The energy is recycled automatically, as the horse becomes more cadenced and collected.

The Metronome-Like Rider

It's the horse's responsibility to go forward in a clear and steady rhythm in walk, trot, or canter, but it's the rider's responsibility to *tell him* that it's his responsibility. Notice the horse's tendency to slow down in corners and speed up on straight lines. When the tempo is too fast or too slow, the horse's back can't swing and the energy doesn't go "through" his entire body. When the horse loses his balance or becomes distracted, you want him to rely on the rhythm to help him rebalance. You want to be the metronome for your horse. Try the Exercise described below.

As your horse's training progresses, pay special attention to the quality of your horse's rhythm. It's a major measure of your horse's training. You'll need to be able to retain its regularity as you work on the next quality for longitudinal balance: monitoring and regulating the horse's energy (see p. 171).

EXERCISES

EXERCISE
Working with a Metronome

Directions Buy an inexpensive portable metronome and ride with it. Find your horse's trot tempo—probably between 138 and 154 beats per minute (bpm). The canter tempo is about 96 bpm, and the walk is about 100 bpm. Keep the same tempo throughout corners, straight lines, and circles. If your horse slows down on bent lines or speeds up on straight lines, you'll notice it immediately. You'll also notice the tempo of your aids. Be sure you give your aids

how two spines meet in balance

A Farmer's Working Pace

The man who built our New England farm in the early 1900s raised his family on it and then moved next door to the smaller house he built for his parents (next to the two homes he built for his aunts and behind the house his wife was born in). Phil Isham was part of a very old Connecticut family. "Goin' to town" meant a day-long drive behind the family horses.

The working paces remind me of Phil Isham because he didn't necessarily work fast, but he worked in endless rhythm. When he was alive in the early days of our farm, he helped us with countless chores, and spreading the manure was one of them. Over time, he would strategically place dozens of small manure mounds over the old cornfield, then one day we'd see him out there spreading with his trusty pitchfork. Scoop, fling, scoop, fling, scoop, fling. He moved slowly but efficiently. What seemed like an endless chore was simply a matter of taking it one scoop at a time in a self-perpetuating rhythm.

Miraculously, he would spread a nightmare's worth of manure in a day with such precision that the field would have an equal depth of rich fertilizer over a very large area. Farmers all over the world know a lot about the working paces. There's nothing hectic about them, but they are energetic, self-perpetuating, rhythmic, and they swing through the entire body. The correct working tempo feels "working" but retains that moment of relaxation during every stride.

in the correct tempo. Some riders unknowingly give their aids too slow or too fast. Always be aware of the rhythmic tempo of your quiet aids.

Essential Information about Rhythm

- Rhythm is your horse's language in motion. The rider can only communicate with her horse in the predictable rhythm of his motion.

- The walk is a marching gait, the trot is a swinging gait, and the canter is a bounding gait.

- The tempo is the speed of the rhythm.

- The rhythm allows the horse to work with a moment of relaxation in each stride: flex-relax-flex-relax

- A dressage horse's gaits are judged on their freedom and regularity. These qualities are almost always perfect when the horse is without a rider.

- Training under the rider systematically adds obstacles that can potentially challenge the horse's balance and cause the rhythm to deteriorate.

- One of the best ways to develop rhythmic relaxation with the right amount of energy is by using cavalletti.

- Cavalletti almost always change gaits for the better by improving the march of the walk, the swing of the trot, and the "jump" of the canter. Cavalletti also make the gaits self-perpetuating.

- The rider is like a metronome for her horse.

- When the gaits have increased power, impulsion, and swing, they become cadenced—that is, the rhythm is accentuated and the movement more expressive.

how two spines
meet in balance

CHAPTER FIFTEEN

Energy

Monitoring and Regulating Power

Energy is the power that allows your horse to work. When you "energize" your horse, you encourage him to work harder. When you calm your horse down, you encourage him to use less energy. The late German master, Walter Christensen, used to say to his students, "*Ruhe*," meaning, "Quiet." "Be calm." He wanted energy that wasn't hectic. Hectic energy is never productive.

Imagine the energy scale like the flame of a gas stove (figs. 15.1 A–C). You can regulate the energy by turning it up or down. Your seat, leg, and hand regulate the horse's energy: The lower leg and seat, together with a following torso and hand, ask for *more* energy. The seat that pushes against the fixed hand in a half-halt asks for *less*.

Brilliance comes from increasing the power, but too much energy, or misdirected energy, makes tension and lack of feeling. You need just the right amount of energy to connect your horse with feeling so his back can swing. Then you can carefully add power without losing the relaxed swing. How do you know when your horse has the right amount of energy?

Not Enough Energy

The horse hangs back and isn't committed or honest to the bit because the energy doesn't reach that far.

- You don't feel the energy travel under your seat; you don't see it in your horse's neck as he steps "through"; and you don't feel it in your hand.

- The contact might feel inconsistent like lights that are flickering or sometimes even going out.

- Your horse doesn't follow where you point your hands.

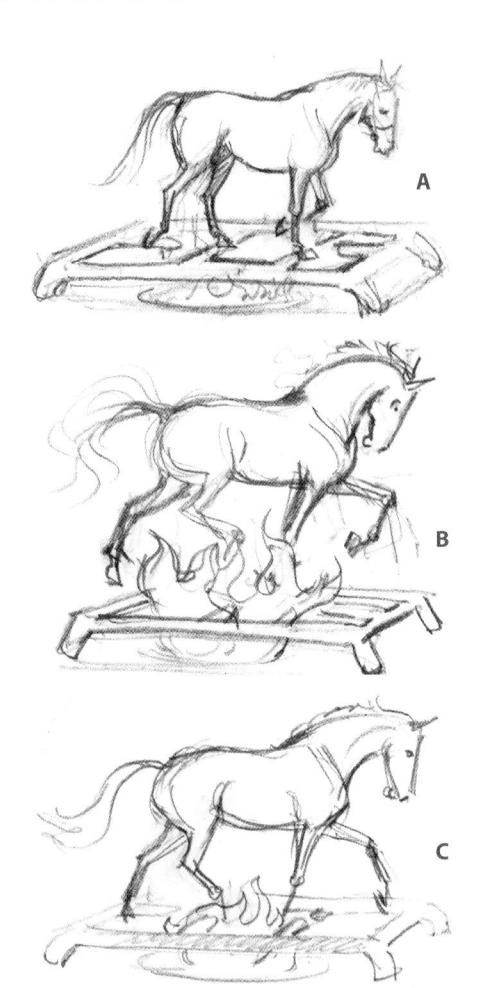

15.1 A–C Imagine the energy scale like the flame of a gas stove. You can regulate the energy by turning it up or down. (A) When there is too little energy, the horse will be difficult to ride because the energy won't reach the bit. (B) Brilliance comes from increasing the power but too much energy can make the horse hectic. (C) You can ask for a little more or a little less energy until you find the right amount.

- His nose might be behind the vertical, but could be above the bit—or inconsistent.

- Your horse can't stop easily.

- Half-halts don't work because his energy doesn't reach your hands.

- Your horse can't bend for the same reason.

- Instead of feeling that the walk, trot, and canter are self-perpetuating, your horse feels like a wind-up toy that winds down too easily. Whereas some "reminding aids" are always necessary, you shouldn't need to remind your horse constantly.

- Your horse's back doesn't swing, and he doesn't "chew" the bit (see p. 112).

If your horse doesn't have enough energy, use exercises that will energize him. Focus on upward transitions that add horsepower. Do exercises that include lengthenings and medium paces. Combine them with suppling exercises—circles, lateral work, half-halts, and downward transitions that help close your horse's frame and recycle the energy so he's in a better position to do the forward, energy-producing exercises. Use of cavalletti (see p. 166) can achieve the right amount of energy without losing relaxation.

Too Much Energy for the Balance
This sometimes happens because too much of his power is coming from the front-end pulling engine instead of the hindquarters. And, sometimes the hindquarters make more power than can be managed in balance. Symptoms of this problem include:

- Your horse is lacking a clear rhythm. It feels hurried or hectic.

- He is too strong in the hand and stiff in downward transitions.

- The working paces feel too powered up and are lacking a moment of relaxation within every stride (p. 166).

- You feel as if your horse is zooming out from underneath you—moving away from your seat rather than staying balanced under it.

- Your horse's back doesn't swing because it's tense.

how two spines
meet in balance

- The neck is sometimes too high but can also be too low.

- Your horse may appear collected to the uninformed observer, but he is actually too short and hollow.

- Your horse has difficulty bending.

- He doesn't chew the bit.

If your horse's energy is coming from the front-pulling engine use exercises that will help your horse think about and use his hindquarters. Circles and voltes shape him in bend. Downward transitions, half-halts, corners, and turns make him softer and better balanced. Leg-yield, turn-on-the-forehand, shoulder-fore, turn-on-the-haunches, and lateral exercises encourage looseness and connection from behind. The turn-on-the-forehand reminds the horse that the leg aid influences the hindquarters, not his forehand.

When the Amount of Energy Is Ideal

- Your horse feels like he is moving with purpose. The terms *working trot* and *working canter* are meaningful descriptions of how purposeful your horse feels.

- There's enough energy to flow through the topline of your horse's spine, reach your hand, push away from the bit, and recycle back to the hind leg in half-halts without loss of rhythm or energy.

- The rhythm is relaxed and metronome perfect. Flex-relax-flex-relax-flex-relax is the rhythm of pumping iron; this moment of relaxation in every stride is vital for the regeneration process. It makes work relatively easy.

- The energy and the rhythm are both self-perpetuating. Your horse doesn't become slower or faster on his own, and he doesn't gain or lose energy on his own. To achieve this, the rider must participate with aids in the right rhythm and tempo.

- His back swings, which is proof that he is working "through" his entire body. The USDF definition of the German term *Schwung* is "The condition in which the energy created by the hind legs is transmitted through a 'swinging back' and manifested in the horse's elastic, whole-body movement." As a result, your *whole-body aids* get a *whole-body reaction* from your horse.

ENERGY

- You have control of the length of stride. Your horse doesn't lengthen or shorten the stride on his own. As a result, you have control of the speed or ground coverage.

- The height of your horse's neck reflects the engagement of the hindquarters with a loose back. His neck isn't too high or too low.

- Your horse is balanced enough so the "Whoa" and "Go" buttons work equally well. He should have the power and suppleness to go forward promptly and to slow down easily. You feel you're being carried forward. It's easy to sit.

Regulating the Energy

To ask for more energy or less energy, how much aid should the rider use? The guideline is always: *As little as possible, but as much as necessary.* Aids come in different sizes or gradients. The rider should always begin with the whispering aid that she considers *as little as possible.* However, that's the ideal situation, and life isn't always ideal. If the horse doesn't respond to these aids, repeat *as much as necessary*, until you get the desired response.

To create more energy, you might need to give your horse a "tap" with the whip or a little machine-gun rat-a-tat vibration with your leg. If that doesn't work, give him a kick with the flat of the calf or a firmer tap with the whip. When you get the desired response, be sure to allow your horse to go forward and praise him, even if he goes *too* forward. Be aware that kicking creates tension, so repeat the process until he gets used to responding in a relaxed way to a light forward aid.

To reduce the energy, use your half-halts and downward transitions consistently and with meaning until your horse understands them.

Follow this simple rule: always return to a light aid. Never let strong aids escalate, and finish the lesson there. The goal is to be able to use light aids. With a balanced, skilled rider the light aids are very specific and meaningful, and in time, the horse learns to respond with equal refinement. When the rider gives precise aids, the horse's response is usually just as specific and prompt.

Directing the Energy

Sometimes the horse reacts to the aids, but the reaction is wrong. He might respond to leg and seat aids with tension in the forehand. Likewise, he may respond to rein aids

how two spines meet in balance

by misaligning his hindquarters. In a nice way, the rider's aids need to be repeated, until the horse understands the correct response to the aids. Never punish him for making a wrong response. You always want him to keep trying.

As you know, when you close your legs, your horse should step to your hands. Your legs, hips, torso, and upper arms channel the energy to the hands, and then your hands point your horse to the place where you want to go, and the horse should follow your hand. Point and shoot.

Riders who jump are better at this than dressage riders who are inclined to lose focus and wander. When they start to ride movements, it becomes easy to lose focus on the line of travel. However, accuracy is what puts the horse on the aids and keeps him there. Jumping riders can point the horse to a fence, and the magnetic appeal of the fence draws the horse's energy solidly into the hand.

The rider on the flat should feel the same honesty to the bit. Without the magnetic effect of the approaching fence, the horse should inflate in front of the rider's leg, fill up the rein, and step reliably to the bit even if your destination point is as boring as a tree or dressage letter (fig. 15.2). If you don't ride a jumper, imagine that you need to jump a fence. Keep the contact, point your hands toward your destination, and ride your horse toward your hands.

15.2 Jumping riders know how it feels when a horse is softly but magnetically attracted to a fence. The rider on the flat should experience the same supple eagerness from her horse, even when the destination is as boring as a dressage letter. Infanta looks pleasant in the contact and her forehand looks inflated in front of Mica's leg.

EXERCISES

EXERCISE
Organizing the Energy

Directions When you ask for more energy, know what you want the horse to do with the increased energy. He can lengthen the stride, or the stride can become loftier. Monitor the rhythm and the length of stride so your increased energy doesn't dissipate. In this exercise you will try to increase the energy without lengthening the stride. Ask for a quicker stride by giving your aid a little quicker.

Step 1 Start on a 15-meter circle in working canter.

Step 2 On the open side of the circle, increase the energy with three quick strides. Count, 1-2-3. Then return to normal.

Step 3 How did your horse react? Did he dance or did he lose the rhythm by becoming unsteady? Did he try to lengthen his stride instead of quickening it? Did he stay relaxed or did he become tense?

Step 4 Try it again. Ask for three quick strides with more energy. Monitor the rhythm and the length of stride.

Praise him if he gives you a nicer feeling. Progress is made in small steps. When you do this exercise a few times, the quality of the normal working canter will improve because your horse will be more in front of the leg and willing to add energy. Be sure to do the exercise in both directions and try it in trot also.

Regulating and directing energy will become easier when your horse is supple. Suppleness starts with flexion of the poll, which I cover in the next chapter.

Essential Information about Energy

- Energy is the power that allows your horse to work. When you "energize" your horse, you encourage him to work harder. When you calm your horse down, you encourage him to use less energy.

- When your horse has too much energy, it is often coming from the front-pulling engine instead of from the hind-pushing engine.

- When your horse doesn't have enough energy, it doesn't reach the bit, and the work is difficult.

- When you can regulate the energy to have the right amount, you can direct the energy. Then you're in a good position to develop a supple horse.

how two spines meet in balance

CHAPTER SIXTEEN

Flexion of the Poll

The Key to a Supple Back

The old masters said that a supple poll was the key to the horse's back. They were right. Suppleness of the poll is a prerequisite to relaxation and suppleness in the entire spine. It enables a swinging back. When the poll is supple, it's easy to flex or "position" it to the left or right. This flexion, left or right, defines the "inside" of the horse, and the opposite side is, of course, the "outside."

Whereas the aid for flexion in the poll is often considered the domain of the inside rein aid, flexion also comes as a result of bending from the rider's leg (fig. 16.1).

The rein aid for flexion is given by the inside fingers and wrist, as seen in fig. 4.3 B on page 43. But the rein aid is never used without the leg aid. The effectiveness of the leg aid should always be greater than the restriction of the rein aid so the horse keeps stepping to the rein. Over-yielding to the inside rein aid is a very common problem.

16.1 Flexion is primarily caused by the rider's inside leg and, secondarily, by the rider's inside rein. Notice how Dancer flexes easily to the left when she feels pressure on her rib cage!

Common Flexion Problems

- Most riders initially want to use their arms to create flexion, which over-bends the horse at the base of the neck, misaligning him in front of the saddle where you want him to be straight, wide, and strong.

- There is usually a side that is more difficult. If your horse doesn't respond to the suppling aids of the wrist and fingers, straighten him and try again. It's different from the leg aid in which you might get strong with him if he doesn't respond. Try a vibrating rein or a steady open rein to explain your aid. You want him to continue drawing on the rein despite your request, so you need to be sensitive. When the crest flips, soften the aid within the contact (see Exercise 1, p. 179).

- When the rein aids are too strong in relation to the leg aids, horses over-yield to the flexion aids. They come behind the vertical, stop drawing on the rein, or tilt as an evasion. Acceptance of the contact is a prerequisite to flexion. The driving aids need to send sufficient energy to a passive rein until the connection is restored. Remember the leg aids are *primary* to the rein aids.

- Some riders are intent on making the horse rounder at the poll, but often the horse needs to be rounder at the base of the neck instead. Demanding hands can damage the poll. Obtaining correct flexion requires a "feeling for flexion," which is quite subtle. Anytime the goal is relaxation (of the poll and jaw) the action needs to be soft. Imagine feeling your horse's tongue. That will encourage sensitivity, which in turn is likely to create a supple poll and correct flexion. Correct flexion causes the horse to chew the bit in acceptance.

When you do Exercise 1 on page 179, you will see that your horse's crest is either flipped to the right or the left. It will only be in the middle for a split second before it flips the other way. This means that there is always an "inside" and always an "outside" of the horse. The "inside" is the direction in which the crest is flipped, so you can tell which way your horse is flexed by examining the crest visually. Although control over the flexion seems a small matter, it is one of the single most important aspects of your ride. Without correct flexion, it is impossible to have correct alignment and bend, so it's impossible to have a correct connection or collection. Without correct flexion, half-halts don't go through, and transitions are ineffective. Correct flexion is nearly invisible, but the educated observer can see it, and the educated rider knows if she has it—or not.

how two spines meet in balance

16.2 A & B The rein aid for flexion is given by the inside fingers and wrist. Annie slowly asks Orion to flex left and right at the halt. This exercise will teach your horse how to respond to your rein aids appropriately. If your horse is like most, he will mistakenly respond by misaligning his hindquarters when you use the rein. This exercise teaches him to stabilize his body and respond appropriately.

EXERCISES

EXERCISE
Monitor and Regulate the Flexion

Directions This exercise will help your horse learn how to respond to your rein aids appropriately. If your horse is like most, he will mistakenly respond by misaligning his barrel and hindquarters when you use the rein. This teaches him to stabilize his body and respond only by flexing.

Step 1 At a halt, use your left fingers and wrists (not your arms) to flex your horse very slightly (centimeters or inches) to the left—keeping a light contact with the right rein. How far should you flex him to the left? Just until his crest "flips" to the left. Stay there for 5 to 15 seconds until he feels comfortable and you have a good visual of how much flexion is required to flip the crest (fig. 16.2 A).

Step 2 Then, with light contact in both reins, slowly position your horse to the center and then to the right. Notice how much flexion is required to flip the crest to the right (fig. 16.2 B). It may not be the same as it was to the left. You will need to know this

FLEXION OF THE POLL

information in the future when you adjust your horse's flexion during changes of direction in walk, trot, and canter.

If your horse is restless during this exercise, be patient. Consider his restlessness a reflection of the degree of agitation he might have in walk, trot, and canter from a simple aid for changing flexion and direction. If he backs up, it's a reflection of how he might back off the connection in walk, trot, and canter during a change of flexion and direction. Just observe, and then you may need to support him with your seat and legs so he *thinks forward* and doesn't back up, fall left, or fall right when you change the flexion. Quietly ask him to step forward and straight; then repeat. At first, he might not understand that your flexing aids are only for influencing his poll and jaw—not his entire body.

When you are successful, you've stabilized his body and made it independent from your rein aids. This is a big step in suppling your horse!

When your horse feels comfortable with changing the flexion at the halt, pay the same attention to flexion in walk, trot, and canter. You may not be able to see it as clearly, but pay attention to it anyway. In time, your horse will stay relaxed and committed to the bridle during changes of flexion and direction.

Essential Information about Flexion

- Suppleness of the poll is a prerequisite to relaxation and suppleness in the entire spine. It enables a swinging back.

- The primary flexion aid is the inside leg and the supplementary aid is the inside fingers and wrist.

- The horse is always flexed either to the right or to the left so there is always an "inside" and an "outside" of your horse. You can determine the flexion by checking to see which way the crest is flipped. The crest never stays in the middle. It is either left or right.

- Over-flexion is common. You have enough flexion as soon as the crest flips. Correct flexion is the basis for correct alignment and bend, which is necessary for correct connection and collection.

how two spines
meet in balance

CHAPTER SEVENTEEN

Spinal Alignment

The Key to Straightness

Most riders have seen a clinician mount a student's horse to demonstrate a point, or assess or fix a problem. Sometimes, the horse instantly looks different. The horse that was, just one moment ago, having a balance problem, is suddenly harmonious and fluid. He seems to have grown and become magically better conformed. What did the trainer do?

Often she has simply flexed the horse correctly (as outlined in the last chapter) and aligned the horse's spine in front of and behind the saddle so he can be better balanced. In front, she centered the horse's neck between the shoulders so he relaxed his neck into a "falling-down" position (see fig. 19.2, p. 202). She flexed right or left—which determined the "inside" of the horse. Then behind the saddle, she "narrowed" the path of the horse's inside hind foot in shoulder-fore so he stepped under his weight. She prevented the outside hind from escaping to the outside. Then she rode him from back to front into equal contact.

Some trainers don't even know they are aligning and equalizing, because it is a habit—a wonderful habit—implemented unconsciously. Adjustments of alignment often take only a few seconds, but they "straighten" the horse.

Before the trainer magically transformed the horse, she was straight herself. Here's how to align two spines.

Alignment of Two Spines

The alignment of two spines is one key to harmony between horse and rider. The buttons or zipper on the rider's shirt or jacket need to be aligned with the horse's crest. Then, the rider's weight falls equally left and right as I discussed on page 24. Both seat bones are down, and the rider feels her heels fall down equally as her hips swing. She has equal influence on the left and right sides of her horse, and she is in a position to shift her weight very slightly to the inside to create bending and turning, without leaning and abandoning the outside of the horse. Once you are straight and aligned with your horse, you can align your horse in front of and behind the saddle (fig. 17.1).

Alignment 101—In Front of the Saddle

The horse's neck and back need to be aligned so they are on one arc. The neck and back are parts of the same spine, so the back can't be relaxed if the neck is misaligned and tense. When the horse's neck comes straight out of the shoulders, he is able to lower it (see fig. 19.2, p. 202). Then the base of the neck gets visibly wider providing both lateral and longitudinal stability.

A common rider mistake is misaligning the horse's spine at the withers by over-bending the neck with the inside rein. Then the energy from the hindquarters goes out the outside shoulder instead of going straight through the body to the bit. When the neck is over-bent at the withers, the horse is unable to relax and lower the neck. He is also unable to bend in the preferred place: the area of the rider's seat-leg aid and the horse's center of gravity—where two spines meet.

Alignment 102—Behind the Saddle

Horses are naturally misaligned behind the saddle, which is not the fault of the rider. Remember that by nature, horses are wider behind than they are in front (see fig. 8.6, p. 100), so when left to their own devices in motion, these wide hind legs push the horse onto the forehand. The right hind hoof of most horses is inclined to step outside the horse's center of gravity (too far to the right) and not track under the center of gravity where two spines meet. Because of its misaligned position, thrust from that right hind foot pushes the horse toward the left rein, which can become stiff or heavy because the left shoulder is being thrust out.

To straighten the horse, the rider asks for shoulder-fore—often called *first position* or *threading* (review information under "The Shoulder-Fore Solution" on page 100). She sits squarely; she "narrows" the path of the horse's inside hind foot and sends him to the rein that he doesn't want to use. The rider needs to take care not to hang on the rein that the horse wants to lean on. In shoulder-fore, the horse will

how two spines
meet in balance

17.1 Mica is well aligned with Infanta: Her buttons are aligned with the mare's crest as she stretches forward-downward. In this photo, you can see Infanta's neck and back are aligned on one arc. The neck and back are parts of the same spine, so the back can't be relaxed if the neck is misaligned.

step under his own weight—under the place where two spines meet—rather than to the outside of it. In this narrowed position, the hindquarters carry the weight squarely under the center of gravity instead of pushing the weight to one side. When you have control of the flexion and alignment, your horse can do shoulder-fore, which is an extraordinary step in your horse's training!

Shoulder-Fore: First Position or Threading

In shoulder-fore (often called *first position* or *threading*), the horse is slightly flexed to the inside—just enough to flip the crest. Remember, his outside legs are aligned and the inside hind steps in the space between the two front feet (fig. 17.2). The rider "threads" her horse's inside hind foot into that space between the prints of the two front feet—like threading a needle. When asking for shoulder-fore, the rider concentrates on the partnership and coordination between her inside leg and outside rein. She also uses the inside rein and outside leg to keep her horse flexed to the inside and aligned behind the saddle. (The horse's outside hind will want to step out.) The horse barely has the suggestion of flexion and bend—just enough to straighten and align him.

17.2 Horses are, by nature, built crooked and on the forehand. To straighten Infanta, Mica has asked for shoulder-fore. You can see that the mare's inside hind foot is stepping between the front feet, directly under the center of gravity. As a result, the mare is in lovely self-carriage.

Caution

If you think of shoulder-fore as a lateral exercise, you might start going sideways. Think that shoulder-fore straightens your horse; keep his outside legs aligned and his neck almost straight.

The key to perfect lateral balance lies in mastering the shoulder-fore, because:

- It asks the horse to step directly under your seat—the center of gravity—and it invites him to come into the outside rein. This situation is balanced and comfortable for both horse and rider.

how two spines
meet in balance

- It helps the horse carry himself proudly because he is confident in his balance.

Threading sets the stage for a connection that leads to collection. When the horse does shoulder-fore equally in both directions, he develops the strength in each hindquarter equally, so he is straight, enabling the leverage needed for collection.

Experienced riders spend all of their riding time aligned in this wonderful balance. Try the Threading Exercise below.

EXERCISES

EXERCISE
Threading

Step 1 Walk straight toward a mirror in a threading position to the right. If you don't have a mirror, ask a ground person to help. Choose a specific destination point and stick with one line of travel. The precision of your line of travel is key.

Step 2 When tracking right, look for:

- Very slight flexion at the poll to define "inside" (the right).

- The inside (right) hind leg "threads" between the two front legs.

- The outside (left) hind leg is aligned on the same track as the left front.

- The horse is comfortably filling up the outside (left) rein.

A Story about Straightness

It was a day for hacking the horses and the weather was less than cooperative, causing Samantha and Igor to spend their walk day in the indoor arena. They were walking down the long side, tracking left, when Samantha became vaguely aware that Igor was tending to drift left—off the track. She repeatedly used her left leg to keep Igor on the track. The results were positive but short-lived, which she blamed on Igor's short memory.

Then she considered the common equine problem of stepping wide with the right hind leg. *Perhaps,* she thought, *it is his outside, right hind leg that is pushing him to the left off the track. Although it is counter-intuitive, perhaps I should be using my right leg.* Sure enough, when she started to use the right leg as well as the left leg, Igor innocently stayed on the track. It seems that the left leg correction was a band-aid, and the additional support on the right was a solution to the underlying problem because it "narrowed" his right hind leg and sent the energy on a straighter path.

U.S. Olympian Sue Blinks likens the energy going through the horse's topline to water flowing in a stream. Just as water flows around a rock in the stream instead of going over it, the horse's energy is inclined to go around the withers instead of over it. The shoulders need to stay aligned so the energy goes over it. Shoulder-fore aligns the shoulders.

Step 3 When you're successful with shoulder-fore right, straighten, and ask for shoulder-fore left. Notice that shoulder-fore isn't just about the front end of the horse, but it is also about stabilizing the hindquarters when you change the flexion. The track of the hindquarters should stay absolutely straight during changes in lateral flexion. Shoulder-fore gives you control over the whole horse.

Step 4 Change directions often, and practice counter-shoulder-fore in your arena—that is, shoulder-fore left when tracking right, and vice versa.

You may find shoulder-fore difficult at first, but be patient with yourself and your horse. When your horse gets the idea, he'll be cooperative because he likes being balanced as much as you do. Once you can do shoulder-fore, your horse can bend easily, and he can turn from your outside aids—even on the stiff side. He comes "through" in the back, which makes both horse and rider comfortable.

Essential Information about Spinal Alignment

- Horses are always more comfortable and appear more graceful when they are aligned within themselves and aligned with their riders.

- Riders who are aligned carry 50 percent of their weight to the left and 50 to the right.

- Their shirt buttons are aligned with the horse's crest.

- Alignment of the horse begins with correct flexion in front of the saddle and "threading" of the hind legs in shoulder-fore.

- Shoulder-fore is also known as *first position* or *threading*. Many people mistakenly think of it as a lateral exercise, but it is a straightening tool that should be used all the time when riding.

- Shoulder-fore is difficult to achieve but relatively easy to maintain because horses love to be balanced and aligned.

how two spines
meet in balance

CHAPTER EIGHTEEN

The Bend

Bend Control Is Horse Control

Bending opens a new world of abilities for horse and rider! All lateral dressage movements—shoulder-in, travers (haunches-in), renvers (haunches-out), half-pass, and pirouette—are based on the horse's ability to bend.

Correct bend on a circle or in a movement leads to balance, connection, straightness, and eventually collection. This means relaxation and improved feeling for both horse and rider. For hunters and jumpers, the quality of the bend in turns improves the horse's self-carriage and balance in approaching the fence.

When the horse is bent, he can more easily carry a bit more weight with his hindquarters and can balance comfortably on the outside rein.

Bending and Turning for a Perfect Circle

A combination of bending and turning aids make the circle (fig. 18.1). First, let's look at the bending aids. The rider's "shaping aids" position the horse in bend. Here are the nuts and bolts of bending:

- The inside leg and rein cause flexion (just until the crest of the neck flips) and bend.

- The outside leg prevents the haunches from going out.

- The outside rein prevents the neck from bending too much; this rein doesn't actually *cause* bend but it does *regulate* it.

18.1 Annie's aids shape her horse in bend. She is riding her own PRE gelding, Icaro.

THE BEND 187

18.2 A & B (A) Think about turn-on-the-haunches: The hindquarters are in one place while the shoulders and the entire forehand revolve around them. Where does the weight shift? "On the haunches."

(B) In contrast, the turn-on-the-forehand requires that the forehand be in one place while the hindquarters revolve around it. Where does the weight shift? "On the forehand." However, turn-on-the-forehand improves the horse's response to the leg, and it also teaches both horse and rider that the forehand must wait and stay relaxed while the hindquarters are activated.

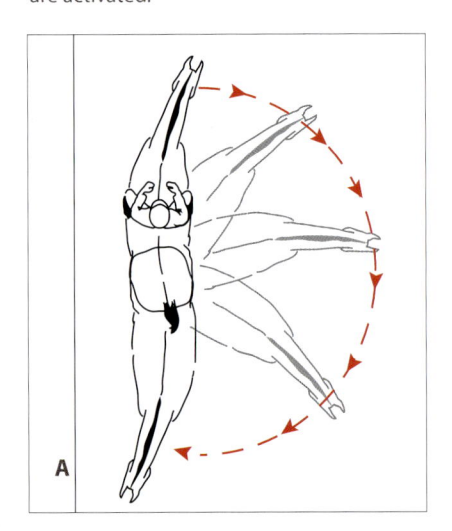

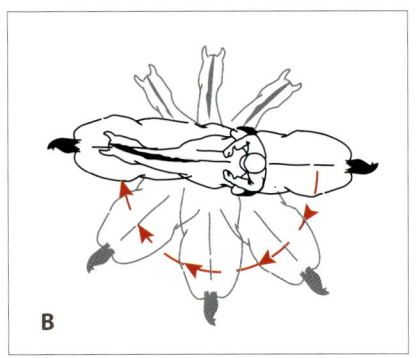

Bend happens in motion, so the dynamics of bend involve diagonal aids and unilateral aids. They work like this:

- Diagonal aids: The horse must be trained to step from the inside leg to the outside rein obediently and without question. The connection between the inside leg and outside rein balances the horse in consistent bend.

- Unilateral aids: The inside Triangle of Aids and the outside Triangle of Aids (see p. 55) align your horse on the precise line of the turn so that the hindquarters follow the forehand precisely. Your horse's tail should follow the same pathway as his nose.

The inside weight, leg, and rein aids *could* be called the aid for turning. One of the first things we teach a young horse is to follow the inside rein. However, most riders are inclined to overuse the inside rein, lean to the inside, and abandon the outside of the horse. Then, of course, their horse over-yields to the inside and loses his upright posture, so it's safer to say that the outside Triangle of Aids is in charge of turning the horse.

The outside Triangle turns the horse by moving his shoulders. The rider's outside leg confirms the connection to the outside rein. As the outside rein surrounds the outside shoulder, it causes the horse to step "through" the topline, creating "throughness." When the horse is in front of the inside leg, he turns easily from these outside aids, and if the bending is well confirmed, he won't lose it during the turn. When watching from the outside of the circle, the cylindrical appearance of the horse's body is evidence of "throughness" (see fig. 8.9, p. 105). It looks like the outside rein wraps around the horse.

Turning and the Value of Moveable Shoulders

Turning teaches horse and rider how to move the shoulders with control. Why is this important? When the horse's shoulders are moveable, he is freer in his forehand—one of your primary goals.

Think about turn-on-the-haunches (fig. 18.2 A). The hindquarters are in one place, while the shoulders and the entire forehand revolve around them. Where does the weight of the horse shift? "On the haunches." In contrast, the turn-on-the-forehand requires that the forehand be in one place,

188 WHEN TWO SPINES ALIGN: DRESSAGE DYNAMICS

how two spines
meet in balance

When the Inside Leg-Outside Rein Connection Is Ideal

As a result of the relationship between your inside leg and outside rein, your horse connects and eventually collects. Once the bridge of muscle is built, leverage causes the front end to lighten as weight is transferred back to the hindquarters (fig. 18.3 and see 11.1, p. 125). Your horse's frame becomes shorter and more uphill. Or, you can release the outside rein gradually, and your horse follows it forward and downward in a stretching frame. When the horse is properly connected, here are some uses of the *outside rein:*

- The outside rein balances your horse, so it's sometimes called a *balancing rein*. Whereas he shouldn't lean on it, he ideally feels solid in it, using it as you would the banister on the stairs.

- Your outside rein is the "brake." It controls the speed.

- Your outside rein is also the "clutch" that half-halts to say, *Wait a second while we change gears,* to make transitions between gaits (different rhythms), and paces (different lengths of stride).

- Your outside aids turn the horse so he can follow your desired line of travel.

The feel in your outside rein enables you to listen to your horse because it mirrors the condition of your horse's back and mouth. You look for the right feel in this outside rein.

18.3 Steffen Peters is riding Floriano here at the 2006 World Equestrian Games in Aachen, Germany. This horse is elegant in his uphill carriage because of what appears to be an ideal balance on the outside rein.

As you know, you always need to be aware of the horse's natural crookedness. In one direction the horse always needs to fill up the outside rein, and in the other direction, he wants to brace on it. However, once you achieve this correct balance on the outside rein in both directions, the reward is high. The outside rein helps monitor all of those balancing qualities: the rhythm, the energy, the length of stride, the height of the neck, the flexion, alignment, bending, and turning.

THE BEND

while the hindquarters turn or revolve around it (fig. 18.2 B). Where does the horse's weight shift? "On the forehand."

A well-executed turn-on-the-forehand has value in training your horse:

- It improves the horse's response to your leg.

- It teaches both horse and rider that the hindquarters can be activated while, at the same time, the shoulders and neck wait and stay relaxed.

The turn-on-the-forehand, however, does not help transfer your horse's weight to the hindquarters. Horses that fishtail the hindquarters are always putting themselves on the forehand, making it impossible for the rider to move the shoulders and steer. Moveable shoulders make for a handy, straight horse so you can build his collection with stable hind legs that carry equally.

A corner is one-quarter of a circle and a great place to learn about bending and turning. Do Exercise 2 (p. 197) to learn how corners can become your friend.

Centrifugal Force

One of the laws of nature works for you on a circle—*centrifugal force*. In everyday life, we notice how the washing machine and the clothes dryer spin the laundry to the outside of the tub. We feel it on the road when the car drifts to the outside of a turn, and we see it on the racetrack as race horses, cars, or dogs are inclined to drift or spin out. Centrifugal force affects the rider, too. She will naturally be inclined to fall to the outside of her horse on circles. Once there, it is impossible for her to give correct bending aids.

Whenever you see a rider sitting correctly on a circle with a deep inner seat and leg, know that she is making an effort to do so. It looks easy, but without the effort, she would follow the force and fall outside. But, here's the good news: You can let centrifugal force act on your horse to help put him on the outside aids. Your inside leg will help send him there, too.

Shoulder-In: De la Guérinière's Great Idea

Over centuries, millions of riders have noticed how bending improves the balance and harmony of horse and rider. Finally, in the eighteenth century, one of those riders, a Frenchman named François Robichon de la Guérinière had a great idea. He developed the notion that he could bend his horse *without* turning him. As a result, we have the movements in which the horse bends as he travels on a straight line: shoulder-in, travers (haunches-in), renvers (haunches-out), and half-pass.

The most basic and most important result of de la Guérinière's thinking was development of shoulder-in—the mother exercise of collection, which I discussed in the chapter "Leverage for Collection" (p. 125). It mobilizes the horse's shoulders and adds weight to the hindquarters, which stay on a consistent, straight line of travel. The shoulder-in demonstrates an 8- or 10-meter bend on a straight line.

To develop shoulder-in, the rider starts in shoulder-fore and mobilizes her horse's shoulders to the inside so that the outside fore is in the same track as the inside hind foot. As the horse's back swings, the rider's inside leg and outside rein leverage against one another to make a springier, more collected stride.

True collection happens when the rider successfully leverages the inside leg and the outside rein. When the horse is correctly connected and swinging through the back, the horse's hindquarters carry more weight, and the forehand of the horse becomes lighter and freer. Turning is easy. When you can ride shoulder-fore and shoulder-in in both directions, you have control of both hind legs and the shoulders, and you are well prepared for whatever you would like to do. Riders are still thanking de la Guérinière for his great idea!

Common Problems on a Circle

All horses find correct bend challenging. Here are a few of the common problems and methods of helping improve the bend.

Problem 1

Overuse of the inside rein is legendary in the horse world. Riders mistakenly turn their horses with the inside rein, and in the process, put the horse on the forehand and misalign his neck. To avoid this common problem, here is a counter-flexion exercise.

Try This
Start on a 20-meter circle in walk, tracking left in left bend. Stay on the left circle, and slowly counter-flex the horse with your right leg and rein—just until his crest flips right. Then, ride him from your right leg to your left rein in counter-shoulder-fore for half the circle. On this large circle, there should be little neck bend. Slowly return to true, left flexion and bend. Your horse will tell you where his neck is aligned, because it will be in a "falling-down" position (see p. 202). Memorize the feeling so you can reproduce it again and again. Do this in both directions, and then try it in trot.

Problem 2

Underusing the inside rein is also common. When riders get too focused on the importance of the outside rein, they sometimes forget that without bend there can be no outside rein, and without inner flexion, bend is impossible. The outside hand sometimes needs to be the passive receiver while the inside rein is active.

Problem 3

When the hindquarters swing in or out on their own, it always puts the horse's balance toward the forehand. Then, he loses his bend, along with a degree of relaxation. Horses don't swing the hind legs in or out with malicious intent. It's a kind of benign avoidance on the part of the horse. It is simply easier for him to avoid engaging. The rider's outside leg defines the bend on the outside of the horse by preventing the hindquarters from swinging out as they are naturally inclined to do when the horse straightens (stiffens) on his own in order to avoid carrying weight.

Problem 4

Sometimes the horse runs away from the rider's bending leg—either because the rider applied it wrong or because the horse isn't educated to respond to shaping leg aids. He thinks that your leg always means "Go." Half-halts given in the shape of bend teach the horse the difference between the bending leg and the driving leg that asks the horse to "Go."

Problem 5

Unfortunately, the rider's two hands are sometimes like partners in a dysfunctional marriage. One partner says "I'll do all the work," and the other says, "Fine with me." Because your horse only has one mouth, he should feel you have only one hand. This problem is compounded by the fact that the horse is naturally crooked and would also prefer to be one-sided.

Try This
If you typically have problems coordinating your hands, try *bridging* the reins—that is, hold both reins with one or both hands (fig. 18.4 A). This helps achieve equal bearing

how two spines meet in balance

18.4 A & B Unfortunately, the rider's two hands are sometimes like partners in a dysfunctional marriage. One partner says, "I'll do all the work," and the other says, "Fine with me." Then we wonder why the horse is heavy in one rein. To help gain equal contact, you can try bridging the reins as you see Annie demonstrating in photo A, or widening the hands as she is doing in B. These techniques will help you achieve equal bearing on the reins.

on the reins. American dressage tests used to require riding with one hand. It wasn't such a bad idea.

Now Try This

If you still have problems getting equal contact, try widening the reins momentarily (fig. 18.4 B). This will give you the feeling of a circular connection between your elbows/hips and the bit. You will feel your right hand in your left and your left hand in your right. Align the horse's neck so that he can meet the reins equally and ride to the rein your horse is reluctant to accept. When you have equal contact, you can feel the result of your inside aids in your outside hand and vice versa.

Problem 6

Sometimes the bent horse over-yields and curls away from the contact—especially on the inside. Then he carries the poll low, he is behind the vertical, and the direction of his energy is onto the forehand. This can be a result of overuse of the inside rein or insufficient leg. Remember that one of the purposes of the inside Triangle of Aids is to put the horse in front of the inside leg. The leg aid is primary over the rein aid.

Try This

Don't ride any circles for 10 or 15 minutes. Ride straight lines in shoulder-fore and counter-shoulder-fore. Concentrate on the upward transitions that send him to steady, solid but passive reins that are like supple side reins. Try different kinds of driving aids to see how your horse responds best: tap, tap, tap with the legs. Or, squeeze him out to the bridle. If he is still evading the bit by coming behind, longeing your horse with correctly fitted side reins without the weight of the rider will usually improve honesty to the bit.

Problem 7

Sometimes on straight lines, the horse loses his flexibility—that is, his ability to be aligned, flexed, and bent so he can balance on the outside rein.

Try This

Do 15- or 20-meter circles at A, B, C, and E with straight lines in between so the horse can learn to carry himself on the straight line in the same balance as he had on the circle (fig. 18.5). When you go straight, retain the very slight 20-meter bend with the narrowed hind leg, which is shoulder-fore. Then go across the diagonal and repeat the exercise in the other direction. Combining circles and straight lines will remind the horse that he needs to stay flexible when he goes straight. He always thinks a circle or

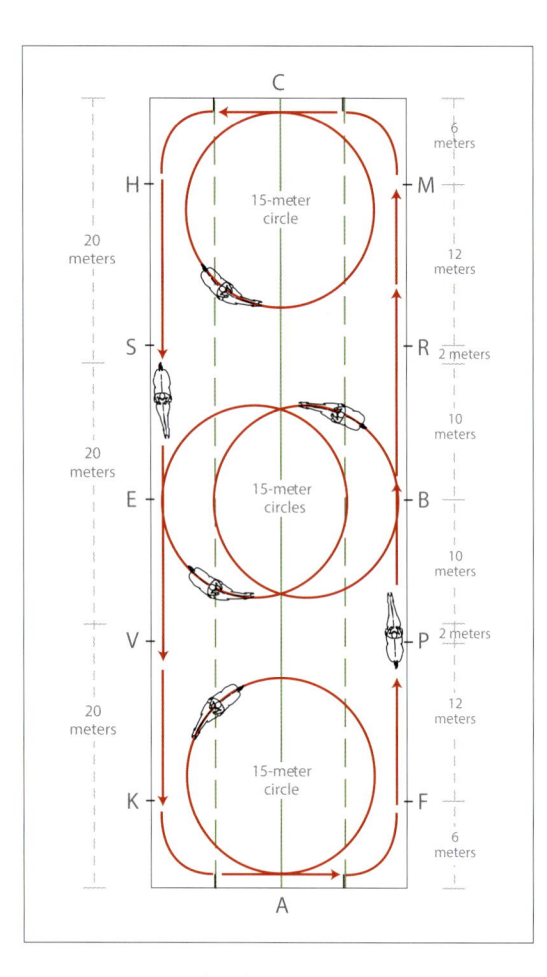

18.5 Horses are inclined to lose their flexibility when they go straight and lose their forward activity in turns and circles. Ride the figures in this diagram so you can combine straight lines and bent lines. Concentrate on keeping the activity on circles and on keeping the flexibility on straight lines by doing shoulder-fore.

Cultured about Bend

The schoolmaster has "culture." He thoroughly understands the meaning of the aids and the results they are intended to produce. Horses that are cultured about bend are very rideable and are able to collect more easily. Whereas schoolmasters are educated about bend, even an Olympic horse will never bend on his own without the correct aids. Even the best schoolmaster will eventually mold himself to his rider's expectations and abilities. That's why the rider also needs to be cultured about bend.

a turn is coming up. If you're in a test, and you can't make a circle with an inflexible horse, you can *pretend* you're going to make a circle. Half-halt, use your 20-meter bending aids, then go straight, retaining the alignment and flexion. This is shoulder-fore.

Problem 8

Sometimes a horse's tempo gets slower as the circle gets smaller or the corner gets deeper.

Try This

Do a figure eight that's in the shape of a snowman (fig. 18.6). Your horse's strides will naturally be shorter on the small circle. To counteract his inclination to get slower in short strides, think of quickening on the small circle. Then make these variations:

- As you come onto the large circle, lengthen the stride halfway around.

- Counteract his inclination to get faster by thinking you want big, slow strides.

- As you come onto the large circle, canter, and then trot before changing direction onto the small circle. Think quick strides on the small circle. Do this exercise in both directions.

BENDING EXERCISES

Large circles, figure eights, and serpentines are nothing new, but they are brilliant exercises that help equalize the use of the horse's hind legs so he can be straight. They also narrow the track of the horse's hindquarters so he's in self-carriage.

German Olympian Hubertus Schmidt, one of the greatest riders in the world, says the execution of a 20-meter circle that puts the horse on the outside rein is not such a small accomplishment. He says that many riders understand the importance of the outside rein, but they are not particular enough about how the horse is put precisely on it in correct bend.

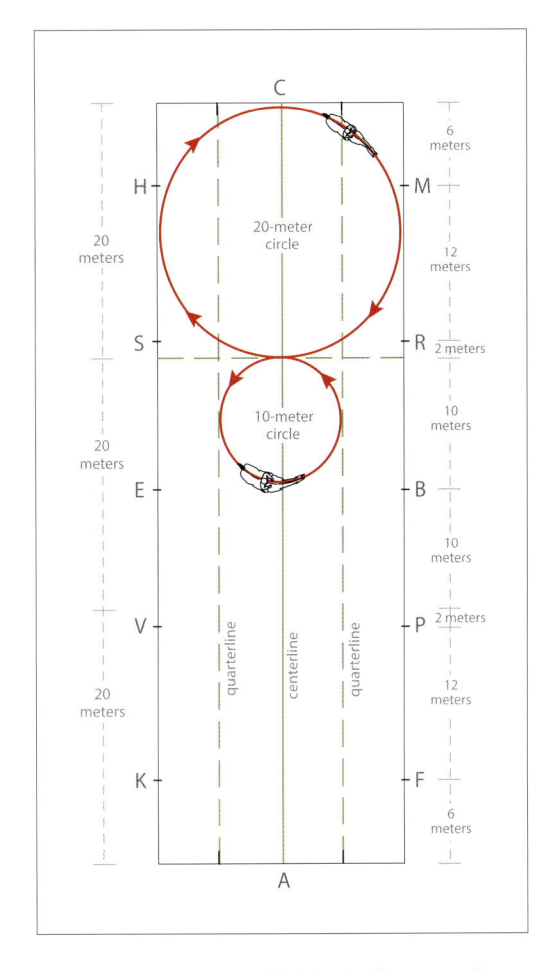

18.6 In the "Snowman Figure Eight," you will feel your horse's strides automatically become shorter on the smaller circle. If you can succeed in keeping your horse's rhythm, tempo, and energy the same on both circles, the smaller figure will help your horse collect.

It's simple in theory, but not easy in practice. Schmidt's persistence in getting correct bend with his horses lays the foundation for his performances that are famous for power and brilliance that look relaxed and easy.

Make it your goal to know the feeling of a perfect 20-meter circle. Then know the feeling of a 15-meter circle, 12-meter, 10-meter, and eventually 8-meter circle. Get cultured about bend by trying these simple but brilliant bending exercises.

EXERCISE 1
Know the Feeling of a 20-Meter Circle

Directions Set yourself up for success by placing cones on the circle points. You'll see how much precision helps!

Step 1 Ride 20-meter circles in each direction with the following ideas in mind:

- Remember that bend happens where your seat is—where two spines meet—not at the base of the horse's neck. Think of turning with your Outside Triangle of Aids.

- A circle requires a combination of bending aids and turning aids. Sometimes think about bending aids, and sometimes think about turning aids.

- Flex (position) and align your horse in front of the saddle.

- Align him behind the saddle by narrowing the inside hind leg in shoulder-fore and preventing the outside hind from going out.

- Keep both seat bones down and your torso aligned with your horse's forehand. Put a touch more weight in your inside seat and stirrup. If necessary, use an active inside leg. This leg might need to be more persuasive than you think.

- Keep an elastic connection with the outside rein. Keep it passive and receiving until the horse goes to that rein. Then it can be useful and effective.

- Your outside leg engages the outside hind leg. It sends energy to the outside rein and prevents the haunches from going out.

Step 2 Next, ride a figure eight and a serpentine—variations of the circle. The frequent changes of direction make your horse equal in both reins with always a touch more connection on the outside rein. Keep these ideas in mind:

how two spines
meet in balance

- Before every change of direction, half-halt or think, *Wait a second,* with the inside-seat/leg-outside-rein connection. If your horse doesn't respond to your half-halts, do a downward transition.

- Keep the energy flowing through your horse's back and through you. Absorb his motion with your body.

- If your horse's neck stays relaxed, it means that the rest of his back is relaxed, too. Look for the connected feeling with a swinging back. When you know the feeling of a 20-meter circle, work on feeling the 15-, 12-, 10-, and 8-meter bend.

EXERCISE 2
Turning and the 12-Meter Corner

Directions Corners are dreaded by inexperienced riders, but are the saviors of experienced riders. In fact, experienced riders "prepare for the corner" when the corner isn't even there—just so they can rebalance the horse.

Try to make friends with your corners. Each time you let your horse "take over" in the corners or fall in, you lose him a little. Each time you can confirm the bend before the corner and then turn him with your outside aids without losing the bend or the line of travel, you improve your horse's balance and the mobility of his forehand.

Check out the geometry of your arena. If you don't have a standard arena, it doesn't matter as long as you have corners. If you don't have corners, create them with cavalletti. The corner letter in a dressage arena is 6 meters—or six average giant steps—from the actual corner where two sides of your arena meet. If you don't have a corner letter, mark a place where the corner letter would be. If you have a cone, put it inside the track there so you can ride between the cone and the wall at that specific point. Then from the corner, pace off 6 meters on the other wall, and mark that place too, ideally with a cone. Both of your marks should be equidistant from the corner.

You will ride an arc through this corner from marker to marker (fig. 18.7). The arc in this corner is one-quarter of a 12-meter circle, which is why we call it a 12-meter corner. Begin in walk:

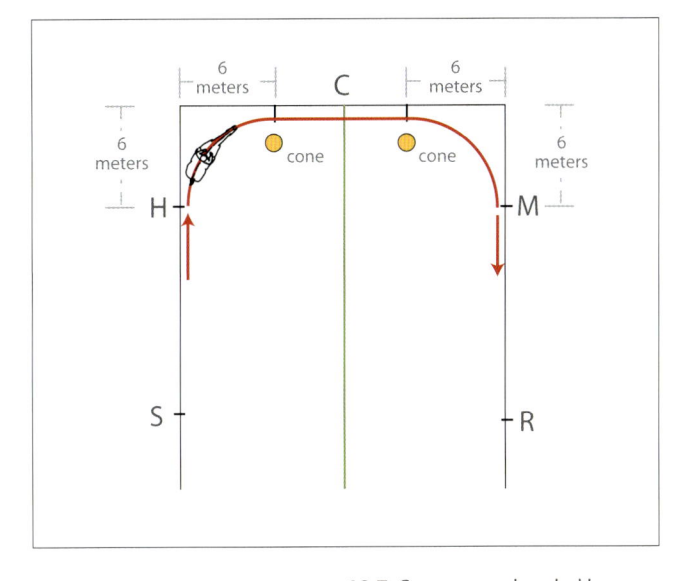

18.7 Corners are dreaded by inexperienced riders but are the savior of experienced riders. This 12-meter corner will help you figure out how to make each corner your friend. Set your horse up in bend before the corner, turn, and finish the corner in shoulder-fore. Follow the directions carefully in this exercise so you leave the track 6 meters from the corner and return to the next track 6 meters from the corner. This exercise will develop your horse's ability to carry himself correctly through turns. You'll love how it feels.

THE BEND 197

Step 1 Ride down the long side in shoulder-fore. This will give you the suggestion of bend and the ability to bend more.

Step 2 Before the corner, half-halt in the shape of bend on a 12-meter arc. Your horse will be balanced on the outside rein.

Step 3 Turn him through the corner with your outside aids. Ride exactly from marker to marker.

Step 4 As you go through the corner, release the inside rein by patting your horse on the neck. Although you may need a little support from the inside aids, be sure you can, primarily, turn with your outside aids without losing the bend.

Step 5 Your corner is complete when your horse's hindquarters reach the second wall, and you are back in shoulder-fore. If your horse retains the bend and balance on the outside rein through the corner, you will feel your horse carry himself in perfect balance.

Step 6 Try the exercise in trot and canter. Ride a square or rectangular pattern with four corners. Be sure to do it in both directions. Be patient but persistent. Mastering this will take time.

Problems abound that cause him to lose his balance. Here are the most common ones:

- If the turning aids overcome the bending aids, he loses the bend in the corner. Repeat in the next corner with more preparation to reestablish the bend beforehand.

- If your horse hurries, he probably isn't responding to the preparatory half-halts. When this is the case, quietly transition to walk, or halt before each corner until he learns to wait for your turning aids.

- If your horse slows down in the corner, be sure to ride the tempo more clearly the next time. You are his metronome.

Step 7 When you feel confident, increase the difficulty. Move each marker one meter closer to the corner, so you can do a 10-meter corner, which is one-quarter of a 10-meter circle. Progress to 8-meter corners if your horse is Fourth Level or more. The

6-meter corner is reserved for the highly collected horse. Don't give your horse challenges that he can't meet successfully.

This exercise develops your horse's ability to carry himself correctly and easily in collection. It's the foundation for self-carriage in all exercises with bend: shoulder-in, travers (haunches-in), renvers (haunches-out), half-pass, and pirouette. When your horse temporarily loses his self-carriage, return to the basics of riding a corner, and he'll regain it.

EXERCISE 3
Theodorescu Serpentines

Directions German Olympian, Monica Theodorescu, daughter of the late dressage master, Georg Theodorescu, rides serpentines and figure eights on the short side of the arena to develop balance and "throughness" in her horses (fig. 18.8).

For *lower-level* horses, Theodorescu rides a 10-meter, two-loop serpentine or figure eight (not shown) on the short side of the arena. Each loop or circle is 10 meters.

- Start at E or B and make the change of direction at X. Or, you can start at K, F, M, or H and make the change of direction facing A or C on the short side. Help your horse by doing this exercise in walk before trying it in trot or in canter. Align your horse in 10-meter bend as you did when you rode your corners. Be sure your horse balances on the outside rein. A mirror helps you notice when you and your horse are misaligned.

- When you have your balance, do the exercise in trot and then in canter with a change of lead through the walk or the trot, or a flying change.

For *Prix St. Georges* horses:

- Do a three-loop serpentine on the short side between H and M. Each loop is almost 7 meters. Do this one in walk first, so you and your horse have time to figure out how to carry yourselves in alignment on the outside rein and make the changes in bend.

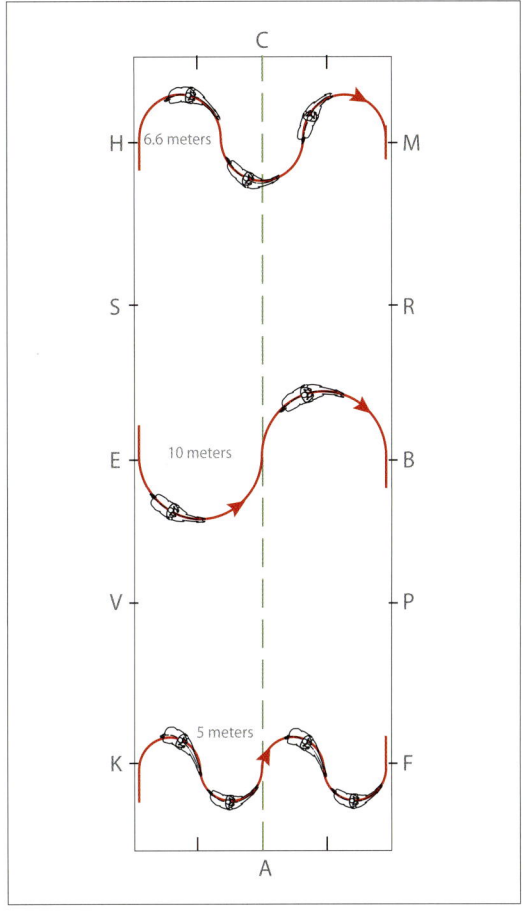

18.8 German Olympian Monica Theodorescu and her late father Georg Theodorescu used serpentines on the short side to supple their horses. The two-loop serpentine is for the developing horse; the three-loop serpentine is for the Prix St. Georges horse; and the four-loop serpentine is for the very highly trained Grand Prix horse. Be sure to master this in walk before you try it in trot or canter.

- Then do it in trot and canter with simple changes through the walk or flying changes.

For *Grand Prix* horses:

- Do a four-loop serpentine with each loop being 5 meters between K and F. This exercise requires a high degree of collection and balance.

- Don't do any exercise that is too difficult for your horse to do well.

Essential Information about Bend

- Correct bend on a circle or in a movement leads to balance, connection, straightness, and eventually collection.

- All lateral dressage movements: shoulder-in, travers, renvers, half-pass, and pirouette, are based on the horse's ability to bend.

- The rider's aids shape the horse in bend.

- Turning teaches horse and rider how to move the shoulders with control, which frees the forehand—one of your primary goals.

- Shoulder-in enables the horse to retain the suppleness of bend on a straight line.

- Correct bend is achieved by a correct connection between the inside leg and outside rein.

- Even highly educated horses who are cultured about bend can't do it on their own. Their riders need to give them the correct aids.

how two spines
meet in balance

CHAPTER NINETEEN

The Height of the Neck

"Throughness" by Nature

By nature, in his normal posture, the horse's neck "falls down" from the withers and his back is raised (see p. 202). When your horse's back is strengthened in this position, he can easily carry a rider. The energy from the horse's pushing engine arcs through his back and his falling-down neck, and it builds a bridge of muscle over the topline. When the rider receives the energy and recycles it, the shape of the bridge is strengthened and stabilized.

But things can go wrong that prevent the neck from being in that falling-down position:

- When the horse is in a state of high alert, his head goes up to assess real or imagined danger. As a result, his withers fall and the weight-bearing bridge breaks (fig. 19.1 A).

- The rider whose weight is not supported by a deep, well-placed leg is heavy in her seat and can challenge the bridge and make the horse's spine become like a hammock (fig. 19.1 B). In this case, the neck goes up because the back and withers are down, and the bridge is broken.

When the bridge of muscle carries the horse and rider correctly, the limbs of the horse are relatively free of stress.

19.1 A & B (A) When the horse is in a state of high alert, his head goes up to assess real or imagined danger, and as a result, the weight-bearing bridge breaks.

(B) When the rider sits incorrectly, she challenges the horse's bridge of muscle and his spine becomes like a hammock.

The Cue to Lower the Neck

The rider monitors and regulates the height of her horse's neck to help develop "throughness." It's the rider's job to find the place where her horse's neck relaxes down naturally from the shoulders. Because your horse's spine is not attached to his

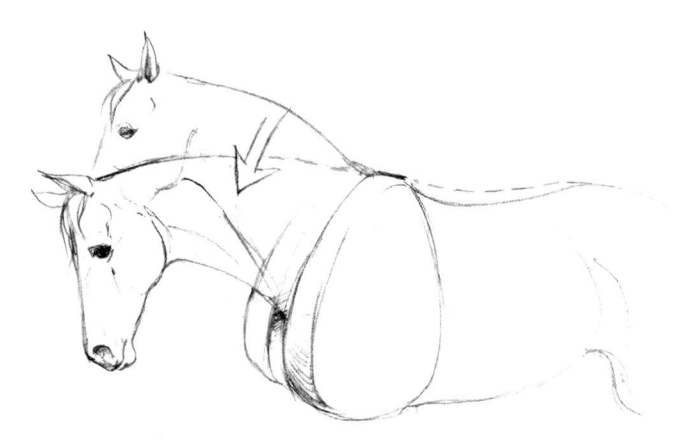

19.2 Your horse's shoulder blades form a "slot" through which his neck can "fall down." In this position, the horse's back naturally comes up. Aligning your horse's neck allows him to lower it, and he will often lower it on his own. If not, try Exercise 1 on page 204.

shoulder blades by bone, his shoulder blades form a "slot" through which his neck can "fall down." In this position, the horse's back naturally comes up (fig. 19.2). To help you find this place where your horse is truly straight and can reach forward and downward, repeat the flexion exercise on page 179.

Aligning the neck allows the horse to lower it, and he will often lower it on his own. But, because tension sometimes causes horses to carry the neck too high, the rider will always do well to know how to ask her horse to lower his neck. This ability will constantly help the horse use his body with integrity as he prepares for figures, movements, or fences. Asking the horse to lower his neck is a reminder to the horse to carry himself with his topline in good posture so the energy can go "through" to make the work as easy as possible, minimize stress on the legs, and maximize longevity. To help your horse lower his neck, try Exercise 1 on page 204.

Release to the Withers

Anatomically, the withers are comparable to the vertebrae at the base of the human neck where nerves gather. Horses take great comfort when the rider touches or

Falling-Down vs. Hanging-Down Neck

There is a difference between a *falling-down neck* and a *hanging-down neck*. The horse's neck, by nature, falls down from the withers and his back is lifted, which makes his shape round. (Imagine him grazing.) In motion, the energy from the hindquarters goes through the topline—through the horse's back, his withers and the top of his neck, which he carries proudly with those topline muscles that enable self-carriage. The horse with the hanging-down neck doesn't carry his own neck, and his back isn't lifted. He has poor posture and no self-carriage, so he wants to hang on the rider's hands. It should be noted that riders often do some hanging of their own. Regardless of the height of the hand, the rider should carry her own forearms and not hang on the horse's mouth. And the horse should carry his own neck. Try Exercise 2 on page 205 if your horse's neck is hanging down.

scratches the withers. If you want your horse to stand still during a halt or you want to stabilize his balance, press your knuckles gently on the withers or scratch him on either side. He'll be inclined to relax. The same is true when the horse is in motion. The energy goes through the withers, so hands that are too high will not necessarily be part of the circle of the aids. When the rider touches the withers in a quiet release, the horse will be inclined to relax and lower the neck (see fig. 13.5, p. 160).

As I've said, the "work place" of the hands is a small area—perhaps the size of a dinner plate—very close to the withers and slightly in front. Touch the withers often as a form of release, and you'll gain greater control over your horse's shoulders. Your horse will be freer in front as he develops self-carriage.

Remember Relative Elevation and the Principle of Leverage

Many small releases encourage your horse to relax in his topline with a falling-down neck. Once that is achieved, the height of the neck is determined by your horse's degree of engagement. When the horse is in "relative elevation," the height of the neck is "relative" to the engagement of the horse (fig. 19.3).

In this ideal situation, the rider rides the neck up or down—from behind by engaging the hindquarters more or less. The hands are uninvolved with the height of the neck other than by providing a flexible point through which the energy flows to the front and half-halts back to the hind legs. When the horse's neck is high because of the rider's hands, he is in "absolute elevation," which is always incorrect and unfriendly to the horse's back. In correct collection, the neck falls down from the withers, but it appears to rise proudly to whatever degree, determined by the degree of the horse's engagement.

Try the following exercises to help you regulate the height of the neck.

19.3 The horse retains the "falling-down neck" even in collection. The neck falls down from the withers but it rises proudly in collection because the shoulders and withers rise as the croup lowers. This is "relative elevation," that is, the height of the neck is "relative" to the engagement of the horse.

EXERCISES

EXERCISE 1
Finding the Falling-Down Neck

Directions Imagine that you're putting a penny in a piggy bank. You can't do it until your penny is aligned with the slot. The relationship between your horse's neck and shoulders is comparable. Once the neck is aligned and coming straight out of the shoulders, it can relax down easily. When the neck is in this naturally relaxed place, he becomes visibly wide in his musculature at the base of his neck.

Step 1 Do a medium walk. Stabilize your horse's line of travel by keeping his hindquarters on one line with your seat and legs. Either ride toward a mirror or straight toward a tree or fence post. The stability of your line of travel is important.

Study the crest of your horse's neck. Use your leg and rein aids to gently flex your horse slowly and slightly in left and then right shoulder-fore. Find the place where the neck can relax down through the shoulders at the base of his neck. Channel your horse's energy to the bit whether he is flexed left or right. Because it's a human inclination to overuse the inside rein, you might be surprised that your horse's place of straightness is farther to one side than you imagined. When you have achieved the falling-down neck, your horse might not be parallel to the long side of your arena. That's okay for now. Although he is not yet "arena straight," he is "axis straight" or straight within himself. Arena straightness comes later.

Step 2 If your horse feels stiff or unbalanced, do a few walk-halt-walk transitions. Always look for and find the place where he wants to relax his neck down from the withers. When the spine is aligned and straight between the shoulder blades, there will be a slight, but even curve in the crest of the neck to one direction or the other. Whereas the neck comes straight out of the shoulders, it won't be straight like a ruler. It will be straight like a horse, which has a very slight curve.

It's important to remember that the horse can only achieve elementary straightness when he is moving forward with relaxed enthusiasm in the energy of the working gaits. Without that forward rhythm, he wobbles like a bicycle going too slowly.

Step 3 You can also try this: When you close your legs, the horse should reach downward-forward toward the contact. Each time you use your seat-leg aid, soften ever so slightly in the hand without throwing the contact away. Your horse will soon learn that there is a little space for him to reach toward the contact immediately following a leg aid. If it doesn't work, be persistent. Repeat it and have faith in the system.

Step 4 Another suggestion: Ride on a large circle, and feel your horse balance on the outside rein. Be sure your horse is correctly and sufficiently flexed to the inside, because that is a prerequisite to going on the outside rein. Then the outside rein helps determine the length and height of the horse's neck. You can lower your horse's neck by riding to the outside rein from your inside leg and then pushing the outside rein a bit forward. If your horse is correctly on the outside rein, he will follow the hand down and out. The horse shouldn't stretch so far that you lose your connection to the hindquarters, however. If your horse wants to get too long or too low, you can use your downward transitions and half-halts to make the amount of reach determined by you, not by your horse.

Step 5 Stretch. Stretching develops the horse's bridge of muscle in a way that encourages the neck to fall down and the back to come up. Lengthen the rein to the precise degree of stretch desired. Horses should stretch as part of their daily work without losing the connection. Half-halts within that stretch complete the circle of aids in the desired frame.

The invitation to stretch feels like a reward for the horse, but it also rewards *you* because the horse comes to a more natural posture that makes him easier to ride. The rider who "holds" the horse on the bit will always need to hold him. Self-carriage happens with frequent, tiny, invisible releases within the contact. Remember Bo Jena's advice: "Many small givings."

EXERCISE 2
Fixing a Hanging-Down Neck

Directions When your horse is hanging, he isn't carrying his own neck. The balance is similar to when your car is stuck in the mud. You need to rock it out of its stuck place.

Step 1 With bend, gently "rock" your horse with downward and upward transitions. The bend supples his neck and entire topline. Downward transitions engage the hindquarters.

Step 2 Release the rein to prevent your horse from leaning on you.

Step 3 Then your leg aids create enough energy to get through the entire spine to the hand, and direct it horizontally instead of downhill. Soften or touch the withers often so he has frequent opportunities to carry himself.

Essential Information about the Height of the Neck

• In nature, the horse's neck "falls down" from the withers. Ideally, the horse's back should be strengthened in this position so the energy goes through the base of the neck.

• Horses often lose "throughness" at the base of the neck. Sometimes the neck comes up (and the withers and back go down) as the horse checks out the environment. Other times the rider doesn't carry herself in balance on the horse's back so it becomes hollow.

• The rider benefits from knowing how to ask her horse to lower the neck.

• Although the neck should be low, the horse should carry it himself with his topline muscles. The horse should never hang on the rider's hands and expect her to carry his neck.

• In true collection, the neck is only high because the withers are high and the hindquarters are lowered. The horse is in "relative elevation" when the height of the neck is relative to the level of engagement of the hindquarters. This is the ideal situation.

how two spines meet in balance

CHAPTER TWENTY

The Length of Stride

The length of stride and the length of the frame should be comparable. That is, as the stride lengthens or shortens, so does the frame. By nature, the horse wants to *increase* the energy level and tempo when lengthening the stride, but that invariably shifts his center of gravity onto the forehand. Also, the horse is inclined to *decrease* the energy and tempo when shortening the stride. However, the big energy of a lengthened stride shouldn't become the small energy of the shortened stride. Rather, that big energy should cause the horse to step higher during the shorter strides and lift him into some degree of collection.

So the rider's challenge during these transitions within a gait is to regulate her horse's rhythm (including the tempo) and energy (figs. 20.1 A & B). If she is successful, she makes her horse supple and elastic. When the horse is in charge of the energy, he loses his balance and his suppleness.

When you're regulating the rhythm, remember the nature of each of the gaits. The *walk* is a marching gait. Utilize the free walk to maximize the marching quality

20.1 A & B (A) By nature, the horse is inclined to *increase* the energy level and tempo when lengthening the stride, but that invariably shifts the center of gravity onto the forehand. When Mica can keep the energy and tempo the same, Infanta lifts into loftier strides of medium trot instead of flattening onto the forehand.

(B) The horse is inclined to *decrease* the energy and tempo when shortening the strides. Mica is successful in retaining the energy and tempo so Infanta steps higher during the shorter strides and lifts into some degree of collection.

in relaxation. When you shorten your stride, try to retain that quality. The *trot* is a swinging gait. Without this quality, the work can never advance correctly. Most horses are inclined to lose some of the swinging quality when they lengthen or shorten the stride. Don't lengthen more than you can do with quality. The *canter* is a bounding gait. Retain this quality as you lengthen and shorten the stride.

Depending on the age and development of the horse, the transitions can be from a working pace to a lengthened stride and back to working. Or the transitions can be from collected to medium or extended and back to collected. Riding to a fence, the rider can shorten or lengthen her horse's stride to the ideal point of engagement and thrust so as to maximize the horse's scope over the fence.

Shortening in a Forward Way

The rider who can bring her horse back by using forward aids is very skilled, but for even the most skilled rider, a swinging back is a prerequisite to being able to ride forward in downward transitions. When the horse's back is swinging, the rider's rhythmic driving and half-halting aids make a bigger circle of aids to lengthen the stride and a smaller one to shorten the stride. The rider's aid is a timely impulse that bounces the horse into bigger or smaller strides.

When the horse makes the common mistake of coming behind the vertical in a lengthened stride, he is not "through," and the back can't swing. The gait integrity—of the swinging trot, the marching walk, or the bounding canter—is lost. The rider should prefer a modest correct lengthening of stride over one that is fast or behind the vertical. Judges should prefer the modest correct lengthening, too. When the horse doesn't reach toward the bit, he also doesn't reach with his hind legs, and if he doesn't reach in the lengthening, he certainly won't reach in the downward transition to a shorter stride. The aim is to keep the horse's neck relaxed and his nose reaching during the lengthening, and ideally it stays that way during half-halts and downward transitions because the rider uses little hand (see "Reach and Roundness," p. 12).

When the transition back is done with too much hand, the circle of the aids is broken, and the horse over-yields in the poll and shortens the neck instead of engaging behind. However, if the horse doesn't respond to the ideal half-halt, a stronger one will be necessary.

The rider methodically brings the hand back, stabilizes it, and pushes into it until the horse comes through. (The hand doesn't "pull" because the seat and leg aid is greater than the rein aid.) During this strong half-halt, the neck may be briefly shortened but the horse, in the next moment, reaches out to the bit as the rider softens the rein and drives to it. The strong half-halt makes the light half-halt possible.

The dressage horse that can smoothly go from extended trot to piaffe and back to extended trot without losing energy, rhythm, or relaxation would get a very high score for suppleness and elasticity, but it doesn't start that way. It starts with lengthening and shortening just a few inches at a time. Play with transitions that lengthen and shorten the stride until your horse can engage from half-halts and transitions. Try the following exercise to help in regulating the length of stride and frame.

EXERCISES

EXERCISE
Lengthen and Shorten the Stride on a Circle

Step 1 Start on a 20-meter circle in walk. The walk is often the best gait to teach your horse a concept because it's slow, and the rider has more time to organize her aids. Be sure your hands follow as if you were part of his mouth, and your horse reaches to your hand. Then, he will notice when you stop following and connect to your seat for a half-halt. Do a few transitions to halt to be sure your horse can "Whoa."

Step 2 Pay attention to the upward transitions back to walk. He should start with a quiet, relaxed step from his hind legs rather than his preferred method of walking away in front-wheel drive. This hindquarter reaction will be important when you ask for a lengthened stride. You don't want your horse to respond with his *pulling* engine to an aid for a lengthening. You want him to lengthen from his *pushing* engine.

Step 3 Experiment with the length of your horse's walk stride. Make half the circle a lengthened stride and the other half a normal walk with a working attitude. The amount of energy and the rhythm must stay the same, but the strides get bigger and then smaller. You need both the seat-leg "Go" aids and seat-hand "Whoa" aids, whether the strides are getting bigger or smaller. Make the circle of your aids bigger (not harder) and then smaller.

Step 4 Use turns-on-the-forehand to remind your horse how to respond to a leg aid—that is, with the hindquarters, not the forehand-pulling engine. The neck stays relaxed.

Step 5 Be sure your horse is walking on his own and carrying you. Do the same in trot and canter and change directions frequently. Soon your horse will be responding to the circle of the aids, and you will need very little hand. Continue to monitor and regulate the energy and rhythm during your lengthenings and shortenings.

Essential Information about the Length of Stride

- The length of stride and the length of the frame should be comparable. That is, as the stride lengthens or shortens, so does the frame.

- When a lengthened stride is shortened, it causes the horse to step higher and lift himself into some degree of collection.

- If the horse increases the tempo in lengthenings, his center of gravity invariably shifts onto the forehand. As a result, regulating the rhythm should be a priority in lengthenings.

- As you regulate the rhythm, retain the marching quality of the walk, the swinging quality of the trot, and the bounding quality of the canter.

- When the horse's basics are all in place and he marches in walk, swings in trot, and bounds in canter, it is possible to shorten the stride in a forward way with little hand. It's a major landmark in the training when the rider can collect the horse without using many rein aids.

how two spines meet in balance

CHAPTER TWENTY-ONE

The Line of Travel

Controlling Your Path for Perfect Balance

Many riders—especially dressage riders—unconsciously have no destination points. They wander. When the rider isn't determining the line of travel, the horse is determining it, and balance always suffers. Although some horses are more naturally balanced than others, none of them balance on their own. Once riders understand the importance of accurate figures and precision on the line of travel, they don't need to be reminded.

Know the anatomy of a dressage arena. Know the precise circle points on a 20-meter, 15-meter, 12-, 10-, and 8-meter circle. Know the points of a 12-, 10-, and 8-meter corner. Know how to ride all your figures accurately (fig. 21.1)

Be True to Your Line

Nothing improves balance more than being true to your line of travel throughout turns and straight lines. So, the rider who stares adoringly at his horse's neck will forever be in his horse's natural balance—or natural *lack* of balance!

Control of the line of travel is the one factor that is outside the horse-rider system. It puts horse and rider in the real world doing figures and lines—whether in the dressage arena, the jumping arena, or on the trail. To be the leader of the dance, the rider's reference point has to be outside the horse—a dressage letter, a fence post, a tree, or a jump. These reference points put the horse on the aids. If your horse falls to the right of the line of travel, he experiences a self-correction by running into your right aids, which will push him back to the center. If he falls to

21.1 The Geometry of the Dressage Arena. Although some horses are more naturally balanced than others, none of them balance on their own. Riding accurate lines and turns improves your horse's balance. Know the anatomy of your arena. Know the precise circle points of 20-, 15-, 10-, and 8-meter circles. Ride your lines and figures accurately.

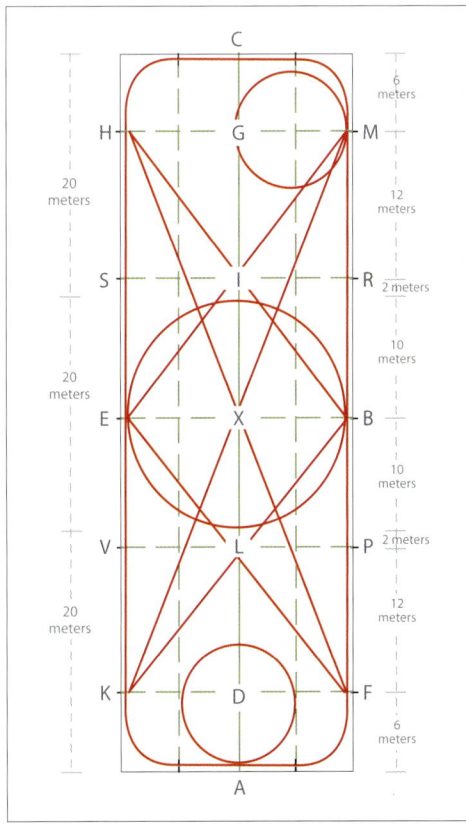

THE LINE OF TRAVEL 211

the left of the line of travel, he will run into your left aids, which will, again, push him back on track.

Whether you're in a dressage arena or on a jumping course, you have a departure point and a destination point. Between these two points there can be only one straight line or an infinite number of bending lines. It's your job to help your horse be true to the line that you choose.

If you choose a figure, such as a 20-meter circle, a figure eight, or a serpentine, the figure itself balances your horse and makes riding easy for both you and him. If your lines are precise, every step will be the same, and the dance will be self-perpetuating. Reliability gives you and your horse mental confidence and relaxation.

If the rider has a problem with the line of travel, then the horse never, under the best of circumstances, can be balanced because the rules will change constantly for him. So, you should ride lines and figures with neurotic accuracy. The rider who has trouble with precise lines of travel should use cones to mark the way.

I used to love teaching flatwork to the hunter riders at the Ox Ridge Hunt Club in Darien, Connecticut. Because I used to jump myself, I had a real appreciation for their task. I remember the magnetic appeal of each obstacle and fascination with finding the ideal point of thrust and the effort to jump over a specific part of the rail. That made the course much easier. I remember how my horse invariably wanted to fall to the inside after a fence in anticipation of the next one. I would neurotically ride straight lines and downward transitions after each fence. I remember the difficulty of keeping the pace steady with an eager horse.

On Mondays, after a weekend show at Ox Ridge, I would ask my students, "What was the course?" Then, in my dressage arena, we would design a comparable "course" without fences. The riders would negotiate the straight lines and bending turns of our "course," and then we'd add poles where the fences were supposed to be (fig. 21.2). Mastering the course without fences wasn't always easy, but it helped when the fences went up again.

With the ability to monitor and regulate your horse's rhythm, energy, flexion, bend, alignment, length and height of the neck, and line of travel, your horse's balance should be quite stable, and

21.2 Mastering the straight lines and bending turns of an equitation course *without* fences can help you and your horse perform better when the jumps are added.

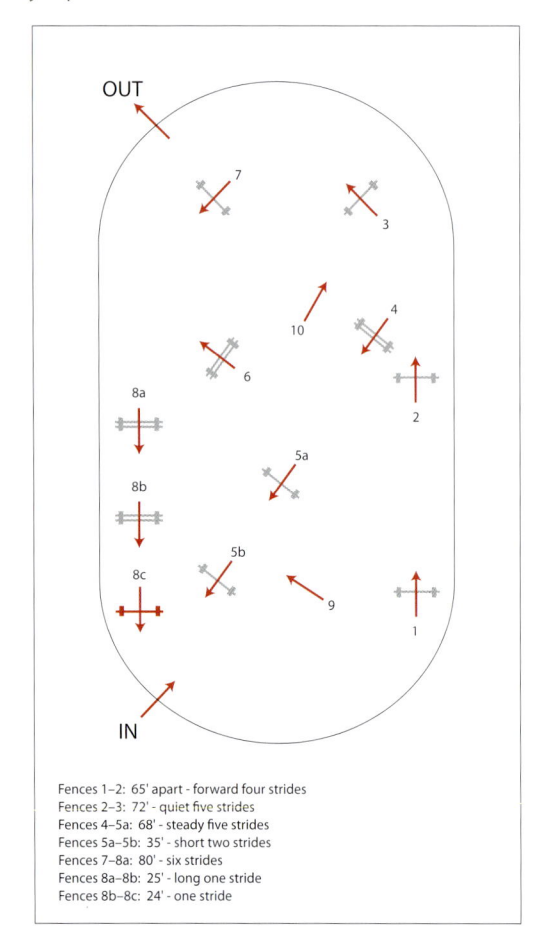

Fences 1–2: 65' apart - forward four strides
Fences 2–3: 72' - quiet five strides
Fences 4–5a: 68' - steady five strides
Fences 5a–5b: 35' - short two strides
Fences 7–8a: 80' - six strides
Fences 8a–8b: 25' - long one stride
Fences 8b–8c: 24' - one stride

you're in a position to develop your horse into an athlete. Figures and movements, with the help of half-halts and transitions, can develop your sport into art. Technique always comes before art.

All riders can, with or without sophistication, use these techniques. Even when they're executed less than perfectly, they usually improve the horse. The hindquarters, instead of just pushing, start, bit by bit, to do a little more carrying. The front end, instead of pulling, starts to push the forehand in an upward, elevated direction. In that better balance, the jumper is set up to navigate a bigger, cleaner fence. The dressage horse moves with more elegance. His rhythm becomes cadenced, his paces improve, and he becomes more beautiful.

Figures shape the horse in bend, and movements give the rider opportunities to position her horse so as to improve the engagement by helping the horse thrust, reach, and engage precisely under the place where two spines meet.

EXERCISES

EXERCISE 1
The Shifting Shoulder-Fore

Directions This exercise helps your horse become attuned to your outside aids so you can stay on your exact line of travel and prevent your horse from "hugging" the rail.

Step 1 Develop shoulder-fore on the long side. Keep your eyes looking straight ahead.

Step 2 With your outside aids, gradually shift the line of travel one meter to the inside.

Step 3 Stabilize your shoulder-fore on this line.

Step 4 With your inside aids, gradually shift your shoulder-fore back to the track.

Step 5 Do this in both directions. If you can, try it in shoulder-in and travers (haunches-in).

Always be sure that your horse can easily move off the rail whenever you wish.

Cones

Years ago, the late Major Anders Lindgren, a great Swedish teacher, visited the United States frequently. Cones were his favorite teaching aids. In the early eighties, he set up a standard arena with cones to guide his apprentice instructors through every movement of an Intermediaire test. There were lots of cones in that arena, but they made that test seem so easy.

Try cones in your arena. If you use them religiously, the day will come when you won't need them because you'll always have a clear idea of your precise path. Those cones will be emblazoned in your mind forever, giving the geometry of your arena tremendous significance.

EXERCISE 2
The Spiraling Circle

Directions Help your horse become aware of your outside as well as your inside aids so you can easily stay on your intended line of travel. Use cones if you have trouble keeping your circles round.

Step 1 Begin in a marching walk on a 20-meter circle in either direction. Pay special attention to the alignment of your body and eyes with your horse's body. Your horse's ears should always be on the line of travel. Keep your body and eyes aligned with them.

Step 2 Let your bending aids shift your horse onto an 18-meter circle. Make the circle line precise. You'll be one meter inside the track of your 20-meter circle. Stabilize your horse on this circle.

Step 3 Let your bending aids shift your horse onto a 16-meter circle, two meters inside the 20-meter circle. Stabilize.

Step 4 Then, shift your horse onto a 14-, 12-, and 10-meter circle. Do this gradually so you make your horse stable in each bend and balance.

Step 5 Gradually move back to a 12-, 14-, and 16-meter circle. Then, finally move onto a consistent 18-meter and 20-meter circle.

Step 6 Do the same exercise in the other direction, and then do it in trot and canter.

Essential Information about the Line of Travel

- When you are not determining the line of travel, the horse is determining it, and balance always suffers.

- Ride lines and figures with neurotic accuracy.

- The rider who has trouble with precise lines of travel should use cones to mark the way.

- Understand the geometry of the dressage arena. If you ride in a different place, even an open field, make conscious landmarks so you can ride straight lines and balanced figures.

- If you plan to ride a course of fences, be sure you can ride "the course" in balance with no fences.

how two spines
meet in balance

CHAPTER TWENTY-TWO

Figures and Movements

A Long-Term Training Plan

Olympian Lendon Gray, and other US dressage pioneers, didn't have great masters to guide them during the emerging dressage years in the United States. Lendon says she learned how to train horses by using the dressage tests. These tests, created by the USEF (United States Equestrian Federation), are redesigned every four years, and they represent the collective genius of generations of great horsemen. They are roadmaps that reliably guide riders in the training of horses. Every country has its own national tests, but they are roughly comparable to one another. For simplicity, this chapter talks about the tests in the United States.

Train with the Tests

Each test level has a "purpose." The figures and movements in each test help the rider achieve the purpose. As an aside, it's amazing that countless riders go to great effort to ride at shows without knowing the purpose of the test they're riding. In addition, they are unaware of the intent of the figures and movements. As a result, to some extent, the training essence gets lost. The "purpose" of each dressage level is printed on the front of each test.

The Purpose of Training Level

To confirm that the horse is supple and moves freely forward in a clear and steady rhythm, accepting contact with the bit.

The figures required at Training Level include:

- *Straight lines on the centerline, the long side, and on the diagonal.* These encourage your horse to go forward in a clear and steady rhythm.

22.1 The Broken Line. Think about the aids that shape your horse and put him in front of the leg when you ride this figure. Each time you change direction, you have the opportunity to put him on a new outside rein from a new inside leg that is meaningful to him. The new inside leg asks him to step up to the plate and go in front of the leg!

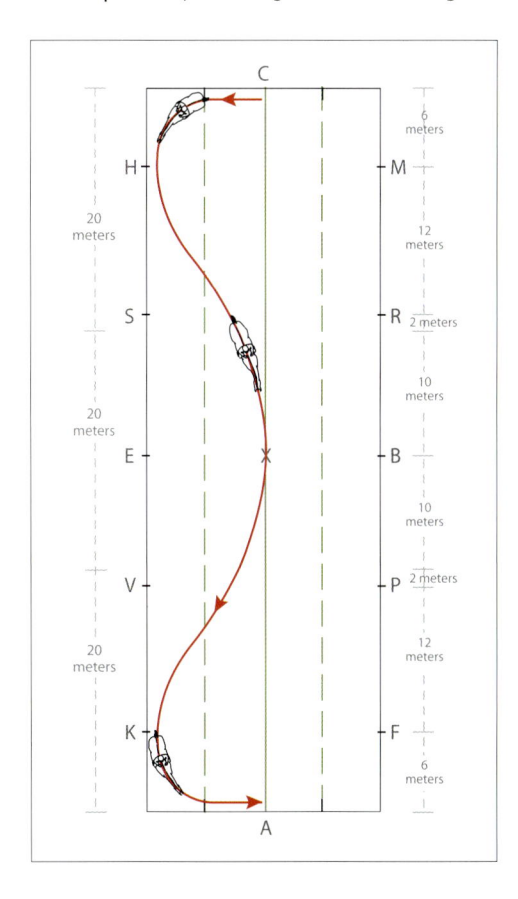

FIGURES AND MOVEMENTS   215

- *20-meter circles* are intended to make your horse supple and loose.

- *Broken lines* also encourage your horse to be supple and loose.

Opposing Qualities

Some of the qualities we need to develop in our horses can be seen as opposing. For example, a racehorse goes forward in a clear and steady rhythm, but he's not supple and loose. A worm is very loose, but doesn't go forward in a clear and steady rhythm. If your horse is inclined to be *racehorse-like*, the circles and bending lines along with downward transitions will help him most. But they're also the most difficult for him.

If your horse is *worm-like*, riding forward on straight lines and upward transitions will be the most helpful for him, but those will also be the most difficult. When you're able to mingle the two, as is required in a dressage test, you make your horse able to do both: He'll be able to go forward in a clear and steady rhythm with muscles that are supple and loose. As a result, your horse will accept the contact in a nice way.

EXERCISE

While training, you can combine exercises in a way that will help him develop forward ability without losing suppleness. For example:

At Training Level, do an accurate 15-meter circle at C, then go straight in shoulder-fore. Do 15-meter circles at B, A, and E. As you go straight, retain the ability to bend at any time (see fig. 18.5, p. 194).

The Purpose of First Level

To confirm that the horse, in addition to the requirements of Training Level, has developed the thrust (pushing power/impulsion) to achieve improved balance and throughness and to maintain a more consistent contact with the bit.

Figures and movements at First Level include:

- *Lengthening of stride in trot and canter.* Lengthenings improve your horse's ability to go forward in a clear and steady rhythm. It's best for the worm-like horse, but it's hardest for him. You need to retain those fine qualities you worked so hard for at Training Level, so that when you ask for more thrust in the lengthened stride, your horse doesn't turn into a racehorse. This is the place where your horse can prove he has developed true impulsion, which retains the relaxed rhythm and demonstrates swing in the back as he reaches for the bit and lengthens his stride and frame.

how two spines
meet in balance

- *The 10-meter circle in trot and the 15-meter circle in canter.* These figures shape your horse and improve his balance and "throughness." They are surprisingly difficult to do correctly, but when you're successful, they encourage the horse to step with the inside hind leg under the place where two spines meet. The outside hind stays aligned with the outside fore and the energy goes through his topline.

- *The broken line in canter* (which requires counter canter) also improves suppleness, looseness, balance, and "throughness," but it mostly develops the straightness that will be required for collection at Second Level. It will help the horse if he's the racehorse type. At the same time, it will be difficult for him. Do you see where we're going with this? We're cleaning that dark closet, going where we don't want to go, doing the things that are hard (but not too hard), knowing that those are the training holes that need filling.

- *Leg-yield* is a movement that improves suppleness and looseness. It improves and tests the connection, the balance, and "throughness" (fig. 22.2).

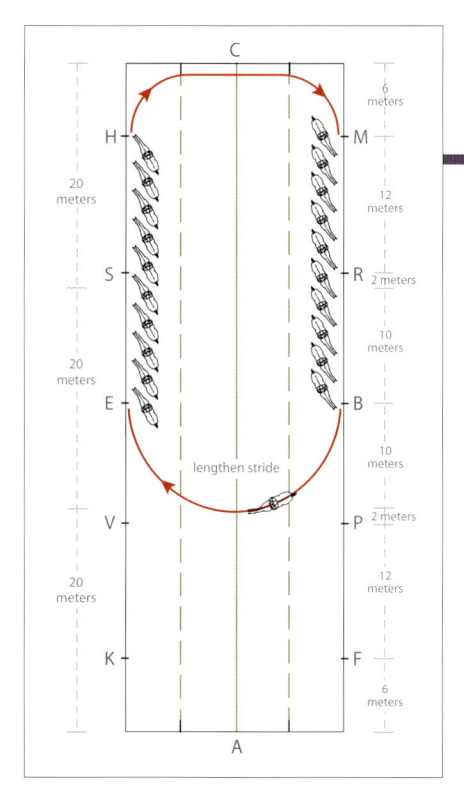

- *The figure eight* and its cousin, the *serpentine,* are both bril-

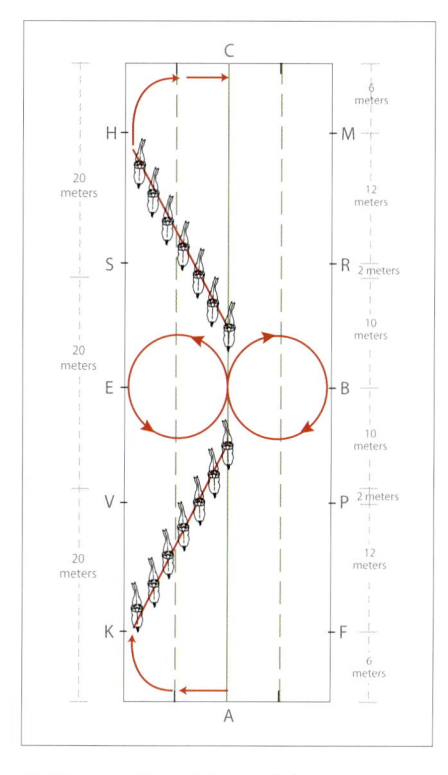

22.2 Leg-yields and figure eights can be combined to create suppleness and straightness in your horse. This exercise engages one hind leg and then the other.

Opposing Qualities

EXERCISE

At First Level, do a head-to-the-wall leg-yield from the corner letter to E or B, then do a lengthened stride on a half 20-meter circle between E and B. Then repeat the leg-yield to the next corner letter. Repeat this in both directions and you should feel that your leg-yield becomes more active, powerful and connected. Your lengthening should feel more supple.

22.3 Help your horse develop opposing qualities by combining exercises that develop strength and power with exercises that develop suppleness. For example, you can combine leg-yields (that develop suppleness) with lengthenings (that develop strength and power).

liant exercises that develop collection by connecting and straightening the horse. The horse engages and develops one inside-hind-leg-to-outside-rein connection and then the other.

The Purpose of Second Level

To confirm that the horse, having achieved the thrust required in First Level, now accepts more weight on the hindquarters (collection), moves with an uphill tendency, especially in the medium gaits; and is reliably on the bit. A greater degree of straightness, bending, suppleness, throughness, balance, and self-carriage is required than at First Level.

That's not just a long paragraph. It's serious homework. Lots of horses and riders struggle or even "dead end" at Second Level. In the Second Level tests, we see figures and movements that improve the horse's straightness and power, and they challenge the horse's basic Training Level skills (rhythm, suppleness, and contact). However, if the horse is, in fact, supple, loose, and going forward in a clear and steady rhythm with impulsion and straightness, collection happens quite easily with the help of wise riding (using half-halts, transitions, figures, and movements).

Figures and movements at Second Level include:

- *The 10-meter circles in canter* put the horse in a shape in which his inside hind leg will carry more weight. Not only does the inside hind connect to the outside rein, but the outside hind leg also connects to the outside rein. In this situation, the figure naturally collects the horse.

- *The three-loop serpentine in canter with no change of lead*, like its predecessor the figure eight, connects and straightens the horse. The required *counter-canter* in this exercise is a straightening tool that encourages and then demonstrates collection. When ridden correctly it puts the horse in better carriage. When ridden crooked, the energy can't go straight through the horse, and it makes him worse instead of better.

- *Shoulder-in*, as you know, is the "mother exercise" for collection: it's the first movement that requires (and develops) collection. The horse has to take the bend of the 10-meter circle that he mastered at First Level and retain it when he goes on a straight line. Then he carries more weight with the inside hind leg if the outside hind leg doesn't escape. This movement is intended to help your horse carry himself better. Ask yourself: When your horse goes straight after the shoulder-in, is he in better self-carriage? Does the rhythm feel more defined? Don't just ride this movement, ride it for a reason: to improve the gaits.

- *Haunches-in* also retains the 10-meter bend and helps the horse carry more weight with the outside hind. It's easy to see why shoulder-in and haunches-in are used together because they complement one another. They work one hind leg and then the other.

- *Renvers (haunches-out)* is also used to complement shoulder-in. In renvers, the shoulders stay in, but the bend changes. Horses are sometimes required to go from shoulder-in to renvers. The transition develops straightness as the horse is required to lift through the shoulders in order to step through to a new outside rein.

- *Medium trot and canter*—here, the lengthenings of First Level are combined with the collection of Second Level to give the horse the ability to lift and carry as the stride and frame lengthen. When the horse retains the collection, the mediums are loftier than the lengthenings were at First Level.

- *Turns on the haunches* encourage collection as the horse is required to keep the rhythm, activity, and bend, and he carries more weight with the inside hind leg. Preparing for a turn-on-the-haunches is good preparation for any movement or transition because it puts the horse in a balanced position—with his inside leg under the place where two spines meet.

- *Simple change* (canter-walk-canter) is a classic exercise that encourages and demonstrates collection. It is a transition that skips a gait, so it allows no trot steps and requires that the horse work from carrying hind legs into a lifted torso.

- *Rein-back* directly engages one hind leg and then the other with clear, diagonal steps. Your horse might initially take exception to the idea of stepping backward after all his forward work, but once he understands, he may have somewhat of a light-bulb moment with regard to engagement. When horses understand rein-back, the forward work often becomes much easier for them.

In the rein-back, the well-balanced horse continues to reach forward toward the bit as he steps back with even and straight steps. The benefit only comes when the rider is able to retain the engaged position of the horse's hindquarters when she rides forward after the rein-back. The result should be greater elevation of the forehand directly because the hind end lowered.

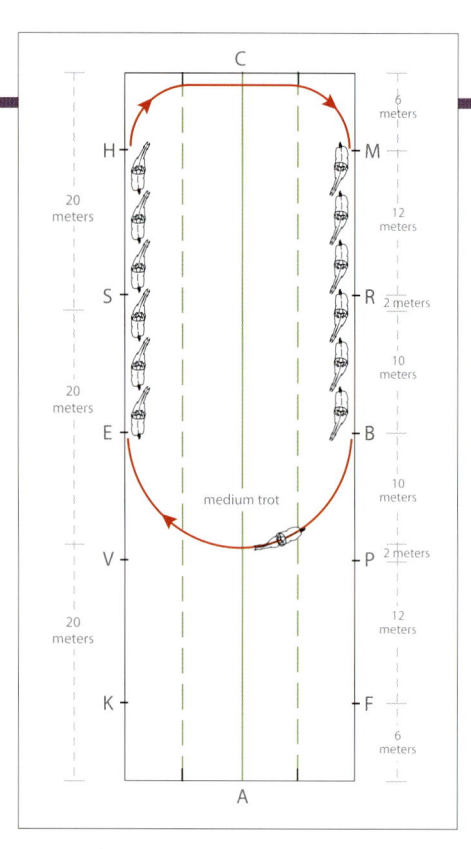

22.4 Help your horse develop power and swing by combining shoulder-in and medium trot. Your shoulder-in will become more powerful, and your medium trots will be come more lofty and elastic.

Opposing Qualities

All of the previously mentioned exercises and movements encourage suppling and straightening. The racehorse-type will need to do the forward exercises with more suppleness and looseness than he'd prefer. The wormy type will need to do his exercises with more power than he'd prefer.

EXERCISE

At Second Level, do shoulder-in from M to B. Then do medium trot on that half 20-meter circle from B to E and then shoulder-in from E to H). The shoulder-in should develop better connection and collection because of the medium trot, while the medium trot becomes loftier because of the shoulder-in.

In the process, your horse will stay supple, loose, and relaxed while he goes more and more forward in a steady and more cadenced rhythm. As you layer more difficult exercises into your horse's work, in addition to being physically developed, he will understand how to develop power while remaining relaxed.

The Purpose of Third Level

To confirm that the horse, having begun to develop an uphill balance at Second Level, now demonstrates increased engagement, especially in the extended gaits. Transitions between collected, medium, and extended gaits should be well defined and performed with engagement. The horse should be reliably on the bit and show a greater degree of straightness, bending, suppleness, throughness, balance, and self-carriage than at Second Level.

Figures and movements at Third Level include:

- *The extended trot and canter* demonstrate the horse's maximum scope as he lengthens his stride and his frame and keeps the balance.

Opposing Qualities

EXERCISE

At Third Level, do half-pass right in trot from M toward K. When you get to the first quarterline, straighten and do medium trot to the next quarterline. Then half-pass right for the last quarter of the diagonal. The medium trot will retain a bit of the collection from the half-pass and it will be loftier. At the same time, the half-pass will become more powerful because of the medium trot.

22.5 As you develop your horse through the levels, stay aware of the opposing qualities of suppleness and strength. When you combine half-pass and medium gaits, your horse will develop power in the half-passes and suppleness in the mediums.

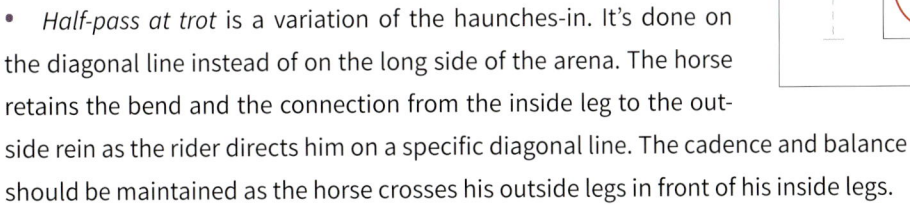

- *Half-pass at trot* is a variation of the haunches-in. It's done on the diagonal line instead of on the long side of the arena. The horse retains the bend and the connection from the inside leg to the outside rein as the rider directs him on a specific diagonal line. The cadence and balance should be maintained as the horse crosses his outside legs in front of his inside legs.

- *Half-pass at canter* is comparable to the half-pass in trot except the horse, because of the nature of the gait, doesn't cross his outside legs in front of his inside legs.

- *The single flying change* must be done from a balanced, quality canter with ample activity, throughness, and regularity. The rider's aid must be timed so the horse can change his leading legs while in the moment of suspension.

- *Überstreichen at canter*—here, the rider gives the rein by extending one or both hands up the horse's crest. This is a test that demonstrates that the horse maintains his balance, bend, tempo, and self-carriage without the aid of the rider's hands.

The Purpose of Fourth Level

To confirm that the horse has developed sufficient suppleness, impulsion, and throughness to perform the Fourth Level tests, which have a medium degree of difficulty. The horse must remain reliably on the bit, showing a clear uphill balance and lightness. The

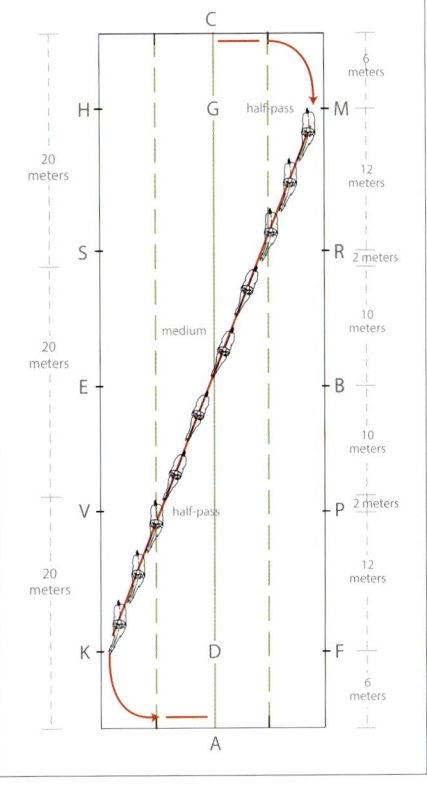

how two spines meet in balance

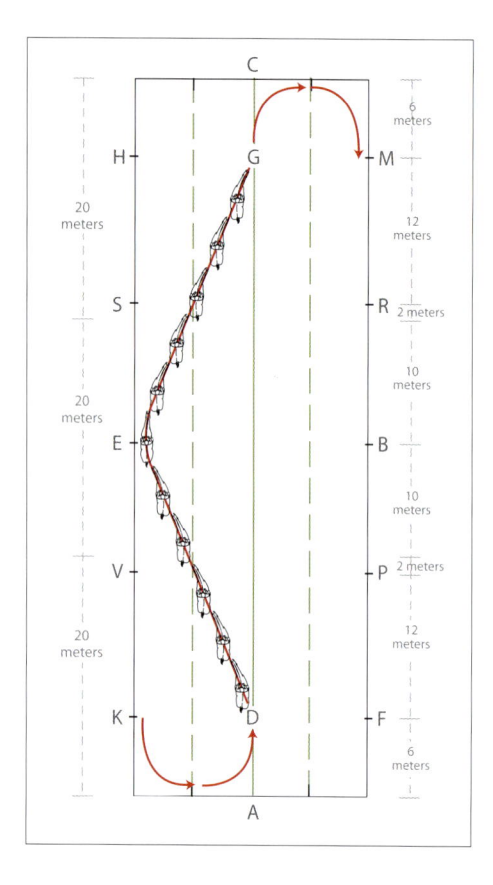

movements are performed with greater engagement, straightness, energy, and cadence, and the hind limbs carry more weight than at Third Level.

Figures and movements at Fourth Level include:

- *The 8-meter circle at trot*—small circles automatically ask the horse's inside hind leg to bend and carry a bit more weight. The circle shapes the horse, which supples and connects him. The figure itself develops some degree of collection, and as the size of the circles decreases, the suppleness, strength, and collection increase.

- *Collected walk* demonstrates greater activity in a marching four-beat rhythm. The hind leg joints bend more, causing the hindquarters to lower and the front end to lift in proud self-carriage. Loss of energy and rhythm are common problems to be avoided at all costs.

- *The very collected canter* prepares the horse for canter pirouettes and has similar problems as the collected walk. Loss of energy and rhythm

22.6 At Fourth Level, the horse is required to do a counter change of hand in trot and in canter: half-pass left and then half-pass right. The half-pass develops the horse's swing and collection; and when you change directions in half-pass, it confirms the straightness and develops even more swing and collection.

The Chicken or the Egg of Tempo Changes

When horses are put in challenging situations such as reducing the size of a circle, they often react by slowing the tempo to avoid the work. If they're required to keep the tempo, they will need to bend their joints and carry more weight with the hindquarters, but that will make the work of the rest of the body easier and more elegant to watch.

At the same time, the tempo of collected gaits *does* get slightly slower as a result of the defined rhythm or cadence. When monitoring the tempo, riders need to ask themselves why the tempo got slower. Did the horse get slower in the corners because he was avoiding collection or because he was dancing in a better rhythm? When the rhythm is self-perpetuating and the circle of the aids is working, the rider usually knows it is right because it feels so harmonious. On the other hand, the rider has to be diligent about noticing if the tempo becomes slower in order to avoid collection.

how two spines meet in balance

are common. It pays to be thinking of the rhythm and activity of gallop as you go to the very collected canter.

- *Walk pirouettes* are done from the collected walk and the quality of the pirouette will reflect the quality of the walk. If the walk is not balanced, active, and rhythmic, you have little chance of success when you add the difficulty of bending and turning in the movement. Pirouettes require even more weight be added to an inside hind leg that keeps stepping in rhythm as the horse bends and turns with the inside hind leg stepping nearly on the spot.

- *Working half-pirouettes in canter*—likewise, the success of the half-pirouette in canter is directly dependent on the quality of the very collected canter. It will be relatively easy to bend and turn with the hind legs on the 3-meter half-circle of a working pirouette if the horse can do a very collected canter with activity, balance, and "throughness."

- *Sequence flying changes*, in which the horse does flying changes every fourth stride, in addition to the skills of the flying change, require that the horse be straighter, more in front of the leg, and responsive to the rider's aids at each moment.

- *Counter change of hand in trot*—when a horse does a half-pass zigzag, he is required to carry rather constantly and equally with both hind legs.

Opposing Qualities

EXERCISE

At Fourth Level, do medium canter on a 20-meter circle. When you get to X, do an 8-meter circle in collected canter. Your collection will have more power and "throughness." You might start to see the possibility for pirouettes.

Use your creativity to make up your own exercises and tailor them to your horse. Help him develop the ability to lift and carry himself—and you—into every movement and figure.

22.7 Develop collection in the canter by doing it with power on the larger circle. Then let the smaller figure help the horse collect naturally. This should give you the feeling that pirouettes are possible.

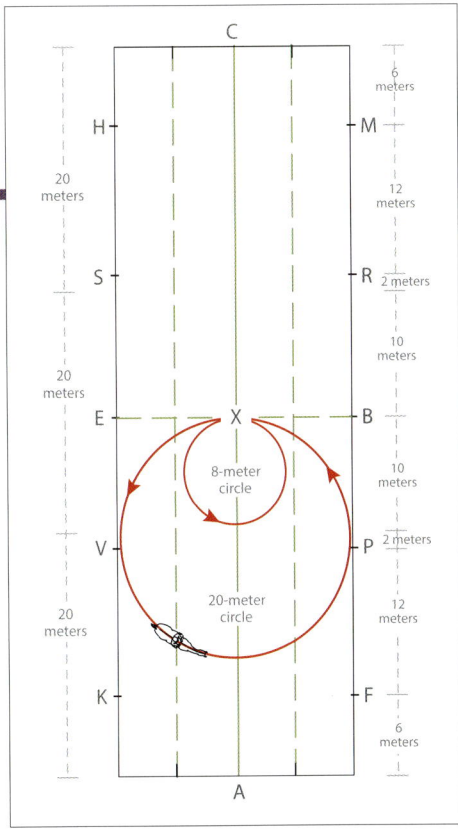

FIGURES AND MOVEMENTS 223

Then the shoulders are free enough to move left or right at a moment's notice. The resulting elevation of the entire front end makes the movement beautiful. It requires exceptional lateral suppleness and acceptance of the aids (fig. 22.6).

• *Counter change of hand in canter* has the added difficulty of requiring a balanced flying change before changing the direction of the half-pass. The benefits of the movement are the same as at trot. The movement engages both hind legs equally, allowing the shoulders and the entire front end to be free and beautiful.

The Prix St. Georges, Intermediaire, and Grand Prix (Olympic-level) dressage tests are developed by the international governing body for equestrian sport, the FEI (Fédération Equestre Internationale). These dressage tests are progressively more difficult as they continue to develop the degree of collection, but the true difficulty at these levels, as it is in the USEF levels, is always to retain and improve the basic qualities of rhythm, suppleness, contact, impulsion, straightness, and collection—the elements of the Training Scale.

Development of the horse as an athlete requires a thoughtful trainer and a thoughtful rider who always have these qualities in mind, along with developing the horse's trust, his mental understanding, and his emotional enthusiasm for his job.

Essential Information about Figures and Movements

• The dressage tests provide a roadmap for training your horse.

• Know the purpose of the test before you ride it so you can consciously prove that your horse has met the requirements.

• Ride the movements and figures for a reason: to improve the gaits. Understand the reason why you do each so you can capture the essential benefit.

• Understand that some qualities are in opposition to others. For example, if you only did strengthening exercises, you would lose suppleness, and if you only did suppling exercises, you would lose strength. The tests try to develop strength and suppleness equally.

Conclusion

The Probability of Magic

The prerequisite for magical moments in the saddle lies in attention to detail: in knowing how your body and your horse's body work ideally; in being endlessly particular about the details of your horse's posture, about your riding position, the refined clarity of your aids, and your horse's understanding of them.

Finnish Olympian Kyra Kyrklund once said that the difference between super riders and all the others is that the super riders never stop concentrating on these basics. They keep working on transitions and half-halts with an explaining, feeling, balancing attitude, and everything improves. When you ride that way, you have the laws of the nature working for you. Balance and harmony are, after all, a matter of science, and it helps to have Mother Nature on your side!

The rider, as the alpha figure of the horse-rider partnership, has a strong responsibility. She is able to monitor and regulate so many aspects of the ride that even those who don't like to use the word "control" have to admit that the rider is in control. With Powerlines and Triangles of Aids, the rider has control over the rhythm, the energy, the height of the neck, the length of the stride, the flexion, the bend, the alignment, and the line of travel. That's a lot of control, but instead of cramping the horse, that ability to control must be used to balance the horse so he can feel free.

The natural byproduct of that balance is lightness of the forehand that allows the horse freedom of self-expression. This is what makes him a happy member of your team. Your horse clears the final fence in the final round because of you. He passages and piaffes down the final centerline with elasticity and vigor because he's proud to carry you, even if he's dog-tired. That's when two minds meet, two hearts meet, and the magic begins.

When two spines meet in balance, two hearts and two minds meet, too. Ashley Holzer of Canada is known for the wonderful partnerships she has with her horses. Here, she thanks Pop Art after a dressage test in Wellington, Florida.